Splintered Worlds

Splintered Worlds

Fragmentation and the Ideal of Diversity in the Work of Emerson, Melville, Whitman, and Dickinson

ROBERT M. GREENBERG

NORTHEASTERN UNIVERSITY PRESS / Boston

Northeastern University Press

Grateful acknowledgment is made to the following for permission to reprint previously published material:

ESQ: A Journal of the American Renaissance for permission to reprint substantial portions of "Cetology: Center of Multiplicity and Discord in *Moby-Dick*," 27:1 (1981), 1–13; "The Three-Day Chase: Multiplicity and Coherence in *Moby-Dick*," 29:2 (1983), 91–98; "Shooting the Gulf: Emerson's Sense of Experience," 31:4 (1985), 211–229.

Harvard University Press for *The Poems of Emily Dickinson* edited by Thomas H. Johnson, Cambridge, Mass.: The Belknap Press of Harvard University Press. Copyright 1951, 1955, 1983 by the president and fellows of Harvard College. Reprinted by permission of the publishers and trustees of Amherst College.

Little, Brown and Company for *The Complete Poems of Emily Dickinson* edited by Thomas H. Johnson. Copyright 1929, 1935 by Martha Dickinson Bianchi; Copyright renewed 1957, 1963 by Mary L. Hampson. Reprinted by permission of Little, Brown and Company.

Library of Congress Cataloging-in-Publication Data

Greenberg, Robert M., 1943–
    Splintered worlds : fragmentation and the ideal of diversity in the work of Emerson, Melville, Whitman, and Dickinson / Robert M. Greenberg.
       p. cm.
    Includes index.
    ISBN 1-55553-167-9
    1. American literature—19th century—History and criticism.
2. Social change in literature. 3. Literature and history—United States—History—19th century. 4. Emerson, Ralph Waldo, 1803–1882—Political and social views. 5. Melville, Herman, 1819–1891—Political and social views. 6. Whitman, Walt, 1819–1892—Political and social views. 7. Dickinson, Emily, 1830–1886—Political and social views. 8. Modernism (Literature)—United States—History—19th century. 9. Pluralism (Social sciences) in literature. I. Title.
PS217.S58G74   1993
810.9'003—dc20   93-7480

Designed by David DenBoer

Composed in Meridien by Coghill Composition Company in Richmond, Virginia. Printed and bound by The Maple Press Company in York, Pennsylvania. The paper is Sebago Antique, an acid-free sheet.

Manufactured in the United States of America

97 96 95 94 93   5 4 3 2 1

This book is dedicated
to my wife,
Nancy,
and to the memory of my mother and father,
Lillian and William Greenberg.

Contents

Acknowledgments

Books are written in a state of productive isolation. Yet eventually a limit is reached; the isolation becomes a burden and one needs to see how others respond to what has been written. I consider myself fortunate to have had friends and colleagues to whom I could go at such a time. Robert R. Smith, dean of Temple University's School of Communications and Theater, and the person with whom I have worked the closest for the past eleven years, has read the four main chapters with interest and has provided helpful comments. His support for my work, throughout these many years as his assistant, then associate dean, has been generous and a source of pride and assurance to me. From Temple's English Department, Miles Orvell, whom I have known since my undergraduate days, has read all of this book. His reading of Chapters 2, 6, and 7 was extremely helpful in bringing the project to completion. Miles' role in the genesis of the book has also been deeper. I can only liken it to that of an older brother, with whom one is somewhat competitive but without whose accomplishments the horizon of one's own aspirations would have seemed less attainable. Glenn "Al" Omans, former chair of English at Temple, has also been a loyal and generous friend and a very careful reader. I appreciate his meticulous reading of the Whitman chapter. Others from Temple's Department of English have been interested and read chapters at various points—Daniel O'Hara helped me with a proposal for the book and read Chapter 1; Jayne Kribbs Drake read the Melville chapter; Sheldon Brivic invited me to read Chapter 1 to the Department's Journal Club and pushed me to make certain key theoretical additions. I also want to thank Philip Stevick and Richard Beards for their interest in my work these past years and Phillip Yannella for sharing his research interest in socioeconomic disarray in New England.

Elsewhere at Temple I owe a great note of thanks to David M. Bartlett, director of Temple University Press, who gave me advice and encouragement as I was trying to place the book and get through the review process. I owe thanks to Temple's Samuel Paley Library for its collection, which rarely let me down, for its liberal loan policy, and for the efforts of the interlibrary loan staff in obtaining certain nineteenth-century texts. In addition, I want to thank Mary Dunn, director of Temple's Information Processing Center, for her patience and intelligent assistance. I also want to acknowledge and thank Marianne Galvin and Deborah Marshall, with whom I work daily; they add to my life a dimension of comradeship, humor, and good judgment without which I would be poorer indeed.

Outside of Temple I want to thank Merton S. Sealts of the University of Wisconsin at Madison for the enthusiam with which he greeted the Melville and Emerson articles that grew into this book. I want to thank A. Walton Litz of Princeton University for the confidence he placed in me during the past decade. Walt's unexpected telephone calls offering writing assignments on subjects other than this book were always good to receive; occasionally, he even succeeded in luring me away for a while. I want to thank Suzanne Smith of Cohasset, Massachusetts, for her letter about my Dickinson chapter; she helped me to anticipate certain feminist responses and to revise accordingly. I want to thank David M. Robinson of Oregon State at Corvallis for his critique of the entire manuscript; it was extremely helpful. And I want to thank Michael and Sally Bailin, my close Philadelphia friends, for just being here and being who they are—intelligent, caring, and loyal people. Mike's companionship and ready ear on our long walks and telephone talks has meant a great deal to me. Finally, there is an immeasurable debt I owe to Marlin S. Brenner of New York City, who always saw my potential.

There are other, older academic debts as well, since this is my first book. Charles C. Walcutt, with whom I studied nineteenth-century American literature and wrote my dissertation at the Graduate School of CUNY, is the person I credit with having taught me how to read American literature closely. Despite his own strong ideas about Emerson and Melville, he let me go my way and find my own thoughts; this, I believe, was critical at a formative period and provided the ideal preconditions for the emergence of this book.

Every writer is lucky to have met one great one. It was my special good fortune that that figure in my case was not only an intellectual titan, but a man of unusual character and purpose. Studying with Irving Howe and reading his work over the years has taught me that literary criticism is an "art" as well as a "science," that quality of mind is as important as methodology, and that sensibility and worldliness go a lot further than theoretical profundities in making criticism meaningful. I hope he can read this book with comfort and pride as I describe him as the closest thing I have had to an intellectual mentor. In addition to Howe, I might cite with appreciation several other figures whose books were, as I look back, important influences, consciously or subliminally: Charles Feidelson, Ian Watt, and Fredric Jameson.

I need to acknowledge the debt I owe to my wife, Nancy, and my children, Jenny and Susanna. Although the book demanded so much of my time and attention, my wife was willing to sacrifice because it was important to me. I appreciate her loyalty and hope she can reap some unpredictable benefit from this book. My daughters felt the pull of this work, beyond them, all too often, I would suspect. I hope it did not deprive them too much and that they can read it someday with pride and interest.

Chapter 3 and 4 contain material that appeared in somewhat different form in articles in *ESQ: A Journal of the American Renaissance*. I would both like to thank the editors of *ESQ* for permission to include this material and to remember fondly the late Kathleen McLean for her conscientious efforts as associate editor.

Finally, I want to thank Temple University for providing a grant to cover part of the production costs of this book. I am grateful to James England, provost, and to Richard Joslyn, acting vice provost, for their support.

Philadelphia
January, 1993

Splintered Worlds

1

Introduction:
Diversity, Democracy,
and the Nineteenth-Century
Literary Imagination

I

This book is about fragmentation in mid-nineteenth-century American literature and about corresponding fragmentation in the social, religious, and philosophical environment. When a literary subject becomes fragmented into multiple manifestations of itself—into multiple moods in the self, multiple views of the Deity, multiple groups on the street—what new angles of vision does such relativism present? What new views of the mind and the world? What new aesthetic and intellectual responses? The answers to these questions comprise the dividends of nineteenth-century literary relativism and are explored in this study. The other major concern of this study is the relationship of literary works typified by multiplicity of representation with their sociocultural environments. In relation to texts of Emerson, Melville, Whitman, and Dickinson, I examine certain historical contexts, both material and intellectual, in order to understand how extrinsic conditions shape different literary works. In this manner, I hope to see the relationship between work and background more deeply, to bring into better focus the sources of the literary imagination and its various relations to general culture, and to arrive at an encompassing image of the culture of fragmentation at midcentury.

Each generation, to some extent, feels it is entering a period of greater diversity and complexity. Each era is challenged to find new unifying ideas, to reform old ones, or to develop a more pluralistic response to contemporary existence. This challenge was a great one for American writers after 1830. The multitudinous image of democracy glimpsed on the streets of cities, the segmenting of religion as a result of revivalism, the rise of empiricism, and the conflicting view of romantic idealism plunged many individuals into a whirlpool of shifting perspectives.

The facilitating idea for those writers and thinkers at the forefront of their culture in responding to the welter of contemporary life was the ideal of diversity, what Arthur O. Lovejoy calls the temporalized principle of plenitude that German Romantics transmitted through their own work and through Coleridge.[1] As guiding ideals in art and life, variety replaced uniformity, difference replaced universality, natural dynamism replaced fixed forms, and spontaneity replaced mechanical rules. This "diversitarianism"[2] provided American writers with a new heterogeneous approach to subject matter and a boldly assimilative and organic sense of form.

In Germany in the 1790s, Friedrich Schiller had envisioned a method of spiritual striving and progressive realization through the artist's contact with a wider and wider variety of phenomenal experience:

> Since the world is developed in time, or change, the perfection of the faculty that places men in relation with the world will necessarily be the greatest possible mutability and extensiveness. . . . The more the receptivity is developed under manifold aspects, the more it is movable and offers surfaces to phaenomena, the larger is the part of the world *seized* upon by man, and the more virtualities he develops in himself.[3]

In other words, the more the individual comes into contact with multiple and far-flung facets of the world, the more the individual discovers about himself and the closer he approaches an intuition of complete reality. Several years later August Schlegel and Friedrich Schleiermacher echoed Schiller's ideas in their writings on art and religion, with Schleiermacher arguing that only tolerance for multiple religions within a culture can bring knowledge of the "unity of the church."[4] In England, simultaneously, Coleridge echoed the German emphasis on the transcendental imagination and on organicism—"the *power* which discloses itself from within as a principle of *unity* in the *many*," or "the principle of unity in *multeity*."[5] And in America even before Herman Melville and Walt Whitman raised the diversitarian impulse to a consummate art form, others were asserting the value of the unfamiliar and the different, were using the categories of unity-diversity or part-whole to organize their experience, and were moving in the assimilative artistic direction that led ultimately to *Moby-Dick* and *Leaves of Grass.*

To cite one figure as an example, diversitarianism helped Theodore Parker defend himself against charges of heresy in the controversy in Boston over the validity of miracles as divine revelation. He could defend his attack on Unitarian dogma by arguing like Schleiermacher that "there is but one kind of religion, as there is but one kind of love, though the manifestations of this religion, in forms, doctrines, and life, be never so diverse."[6] And functioning differently, it could help Parker later in his life bring order to his description of urban change and estrangement: "In your busy, bustling town, with its queerly-mingled heterogeneous population, and its great diversity of work, I soon learned to see the unity of human life under all this variety of circumstances and outward conditions."[7]

The most explicit manifestation of the influence of European Romanticism on the developing artistic thought of the period is Ralph Waldo Emerson's prophetic complaint in "The Poet" (1844) that we do not yet "chaunt our own times and social circumstances," that "all things await" "yet the timely man, the new religion, the reconciler."[8] And a still somewhat earlier expression of this new interest in the diversity of the times can be found in the declaration jointly written by Margaret Fuller and Emerson for the first issue of *The Dial* (1840).[9] Most striking about their declaration is the egalitarian conviction that they must discover new authors, subjects, and audience for this new approach, and that this "new spirit" in literature will be found not in business and politics, nor in the work of professional writers, but in those peripheral individuals of society—farmers, women, closet poets, and mystics for whom the truths of humanity and the influx of nature have not been obstructed by participation in the mainstream. New voices, they seem to be saying, are likely to be found in alienated and economically marginal individuals; and, as if a rock of social and psychological repression were being lifted, the new literary organ would enable these voices to issue forth. Furthermore, the aesthetic implications of Fuller's and Emerson's egalitarianism, implicit in their extensive use of lists of parallel phrases or "catalog rhetoric," involve looking for subjects as well as readers in out-of-the-way places, that is, in assimilating the economic, social, and regional diversity of America. "Historically," Lawrence Buell observes in *Literary Transcendentalism*, "the catalogue is that aspect of the grammar of Transcendentalism which most differentiates it from all the British romantics except

Blake."[10] Lacking the sense of natural abundance and social diversity, British Romantics were not compelled to create an inclusive catalog form. In *The Dial* manifesto, on the other hand, we see clear evidence of this diversitarian impulse entering American artistic theory by 1840.

II

Complementing the romantic ideal of diversity, the other major influence on how the world was perceived and described by midcentury writers was American democracy itself in both its political and cultural manifestations. Politically, the framers of the Constitution had endorsed self-interested diversity; and culturally, Americans drifted away from a sense of psychological dependence on an educated elite and toward an endorsement of the wide diversity of standards (or lack of standards) of the masses. Following the War of 1812, cultural nationalism, especially against England, had begun to assert itself; and with the election of Andrew Jackson in 1828, it had become increasingly dominant.[11] The frontier states and the lowly individual were embraced with egalitarian enthusiasm; attitudes of youthful expansiveness and populist inclusiveness grew prevalent. A sense of superabundance about natural resources linked up with an increasing sense of human plenitude; and there developed, with these changes, the potential for new materials and new directions in literature.[12] Presciently listed by Emerson in "The Poet," there were many "unsung" subjects awaiting literary treatment: "our logrolling, our stumps and their politics, our fisheries, our Negroes, and Indians, our boasts, and our repudiations, the wrath of rogues, and the pusillanimity of honest men . . . the western clearing, Oregon and Texas."[13]

In addition, American democracy, based on the assumption of natural rights, resulted in an opinionated quality on the part of the common man that colored the political and cultural climate and had a formative effect on how writers began to approach their themes. "Equality begets in man the desire for judging everything for himself," observed Tocqueville in *Democracy in America* (1838).[14] Lacking social superiors or humbling reminders of a higher tradition, Americans tended to believe that each individual could formulate an important opinion on any question, practical or abstract. Augustus Brownson in 1836 remarked on how Americans "have a strong tendency to profound and philosophic thought, as well as to skillful, energetic and persevering action." He added that "this is written on almost every man's brow" and "fits us above all other nations to bring out and realize great and important ideas."[15] This penchant for expatiating on all matters, abstruse or pedestrian, as if God intended it that way, helps in part to explain why American writers sought to create works that approached reality from multiple perspectives.

Added to this opinionatedness was the pressing multiplicity of issues and media utilized for debate. Greater capital investment and new technologies in publishing had resulted in a rapid increase in the number of books, newspapers, magazines, and pamphlets. And both reflecting this increase in printed material and creating a need for still more of it was the great clamor of social, religious, political, and even philosophical issues that filled the air of the 1830s and 1840s. Harsh and persistent were the conflicts over slavery and free-soil, nativism and immigration. In the domain of religion, a rapidly growing array of religious newspapers and periodicals attacked the methods of the revival ministers, while at the same time the revivalists counterattacked in their own journals. In the orbit of Boston, biblical interpretation and the Transcendentalists' quest for direct knowledge of God were explosive issues.

In sum, a space of public consciousness, filled with contending values and viewpoints, grew larger and more turbulent in American society.[16] And this sense of warring points of view on vital issues, of all positions being subject to challenge and open to debate in the democratic marketplace, ultimately motivated American writers to want to find new ways—new, explicitly *American* ways—of defining and thinking through problems in their writing. Each point of view had to be given its due; each had to survive the time and attention given to competing perspectives; each had to justify having a place in the big picture. For these new kinds of pluralistic problems a new approach to form and subject was required.

The thesis of this study, then, is that American writers would not have been able to deal with the fragmentary aspects of change and transformation in America between 1830 and 1865 had it not been for the ideal of diversity amplified by American democracy, politically and culturally. The ideal of diversity and American democracy exercised a powerfully reciprocal influence on each other, with romantic diversity reshaping our literary image and conception of the self and society, and American democracy giving to European Romanticism a fresh particularity and formalistic revisioning grounded in the ideals of individual self-sufficiency and cultural multiplicity.

In American literature, the normative thought-form of unity-in-diversity, which lies at the center of romantic thought, made possible not only Emerson's claim for the spiritually unified man or Whitman's vision of democratic oneness; it also provided a warrant for exploring the unfamiliar, the conflicted, and the alien elements of life within and without. Deviations from the norm were permitted by the norm's presence, just as the ideal of democractic unity provided Whitman the freedom to lose himself in human variety. When deviation led the writer into unrelieved multiplicity or radical disjunction between mind and world, then these writers were faced with a still more extreme challenge that had to be dealt with on more spiritually attenuated, protomodernist terms.

In addition, because it provided an organic approach to social as well as internal realities, romantic diversitarianism enabled American writers to yield their imaginations to a dynamic interaction between external and internal worlds, and to sustain their confidence in discovering an ultimate form for their complex, evolving explorations. Romantic diversitarianism also provided a way of presenting life as occurring in rapid and changing combinations, and a way of envisioning the deep structure of reality as a shifting fragmentariness, characterized by metamorphosis, changing ratios of subject and object, and indeterminacy.

I have reserved the terms "diversity" and "multiplicity" for times when connotations of fullness and affirmation are intended in my argument, or when variety leads to a sense of unity. Much of this study, however, is concerned with highly self-conscious and experimental departures from the romantic paradigm of unity-in-diversity, and for these instances I have tended to use "fragmentation," with its connotations of disjunction, disarray, and disunity. Use of the modernist master-term "fragmentation" has also helped me specify the evidence of continuity between American Romanticism and modernism and to delineate the protomodernist tendencies of the writers examined.

III

The portion of this book devoted to literary analysis is divided into two parts and reflects a distinction between two types of fragmentation: segmentary fragmentation and atomistic fragmentation. These two types of fragmentation, moreover, correspond to the two forms of the diversitarian impulse described by Lovejoy. Lovejoy divides the ideal of diversity into both the impulse to extend the range of experience to encompass the widest possible variety and the impulse for individual uniqueness.[17] When these efforts fail, two very distinct and different types of fragmentation result. Being awash in variety without any unifying principle results in segmentary fragmentation, and being chilled with isolation by one's unique individuality results in atomistic fragmentation. As the literary acknowledgment of democratic variety and individuality occurred, so did the necessity to treat the consequences of their extremes—to deal with the feeling of being overwhelmed or pulled apart by too much variety and choice, or to deal with the feeling of lonely isolation, of disconnection from the group, when too exclusive an individuality was asserted.

By segmentary fragmentation in a literary work, therefore, I am thinking of multiple manifestations or views of the same phenomenon, such as the multiple immigrant groups in cities, or the multiple and shifting views about God and other religious questions within an individual. Regarding Emerson and Melville, who are examined in Part 2 under this rubric, I am interested in their struggles with multiple views of God and human nature and in their difficulties in retaining a unified conception in each sphere. Hence I view their writing primarily with an interest in the themes of segmentation, relativism, and indeterminacy of viewpoint. On the other hand, in Part 3 on Whitman and Dickinson, I am more interested in the atomistic aspects of fragmentation, that is, in their sense of loss of contact with a larger whole and in their vision of life shaped by feelings of incompleteness and isolation—whether they occur on the streets of large cities or in a bedroom in a New England town. While my view of Whitman seeking to regain wholeness does not contradict his celebration of the unity of the world as a "song-of-myself," it does underscore a reactive element in his impulse for celebration; and it does begin to account for the explicit loneliness that emerges in his major poems between 1855 and 1860.

Thomas McFarland's *Romanticism and the Forms of Ruin* (1981) treats atomistic fragmentation. "Incompleteness, fragmentation, ruin," he asserts, "not only receive special emphasis in Romanticism but also in a certain perspective seem actually to define that phenomenon."[18] The absence of a segmentary fragmentation in his study—or rather, its presence in mine—reflects a difference between English and American society.

More precisely, it reflects the greater degree of diversity within various cultural domains and the greater instability of viewpoint this proliferation of variations produced. If we consider religion, for example, English society also saw the advent of increased demands for emotional latitude in religion and saw the resultant splintering into new denominations that drew members from an established church; but in America the rate of emergence of new denominations and sects, the rate of reaffiliation of ministers and members between them, all suggest a degree of fluidity and segmentation that is not quite duplicated by British society.[19]

Unquestionably, both a segmentary and an atomistic view of existence occurs in each of the writers I treat. However, as assumed by my organization, one pole of their sensibility predominates and provides the key for grasping the fundamental ingredients of their vision of life and art. The exception may be Whitman, whose impulse to unify his country seems to rise as well from a deep-seated loneliness in the crowd. The atomistic sense of self repeatedly emerges as a subject in Whitman, equal in force to variety and segmentation; however, Whitman has difficulty dealing with it, and until he is fully able to, he fails to integrate the twin principles of the self and the democratic mass that he announces as his goal in the opening lines of *Leaves of Grass*. Eventually, in "As I Ebb'd with the Ocean of Life," Whitman finds a way for the painful and lonely atomism of the individual to be fully reconciled with his more easily asserted merger with the diversity of the times. And at that point, his segmentary and atomistic vision of existence, reflecting his struggles with the inclusive and individualistic tendencies of American society, are fully united in a bipolar vision.

IV

The writers I have chosen to study are ones for whom diversitarianism is an enabling idea. Each is able to create new artistic order from social and psychological disorder. Each explicitly grapples with diversity not only as an artistic problem, but as a philosophical problem (relativism and uncertainty) and as a social and psychological problem (multiplicity of cultural viewpoints and selves). Moreover, each writer is working self-consciously to develop formalistic analogies to the diversity of the times in the treatment of material and viewpoint. If their work is conceived, to some degree, in a self-referential, symbolist mode (such as *Moby-Dick*), it is also intended to be representational or expressive of contemporary cultural patterns.

I begin with Emerson's essays because he is seen as a "seer of Unity"[20] whereas his essays reveal an interest in the segmentary fragmentation of moods that undermines an assumption of spiritual unity. By confining my discussion of Melville to *Moby-Dick*, I hope to offer a large, coherent picture of diversity, in its positive and fragmentary aspects. Instead of the towering instance of individuality and atomistic isolation in Ahab, I am interested in Melville's aesthetic and philosophic goals beyond the reach of plot and character. These goals are to represent the segmentary interactions of mind and matter and to convey a condition of epistemological fragmentation and disarray. Whitman's poetry arises, as I indicated, from his solitary condition in a social matrix—from a combination of his overwhelming loneliness with the overwhelming plenitude of city life. Ostensibly, he achieves wholeness through optical and imaginative merger with the procession of modern life. Yet the undercurrent of isolation grows greater throughout his major phase, until he explicitly describes, and must come to terms with himself, as a fragment in a contingent universe. Dickinson offers both partial contrast and advance of my protomodernist theme. Her body of poems, devoted to exploring segmentary views of God, nature, death, immortality, psyche, womanhood, and soul does not reflect as prominent a romantic influence as the other writers I consider; nevertheless her poems advance a view of the atomistic fragment as an authentic spiritual response to existence. Dickinson's poems are fragment poems not in the sense that they are unfinished or are intended to appear unfinished, but in the sense that they speak about disconnection from culture and society and about a highly individualistic reconnection to life through poetry. Religious disconnection, psychological disconnection, and literary (formalistic and mimetic) disconnection are transformed by Dickinson into opportunities to forge new connections to life and to create a poetry of atomistic fragments that are expressive representations of her condition.

Each of my four literary chapters contains one or more anchors of sociocultural material that play a constitutive role in the particular work I examine. These anchors derive from the wider fields of contextual material described in Chapter 2. It will be the role of the anchor to provide, within the author chapters, instances of different direct relations between text and context, while the broader context material in Chapter 2 will delineate the more general cultural realities, relevant yet discontinuous

from the artworks in question. The anchors will enable me to illustrate
different kinds of interdependence between cultural and literary fact—
some materialist, most idealist. In Whitman, for example, New York City
streets are established as a prominent cultural anchor; in Dickinson, Protestant religious revivals in Connecticut and Massachusetts are fore-
grounded. The more removed context material in Chapter 2, on the other
hand, will enable me to demonstrate the pervasive fragmentation in the
general culture, to indicate the broader source of the immediate influence
in the anchor, and to ultimately have a basis for considering the nature of
the representational relationship between literary work and cultural
background. Fredric Jameson in *Marxism and Form* (1971) says about the
relation of the individual work of art with social reality that the "work
itself" can "be thought of as a *reflection* or a *symptom,* a characteristic
manifestation or a simple *by-product,* a *coming to consciousness* or an imagi-
nary or symbolic *resolution.*" I share Jameson's sense of the manifold relations a literary work may share with a sociohistorical context; however,
in the "dialectical method" I employ, the individual imagination shares
the "ontological ground" with the encompassing social reality that Jameson sees as the only constitutive source.[21] In my study, in other words,
the romantic ideal of diversity is a specific and necessary ordering principle for the literary forms describing environmental fragmentation.
Without a subjective imaginative agency that includes a nonmaterialist
ordering principle, the fragmentary forces of culture would not find a
form with which to manifest themselves; they would pile up layer upon
layer of repetitive material. To approach Melville's or Hawthorne's ordering vision largely as a product of social or political history[22] exaggerates
a partial truth because it omits the view of existence from *inside out*—that
is, from the originating center of perception, imagination, and form out
of which literature rises.

In the face of pervasive fragmentation, the ideal of democratic diversitarianism, brought to bear by certain imaginative writers, played a
major role in the reconstruction of the self and social reality in America.
In the metropolitan context, diversitarianism provided both a rhetoric of
plenitude for describing the overwhelming variety of city life and a rhetoric of exploration that optimistically fed off plenitude to confidently document urban disorder, poverty, and vice. In the psychological sphere, the
ideal of diversity enabled evolutionary theory about man's diverse animal heritage to animate new conceptions of the self. And in the religious
sphere, democratic diversitarianism supported the upsurge of new and

sometimes warring denominations and sects, while at the same time it reinforced the constitutional emphasis on religious tolerance. In the face of disintegration in various social and intellectual domains, the ideal of diversity, formulated differently in different contexts, therefore played a major role in constructing new views of the self and society; and those essayists, poets, and novelists who employed it were in the forefront of the effort to respond innovatively to social change.

Let me develop this connection between the romantic thought-form and a cultural context in more detail by illustrating my method with regard to one cultural force. The psychophilosophical context described in Chapter 2 involves certain philosophical trends in the nineteenth century—on the one hand, the German pre-romantic attack on Locke and Hume through emphasis on intuitive knowledge; and, on the other hand, the extension of Lockean empiricism in American Common Sense philosophy and evolutionary science. Two parallel views of human psychology emerge as well—a romantic-Transcendentalist view of the individual comprised of Coleridge's faculties of sense, understanding, and higher reason, and an evolutionary naturalistic view of the psyche. Romantic diversity, allied with romantic correspondence, I argue, had an influence on both the romantic and the naturalistic psychological trends. American Transcendentalists extended the Coleridgean position that reason was to be equated with Christian spirit by diffusing and universalizing their notion of spirit. They conceived it as flowing through phenomenal consciousness and revealing correspondential relations between man and nature. Growing out of nineteenth-century science, the other approach to individual psychology is the view that culminates in Freud's conception of the unconscious energized by animal drives—a view that was implied by Darwin when he established the continuity in man between higher and lower natures. Here the formative influence of romantic ideas of diversity and correspondence is perhaps less obvious. Man changed, for one, from a potential spiritual unity to a creature with diverse basic drives. Second, the dividing line between reason and passion that was so clearly demarcated by the schema of the "great chain of being" was permanently blurred by the romantic notion of power and imagination having their source, partially, in these unconscious depths. Finally, man was discovered to be a creature with a profound correspondential relationship with the animal kingdom. If ontogeny recapitulates phylogeny, then finding correspondences for human behavior, from man's sharkish aggressiveness to his nurturing maternality, was an appropriate angle of artistic exploration.

This is a partial summary of the entwined philosophical and psychological context especially relevant to Emerson and Melville. What, then, are the anchors that will more directly link background to writer, specifying the elements out of which the writer's work may be seen as a heightened manifestation, expression, or working-out of culture? Rather than give away too much of my argument, let me confine my answer to one aspect of Melville. The midsection of *Moby-Dick*, which studies the whale and its technological processing from every practical vantage point and philosophical perspective, is intended, I argue, to convey a sense of epistemological disarray. Its purpose is to mirror the disarray in the general culture among religion, poetry, and science. To be sure, the tension between evolutionary fact and religious faith is articulated in other works of literature such as Tennyson's "In Memoriam" (1850). But where did Melville get the idea of dramatizing the sense of opposition that existed in the philosophical and literary culture of his era between different warring epistemologies and their working methods? Where did he get the idea of showing that neither empiricism, intuition, nor poetic symbolism can know the whale—Melville's comprehensive symbol for the physical and spiritual realities of life? The answer is that, to an important extent, he got it from the pre-Darwinian evolutionary writings and ideas with which he was familiar, either directly or indirectly, such as Charles Darwin's *Voyage of the Beagle* (1839, 1845), Charles Lyell's *Principles of Geology* (1830–33), and Robert Chambers' *Vestiges of the Natural History of Creation* (1844). Melville realized from the angle of literary need with which he came to the naturalists' writings that he could not only dramatize, in satirical fashion, the warring approaches of empiricism and transcendental intuition, but that he could automatically awaken deep and troubling theological associations as he discussed the origin and nature of the *Cetus*. While the naturalist understandably eschewed the incendiary implication of their research about God and creation, a free-wheeling satirical philosopher-poet was able to draw out of his whale material the powerful, ambiguous web of naturalistic fact and theological implication. Ishmael's and Ahab's quest to know the Deity through the largest natural creature on the globe could be made to resonate with, and to dramatize, the philosophical and theological conundrums of the mid-nineteenth century.

Two important motives exist, therefore, for my practice of specifying particular sociocultural anchors in the literary text. One is to substantiate the direction and emphasis of my literary analyses by providing evidence of extrinsic forces that are congruent with the intrinsic formulations of mind and world in the text. The other is to demonstrate powerful congruences between extraliterary and literary realms. If I can offer instances of literary works behaving as focal points, as highly individualized expressions, of cultural realities and problems, then I can examine the kinds of relationships a writer's text may have to culture and the kinds of unusual cultural activity they accomplish.

V

In broadest terms, I am suggesting a representational relationship between the splintered worlds in certain literary texts and the splintering historical scene.[23] I have not tried—for reasons that will perhaps be clearer at the end—to formulate a unified theory of cultural representation. Rather I have been content to think more loosely and variably in terms of representation and expression, and of the coalescence of both practices, in imaginative literary projections that both give and take form from the cultural milieu in which they arise. Regarding a higher level of representation, however, I do claim that the writers I have selected are deliberately trying to represent or simulate patterns of multiple and conflicting viewpoints typical of the public sphere in mid-nineteenth-century America. This creation of a representative analogy of their times is a common goal, although in Whitman and particularly in Dickinson the creation of an expressive representation of their atomistic conditions is equally significant. Melville sought to create in the cetology chapters a sense of a "world of mind"[24] swinging between heterogeneous realities without any stable point of reference or unified theory of knowledge. Emerson sought to dramatize how moods, opinions, and events confront the individual in disjointed succession, posing a threat to a coherent or continuous sense of self. Whitman ultimately conceded that man was like "drift" and "debris": "fragments, / Buoy'd hither from many moods, one contradicting the another."[25] Dickinson enacted a spirited byplay between disconnection and reconnection, deprivation and compensatory gain, finitude and infinitude. In each case, they are creating patterns that evoke and dramatize the structure of reality socially as well as psychologically—patterns that I show are representative or expressive of experience in the mid-ninteenth century. In the final analysis, these literary texts are themselves profound cultural facts that complete the picture of encompassing cultural fragmentation, and that speak of "homologous" or similar structures in various literary and cultural areas.

VI

Paul Ricoeur's helpful work in reader-response theory argues in favor of a relation to the text that retains some degree of transparency and spontaneity. While Ricoeur accepts the idea that interpretations are inevitably the "appropriation" of a text by the reader's "self-understanding," he argues that responses need not be viewed as "a circle between two subjectivities" nor as the "projection of the subjectivity of the reader into the reading itself." His solution is to alter the discourse from a "subjectivist level to an ontological plane," that is, to see a text as "the coming to language of a world" that "the reader understands himself in front of" in a way beyond self-knowledge. "To understand oneself in front of the text," says Ricoeur,

> is quite the contrary from projecting oneself and one's own beliefs and prejudices; it is to let the work and its world enlarge the horizon of the understanding which I have of myself. . . . The circle is between my mode of being—beyond the knowledge which I may have of it—and the mode opened up and disclosed by the text as the world of the work.[26]

If literary discussion can enable readers to open themselves to texts "beyond the knowledge" they have of themselves, and if the scholar-critic's definition of relevant historical contexts can further saturate that reception, then the goals of literature and interpretation, of providing new orders of experience and knowledge, will be served.

Such a ponderous declaration of purpose is perhaps justifiable only in light of the contemporary school of historical, ideologically oriented literary scholars. For these scholar-critics, who view interpretation as "interested study" of "interested art," ideology has become the key term that "demarcates the limits of individualism and the imagination." They want to escape the powerful sway of an author's imaginative vision, to be able to step outside a deep, encompassing interaction with the text, in order to discern the narrowness of class, gender, or racial interest that subsumes artistic endeavor. And the consequence of this assumption has been a polarization between ideological and nonideological approaches, with the nonideological interpreter having to defend himself against charges of naïveté. "The work that presents its conception of the world as natural through the apparent spontaneity of character and story," explains Myra Jehlen, should be approached for the ways it "conceals . . . 'its real ideological determinants,' which it is the critic's task to reveal."[27] On the other hand, I would argue that the "naïve" interpreter enjoys a deeper and wider range of responses to the world of the text; he or she has the freedom to utilize an array of critical approaches as well as to pursue aspects of sensibility that emerge only through synchrony with the text. If the danger lies, on the one hand, in a laxity of sentiment and in ahistoricism, on the other hand, it lies in alienation from a full response to the text and in the willful assertion of political prejudices and predispositions in the service of contemporary political needs.

Reacting to an overly willful approach to literary texts, Daniel T. O'Hara in his book on Lionel Trilling has indicated a need for a more "magnanimous" critical spirit.[28] Bashing dead, dated critics such as F. O. Matthiessen, whose only real error may be that they wrote the most influential books of their day; ignoring evidentiary obligations when making claims of identity between literary and historical motivation; maligning writers based on how the critic thinks he or she would have acted if he or she were the writer; or, really no better, praising writers for a presumed attack on social evils—all these practices constitute two steps backward for one step forward.[29] Ideologically oriented historical scholars seem to lose sight of the fact that a writer's vision is largely inevitable or "fatal"; and they confuse a writer's vision with their own critical responses, which are more elective and willed.

Also, the impulse of nearly all writers to distance, to some degree, the worlds of their imaginations from their contemporary political views requires a more honest recognition.[30] Ideologically engaged scholars need to be able to see that artistic imagination and historical context are, as Jameson nicely puts it, "discontinuous realities . . . *somehow* implicated with each other."[31] The "implication," however, differs for each writer and cannot be imposed by critical legerdemain. In order to understand this implication, literary scholars need not only historical knowledge but imaginative sympathy—that is, a yielding of one's being to the historical text. My skepticism is not over whether political or ideological views are inscribed inescapably in a writer's vision, but how the literary scholar can possibly stand back to capture those views and yet retain an open relation to the text. The attempt at critique from outside the confluence of the writer's and the reader's cultural interaction is a sterile illusion in which more is lost than gained.[32]

VII

Having questioned the explicit injection of politics into literary interpretation, let me anticipate a possible line of attack on the implicit ideological premises of my own study. For if this book treats early manifestations of the modernist sensibility of fragmentation and disjunction, it is not entirely an embrace of the alienation of cultural individualism as Donald E. Pease would claim.[33] It emphasizes as well in its interest in romantic correspondence a vision of interdependence that is pervasive in American literature, American political theory, and even contemporary urban American life.

Pease has attacked twentieth-century modernist critics such as Richard Chase who read American Renaissance writers for their connection with the modernist critic's own dislocated sensibility. Pease urges critics, instead, to see mid-nineteenth-century writers as trying to close the gap between private and social, cultural and political spheres. Rather than emphasizing the self-reliance of the individual, Pease wants to focus on efforts to define a new social compact and civil self. Yet closing this gap between literature and history, the self and the society, ought not involve a repudiation of the romantic-modernist approach to nineteenth-century literature. There are important romantic efforts to define areas of interdependence and deep common ground, politically and psychologically, between the self and the other. In fact, in Pease's superb chapter in *Visionary Compacts* on the pursuit of a "fusing relation" and a "crowd identity" in Whitman, Pease illustrates such an effort in *Leaves of Grass*.[34]

America's Founding Fathers conceived of multiple individualities not only as the goal of democracy, but also as the only practical means of insuring its protection from the tyranny of a majority. In addition to the inherent checks and balances of a tripartite government, they believed that because "society itself will be broken into so many parts, interests and classes of citizens, that the rights of individuals, or the minority, will be in little danger from interested combinations of the majority."[35]

Of course, as Myra Jehlen puts it, America has been "a heterogeneity that pluralism did not always reconcile."[36] Liberal democracy can mean not only freedom of action and structural absorption of conflict, but eruptions of behavior that violate the limits of the social compact and warn of approaching anarchy. In America, variations of this warning have been a perennial phenomenon, and from any number of viewpoints have not been entirely alarmist. In 1843 an observer contrasting the behavior of Bostonians and New Yorkers claimed that in New York City, "every man you meet in our city walks, with his countenance free of any sense of observation, any dread of his neighbors. . . . He is an integer in the throng, untroubled, with any influence beyond the risk of personal accident."[37] Ever since, New York and then other American cities have burst with thousands of individualities packed into the streets and bristling with a threatening immediacy. As early as the mid-nineteenth century, however, the realization existed that the city also exerted a cosmopolitan influence on each "integer." The city, said another observer, "will not let a man harden inside his own epidermis. He must affect and be affected by multitudinous varieties of temperament, race, character."[38] The city dweller, in other words, cannot escape proximity to difference—difference that is often deliberately accentuated so as to stand out from the crowd and compete with other claims for distinction. Certainly for the past twenty-five years, a characteristic of so many large American cities has been a species of postmodern street theater, with an exhibitionistic segment of the population combating estrangement and otherness with the peacock approach to identity and many other segments of the population not only enjoying the extravaganza but slowly being drawn into the orbit of experimentation.

Individualism, in other words, particularly in large, diverse cities, has as its complementary effect the creation of a social diversity that can counter and redirect the egotistic tendencies of the self. Correspondence is generally associated with reciprocal relations of man and nature, an antidote to the friction of industrialized existence. Yet correspondence, as Whitman glimpsed, occurs in cities as well. It links the individual with the other individuals on the street, subtly but continuously combining them in the field of each other's vision. It leads inevitably to a psychological deepening. And it leads to a tacit agreement in the value of diversity as often as it leads to polarization and suspicion. True, one cannot have correspondential relations with the poor if they are living in another neighborhood, nor if one's fear of their hostility is stronger than one's interest. On the streets and subways of all American cities the collision of eyeballs, if not of fists, is as liable to occur as a more generous pressing of flesh. However, the history of cities, as many an American or European novel attests, is the story of people coming to discover not simply their fortunes but themselves. In confronting individuals with different ideas, experiences, and characters, cities enable people to discover dimensions of their being that they could not otherwise know. In the theater of city life, visual correspondence has the potential to become deep transaction.

What I am trying to suggest is that my theme of life as a drama of diversity or multiplicity cannot be reduced to an implicit ideology of laissez-faire individualism, social indifference, and cultural alienation. Jefferson feared the effect of industrial cities on his dream of individual self-realization. Franklin came somewhat closer to an understanding of the rich potential of city life, at least at the institutional level. However, it is important to realize that their vision of a nation of freely developing individuals, especially within an urban context, implies not merely the pursuit of individualism but the discovery of the self through encounter with the unfamiliar.

American life explored as multiplicity in the writings of major nineteenth-century writers does not offer a politics or ideology. It does, however, involve a correspondential view of psychology, with a powerful basis for ties between individuals. And, consequently, it also involves an aesthetic with a vision of life that is immediate, stirring, democratic in a broad cultural sense, and perhaps for some even transformational.

PART ONE

Splintering Worlds

Fragmentation in American Social and Intellectual Life

I The Metropolitan Context: New York City

In the context of the city, particularly New York City, the romantic ideal of diversity underwent what might be called a "metropolitanization." It was appropriated by writers trying to describe a newly emerging social reality characterized by multiplicity and discord. One obvious use of this romantic ideal was the energized description of the abundant variety of urban life, including the varied detail within each group of people or scene—an excited rhetoric of urban plenitude that celebrated the incomparable democratic mix. Another quite different use was the recognition of the estranged perspective of the individual in the crowd, the sense of isolation that was often inescapable amidst a sea of strangers. If the writer brought to the urban setting the artistic lens crucial for unifying the many in the one, then the writer also had to acknowledge that sometimes the individual felt one of the many, atomized and powerless to find a link with the multitude. At the heart of urban life at midcentury was both multiplicity and individual separation, the sources of the two prototypical literary responses that I have categorized as segmentary and atomistic fragmentation.

Between 1840 and 1860 New York City began to experience the first stages of an extraordinary growth and transformation. The population rose from approximately three hundred thousand in 1840, to five hundred thousand in 1850, and to eight hundred thousand in 1860.[1] This growth was largely the result of immigrant groups flooding the City: by 1855 more than half the population of New York City had not been born in the United States. The largest immigrant group was the Irish, then came the Germans, then those from Great Britain, then those from France.[2] In addition, sixty thousand to seventy thousand of the native population in the 1850s did not originate from New York City,[3] but from Upstate New York or from other neighboring states. The City's commercial capacity also expanded rapidly. By one measure of economic growth, imports and exports, the economy of New York City grew by 400 percent during this period.[4] And as the City grew in people and commerce, it grew physically also. Residential populations, especially the well-off, moved higher and higher up the avenues. By 1858 Lower Manhattan was nearly entirely commercial, and residential homes extended as far as 36th Street on the East Side and 50th Street on the West[5]—with the exception of Fifth Avenue, where the line of mansions reached all the way to Central Park.[6] The results of this transformation were economic and social opportunity, a growing middle class, a surge of wealth and ostentation on the part of the new upper class, and a new sense of economic and cultural freedom and confidence. Yet the negative consequences were at least as numerous: slums and dirt and congestion, class and ethnic conflict, poverty and disease, economic cycles and strikes, and governmental incapacity, mismanagement, and corruption.

New Yorkers felt themselves to be living in a huge, changing environment, haphazard in its expansion. A combination of wonder and fear filled them at the profusion and contrasts of life around them—at the City's ethnic multiplicity, at its evidences of individual wealth and nearby poverty, and at the growing sense of economic and historical forces that were rendering the City increasingly alien each year—bigger, more diverse and strange, and more dissonant. By 1860, Edward Spann says in *The New Metropolis*, New York City "had become a vast and complicated society whose variety and complexity was beyond human vocabulary to describe and beyond human mind to comprehend."[7]

Some nonetheless did feel challenged to try to comprehend the City. Perhaps most noteworthy on the literary front—other than Walt Whitman—was journalist George G. Foster,[8] whose books *New York in Slices* (1849), *New York by Gas-Light* (1850), *Fifteen Minutes Around New York* (1853), and *New York Naked* (1854) were a mixture of exposé, celebration, and insider's guide. Familiar, expansive, cosmopolitan, Foster gave New Yorkers brief "slices" of their kaleidoscopic environment. Broadway, the markets, the eating houses, the omnibuses, the liquor groceries, the balls of Tammany, the Boys, and the dandies of the Bowery are some of the worlds into which he peers in *New York in Slices*, the freshest of his series along with *New York by Gas-Light*. And prominent among the characteristics of his "slices" are those elements important to this study — multiplicity, abundance, and discord.

As in Whitman's poetry, the rhetorical device of the catalog helps Foster document the diversity of the City. Yet where free verse enabled Whitman to suggest a synchronous assimilation of abundant variety, Foster's representation of New York City suggests overclose and overwhelming variety — of there being too many instances, too much new detail, and too little frame for any subject. In Foster's fragments things often seem to spill over, to overflow. Little is containable on the basis of fixed subjects, classes, neighborhoods, limits, traditions. A democratic vitality pulsates through Foster's multiplicity, greater than the sum of its parts. Here is Foster's description of an eating house at lunchtime in the mercantile and financial district. In the first lines, the waiters are fielding orders from their many customers:

> "Readynminitsir, comingsir, dreklysir . . . ricepudn sixpnce, eighteen-pence . . . lobstaucensammingnumberfour—yes sir!" Imagine a continuous stream of such sounds as these, about the size of the Croton river, flowing through the banks of clattering plates and clashing knives and forks, perfumed with the steam from a mammoth kitchen, roasting, boiling, baking, frying, beneath the floor . . . and you will have some notion of a New York eating-house. We once undertook to count these establishments in the lower part of the City, but got surfeited on the smell of fried grease before we got half through the first street. . . . We believe, however, that there can't be less than a hundred of them within a half mile of the Exchange.[9]

The variety of individuals found in City markets is also a subject of Foster's:

> Every face you meet is a character, every scene affords a piquant contrast. Talk of your Eastern bazaars and Parisian arcades! of your white-footed oriental gazelle and your brown-cheeked, mischief-colored grisette. . . . Why, they are the merest common-place people, place them side by side with the butcher-boy of the market; the old huckster-woman who implores you in all weather to buy her vegetables, although

she has a handsome house at home and fifty thousand dollars out at interest, (we hope not in the Moonshine Insurance Company,)—the pretty, bare-armed girl who comes to buy breakfast for the mistress and must av coorse have the best of everything—the modest mechanic's wife, who surveys the aristocratic turkey and the lordly sirloin with a sigh, and then, with a timid glance at the little stock of change, is fain to put up with a lean joint for dear John's dinner.[10]

If the encyclopedic method, the exhaustive commitment to detail, and the emphasis on variety and abundance begin to sound like Herman Melville in the cetology sections of *Moby-Dick*, Foster's description of the manifold labors and energy of the New York journalist will reinforce the echo of the "tumultuous business of cutting-in" where "there is much running backwards and forwards among the crew" and where "there is no staying in any one place; for at one and the same time everything has to be done everywhere."[11] For the journalist trying to make a living from his pen, just as for the cetologist who endeavors to describe the cutting-in, exaggeration is necessary to suggest a gigantic theme and the great energy needed by its recorders:

Talk of the power of abstraction and individualization in Shakspeare— what is it, compared with the same power as manifested by the accomplished New York journalist? It was comparatively easy to put appropriate words into the mouths of Miranda, and Prospero, and Hamlet, and Cleopatra; but suppose your Shakspeare had been called upon to hammer out a leader for the *Courier & Enquirer* on Monday; condense an almanac for the *Journal of Commerce* on Tuesday; revolutionize Cuba for the *Sun* on Wednesday; prove in the *True Sun* of Thursday that Martin Van Buren was no Democrat; conduct the country through a "tremendous crisis" in the *Herald* on Friday; and correct *all* blunders of the *Express* for *The Tribune* on Saturday—to say nothing of spinning out half a dozen yards of gutta percha for the *Evening Post*, making hourly observations on the state of the mercury for the *Commercial*, and treating the subscribers of the *Evening Mirror* to mock turtle with their muffins— what think you the world would have ever heard of the Bard of Avon? And yet there are at least half a hundred journalists "attached to the press" of New York, any one of whom could do all this, besides finding time, at odd spells, to contribute a couple of columns to the *Sunday Dash*, write a love-story for the *Sky-blue Mirror*, carry on a daily correspondence with two or three papers at the South or West, and get up a prize tragedy or a satiric poem, according to the state of the market. *Indeed the*

amount and variety of intellectual and physical labor performed by a thorough-
bred New York journalist is unparalleled and incredible.[12]

Abundance and variety are everywhere in New York City life—not
unlike Melville's whaleship. I would argue, in fact, that New York City
life and the diversitarian journalistic style it elicited from its recorders
were conceivably an influence on Melville, with the emphasis on scale,
vitality, and variety stimulating his approach to the sea and its creatures.
Jonathan Arac, in a discussion of the imprint of urban life on Conrad's
treatment of the sea, suggests in passing the related possibility that the
urban crowd directly imprinted a way of seeing on Melville's description
of maritime experience.[13] Certainly, Whitman's 1856 article for *Life Illus-
trated* about Broadway evidences an urban journalistic style in which the
imprint of City life is reflected in his emphasis on scale, vitality, and variety.[14]

The greatest challenge to the sensibilities of midcentury writers,
some have argued,[15] was posed on the level of national politics and culture. In the issue of slavery and the problem of Union in the 1850s, they
argue, lie the origins of American Renaissance writing. What I am suggesting here is that there were other, more local and more immediate
experiences of fragmentation affecting Melville and (obviously) Whitman
that might have played as great a role in defining social, political, aesthetic, and ontological realities for them.

We find evidence in Foster also of how variety brought with it an
inevitable sense of discord—another theme of Melville's *Moby-Dick*. Foster
does begin *New York Slices* in an urban Transcendentalist vein, speaking
of "a great city" as "the highest result of human civilization," which
enables "the Soul" to "put forth all its most wonderful energies . . . developed to their utmost power, and excited to their highest state of activity by constant contact with countless other souls, each emulating, im-
pelling, stimulating, rivalling, outdoing the other." But "reluctantly" he
then turns our gaze from lofty vistas down to where "our dreams will be
soon enough broken" "in the far-reaching sweep of the street, termi-
nated by a confused cloud of moving wheels, fronts of houses, and thick-
ened air."[16] And it is then, as he moves from his introduction to "Slice
I—Broadway," that the aesthetic problem inherent in variety is articulated: the inevitable discord that emerges from a lack of encompassing
cultural vision:

Broadway narrowly escapes being the most magnificent street in the world. If the money expended upon it, architecturally, had been guided by half a grain of true taste or even common sense, the effect would have been perfectly glorious. As it is, we have chaotic elements of a noble avenue, the contemplation of which gives us more pain than pleasure. We admire variety, as well as another; and especially in city architecture should monotony and tameness be avoided. But the laws of diversity are as strict and as imperative as the requirements of good morals or a good dinner; and the moment the eye is offended with an unmeaning incongruity or unsymmetrical abruptness, that instant we have left the realm of taste, and crossed the boundary of chaos. In music there are nearly as many discords as concords; but the proper distribution of discords, according to the immutable laws of proportion, is all that distinguishes harmony from the tuning of the instruments.[17]

On the cusp of, but not quite able to grow into, the protomodernist aesthetic of heterogeneity and discord, Foster complains about the "unmeaning" and "unsymmetrical" discords of Broadway. "Hastily erected to meet the emergencies of trade and traffic," buildings lack the guiding hand of taste. A shared sense of proportion, something that might serve as a bulwark against unplanned development, is absent.

To many people besides George Foster, Broadway was a crystallization of the diversity, size, and discord of the City itself. Especially in the mile between Bowling Green and Canal, Broadway provided local commentators and visitors with a chance to put their finger on the pulse of the City. One man counted the number of vehicles that passed in an hour.[18] Francis Trollope and Charles Dickens marveled at the profusion of elegant shops and colorful clothing and carriages: "plenty of hackney cabs and coaches too; gigs, phaetons, large-wheeled tilburies, and private carriages. . . . Negro coachmen and white; in straw hats, black hats, white hats, glazed caps, fur caps."[19] Another observer compared the sound produced by iron wheels on granite pavement by the commercial wagons and public omnibuses to Niagara Falls—a "great corroding roar."[20] Broadway was lined with retail stores, hotels, Stewart's famous department store, saloons, and entertainment such as P. T. Barnum's American Museum. "It was," says Spann, "the fashionable street of the nation, *the* place in democratic America for the successful to display their superior social status. . . . Wealthy women, conveyed down Broadway in their private carriages, came . . . to see and be seen . . . [and] to buy the best and the latest."[21] Broadway took on mythic status. Not only did all visitors have to see it, but New Yorkers swelled with pride at its magnificent chaos. In a *New York Evening Post* article concerned with a proposed horse-drawn railroad that would ruin Broadway, the avenue's vices become points of pride:

> The more the noise, the more the confusion, the greater the crowd, the better the lookers on and crowders seem to like it, and the world from the match-boy to the gentlemen of leisure, resort there to see the confusion, the uproar, and the sights while all enjoy it alike. The din, this driving, this omnibus-thunder, this squeezing, this jamming, crowding, and at times smashing, is the exhilarating music which charms the multitude and draws its thousands within the whirl. This is Broadway— this *makes* Broadway. Take from it those elements, the charm is gone.[22]

If Broadway served as a proud, unifying symbol of American life in which variety, even in its chaotic manifestations, was celebrated, nearby were other realities that exemplified growing estrangement. In his study of the industrial town of Newburyport, Massachusetts, Stephan Thernstrom has shown that the "warmth and security" of an "organic community" gave way in the 1840s to "the factory, the immigrant, the reign of the market."[23] One result of the armies of workingmen drifting from city to city in New England, finds Thernstrom, was the loss of "social knowledge of each other's residences and occupations."[24] Even in the small, "idyllic" town of Thoreau's Concord, there was social and economic disarray in the 1840s and 1850s.[25] Given such changes in smaller centers, the consequences of immigration, industrialization, and urbanization in New York City were naturally more dramatic. Comprised of both native and foreign-born individuals, the floating population residing in New York City in rented rooms or boarding houses was huge, with many in their twenties.[26] In addition, there were an estimated three thousand vagrant children on the streets of the lower City, and perhaps as many as fifty thousand not in school who should have been.[27] Many of the rootless, "floating" population of sailors, laborers, carters, porters, and drifting businessmen participated in the masculine culture of the Bowery—a culture known for its drinking, boisterousness, and public disorder, its gangs, "B'hoys" and "G'hals,"[28] its fire company rivalries, and its mob spirit in the theater.[29]

Edward Spann gives a vivid picture of the rootless population of New York City:

> In bad times and even more in good times, the city seemed to be in a state of flux, its people floating atoms in turbulent space. The rootless character of individual life was dramatically illustrated annually on May 1, the great moving day, when the streets were filled with people who, having given up or lost their annual leases . . . now all at once were caught up in the frenzy of moving their possessions to some new place in town, temporary nomads in the upheaving city. . . . Perhaps in no other city were even citizens so much strangers to each other.[30]

The atomism and estrangement experienced by New Yorkers had various other causes. One was the constant physical building and re-building—a result of the movement of private residences uptown, galloping commercial needs downtown, and a lack of respect for things old. In 1856 the editor of *Harper's Monthly* bemoaned the absence of past things: "New York is notoriously the largest and least loved of any of our great cities. . . . It is never the same city for a dozen years together. A man born in New York forty years ago finds nothing, absolutely nothing, of the New York he knew."[31] Another cause of the estrangement that engulfed New Yorkers—naturally there were differing versions of alienation for different groups—was the economic mobility and instability of the boom and bust economy. The rise and fall of merchants, speculators, and landholders tended to magnify the American absence of rigid social structure, so that there were in the course of a decade few fixed references of taste, value, or social identity.[32] Still another cause of estrangement, related to the floating population already mentioned, was the developing immigrant slums of the 1840s, particularly in the Fourth and Sixth Wards, which ran from a portion of the East River to Broadway. The Sixth Ward included not only City Hall and the fashionable portion of Broadway but Five Points, the most infamous slum in the nation. In 1850 the population density of a particular quarter of a square mile of Five Points was an estimated 45,000 people, an average of 18 people per house often crowded into unheated and unventilated attics or basements.[33] And the variety of different nationalities—typifying the problems of social fragmentation—was staggering. One block in Five Points in the 1850s contained 812 Irish, 218 Germans, 186 Italians, 189 Poles, 12 French, 9 English, 7 Portuguese, 2 Welsh, 39 Negroes, and 10 native Americans.[34]

Given the political decentering of the old Whig elite, the economic and social instability of the newer middle and upper classes, the multiplicity of ghetto cultures, and the persistent physical changes of the City, there was a growing and inevitable sense of relativism and alienation, in which each New Yorker, or group of New Yorkers, perceived a different face of otherness menacing to their self-interest.

In reaction to such fragmentation and estrangement, it is not surprising that a spirit of cultural conservatism and longing for homogeneity emerged in the breast of some native citizens—"a longing," in Sean Wilentz's words, "for a supposed golden age, before poverty, before immigrants, before social conflict."[35] In addition to nativism, another response to such massive uncontrollable growth was the emergence in the late 1850s of a strong city government in the person of Mayor Fernando Wood, who believed that only centralization and power in one man could bring order where there is "no such thing as *one* public mind."[36] And still another symptom of estrangement and moral fatigue was the success, somewhat earlier, of Charles G. Finney in bringing religious revivals to New York City.[37] Yet the nativist response to cultural fragmentation was doomed from the start, seeking, as it did, to turn back history. Fernando Wood's response of seeking expanded executive power was equally futile given the City's intensely local political tradition. Only evangelicalism seems to have tapped the substratum of urban experience for rich and poor alike and to have provided, for some at least, a unifying experience that answered their insecurity and disquietude.

II The Religious Context:
The National Scene 1800–1860

The social and material realities of city life were not the only influence on the style, substance, and organization of certain midcentury literature. The many religious denominations that competed for the spiritual and intellectual membership of Protestant Americans contributed also to the increasingly fragmented picture of national life.[38] Splintered by the upsurge of popular religious sentiments that grew to new sects and mass movements, religious life in America took on an extreme fragmentation; and this fragmentation of doctrines and movements, was, like the urban experience, a prominent motive for certain writers to create an analogy of the times in the mimetic and organizational properties of their

literary works. Not only are the many metaphysical viewpoints dramatized in *Moby-Dick* suggestive of the splintering going on in the religious
sphere in America, but even the idealist Emerson's immersion in the
problem of rotating moods and opinions cannot be separated from the
religious divisiveness that was occurring around him.

Two factors figure most prominently in the multiplication of religious
denominations and sects in nineteenth-century America: the democratic,
Enlightenment-based rationalism consolidated by the American Revolution and the emotionally oriented evangelicalism that arose from the
democratic masses drifting westward. As Nathan O. Hatch has put it,
"America's nonrestrictive environment permitted an unexpected and often explosive conjunction of evangelical fervor and popular sovereignty"
and it "was this engine that accelerated the process of Christianization
within American popular culture, allowing indigenous expressions of
faith to take hold among ordinary people."[39] Before the Revolution, the
American colonies already possessed a strongly "antiprelatical"[40] and antiauthoritarian bias. Afterward, the emphasis on individual free choice,
the separation of church and state, and the continued alienation of
"many common folk from gentry culture and its churches"[41] contributed
to the religious reformation that occurred.

The onset of Protestant revivalism and the emergence of sharp sectarian conflict are often associated with the Cane Ridge frontier revival in
1801. For a decade or two after the ratification of the Constitution, social,
political, and economic gains were the primary concern of most Americans. Church membership was low and religious activity uninspired.
There were, at this time, some sporadic revivals such as those in Connecticut.[42] Also, there were unmistakable signs of a more tolerant attitude
developing on the part of some Congregationalist and Presbyterian clergy.
Terrified by the atheism and religious rationalism of the Revolutionary
era, they began to consider a conversion experience, produced by a revival, as the basis for establishing church membership. And then, in the
old southwest, where the first awakening never really died, there occurred the famous revival at Cane Ridge, in Bourbon County, Kentucky,
which produced distant reverberations and which probably helped spur
the Second Great Awakening in New England.

The Cane Ridge revival lasted for weeks. It drew ministers from all
denominations who preached from stands to different sections of a crowd
of thousands and brought them to extreme states that included falling or
jerking or dancing when seized by the spirit.[43] "From this camp-meet-

ing," says Peter Cartwright (a prototypically vigorous frontier preacher who was a Kentucky teenager at the time of Cane Ridge), "the news spread through all the Churches, and through all the land, and it excited great wonder and surprise; . . . it kindled a religious flame that spread all over Kentucky and through many other states."[44] Cartwright also describes the ensuing internecine struggles in the Presbyterian Church between the old order and the "New Lights," which were typical of the sectarian fragmentation that revivalism also ushered in.[45]

The rise of Methodist and Baptist churches during the first half of the nineteenth century and the corresponding weakening of the Episcopal, Congregational, and Presbyterian churches were outgrowths in large part of the flood of migrants swarming westward and the religious opportunities opened by the new territories. Alone in a vast land, not only were these frontier folk spiritually needy, but their lack of education and uprooted condition meant that they were susceptible to a more emotional kind of appeal. In addition, there was the inescapable fact that the great number of ministers needed to preach to them could not possibly be met by intellectually trained ministers of the eastern seaboard divinity schools. In both number and level of appeal the more fiery sermons of the Methodist and Baptist churches triumphed. Methodism, as a result, no more than "a small and highly suspect adjunct to Anglicanism before the Revolution" with perhaps 65,000 members, had by 1844 become the largest religious body in America, with a million members, 4,000 itinerant preachers, and 7,700 local preachers. Even in New England, Methodism had become the second largest religious denomination.[46] The story of the liberal or "Free Will" portion of the Baptist movement, reacting against the Calvinism of the Regulars, was the same, with great gains especially on the frontier.[47]

This broad, sweeping assertion of newly vitalized denominations led to the diversitarian vision of religious life in America denoted by the term "denominationalism." On the one hand, denominationalism signified the realization of Enlightenment tolerance for all religions as equally valid.[48] On the other hand, it set up a competitive and antagonistic situation. In a liberal individual, it might elicit an ecumenical or transcendental spirit of the type reflected in William Ellery Channing the Younger's poem, "Wachusett":

From every village point at least three spires,
To satiate the good villagers' desires,

> Baptist, and Methodist, and Orthodox,
> And even Unitarian, creed that shocks
> Established church-folk; they are one to me,
> Who in the different creeds the same thing see.[49]

In a theologically conservative individual, it might elicit a dismay that the old doctrines and founding Protestant traditions had been splintered by new European groups and their sects. Philip Schaff, a prominent German Reformed Lutheran writing in 1845, questions the *"sect system,* which reigns especially in our own land, favored by its free institutions and the separation of the church from the state." [50] He goes on to say:

> Thus we have come gradually to have a host of sects, which it is no longer easy to number, and that still continues to swell from year to year. Where the process of separation is destined to end, no human calculation can foretell. Anyone who has, or fancies that he has, some inward experience and a ready tongue, may persuade himself that he is called to be a reformer; and so proceed, at once, in his spiritual vanity and pride, to a revolutionary rupture with the historical life of the church, to which he holds himself immeasurably superior.[51]

What this volatile sectarian atmosphere was like for the individual asked to choose among competing ministers, churches, and doctrines, and how this atmosphere influenced certain American writers, we will come to shortly. First, I want to complete the picture of religious fragmentation by moving to the situation of the established churches.

In the northeast among the established churches the tide of liberalization and revivalism, for the most part, meant weakening and fragmentation.[52] The historical record indicates many defections from Congregational ranks: of the wealthy to Episcopalianism, of the extreme evangelicals to Baptism, of the Boston liberals to Unitarianism, and of northwesterners to Presbyterianism. Presbyterianism did far better at holding members because of the far-reaching church organization of congregation, presbytery, synod, and assembly. Yet schism divided the Presbyterian Church as well. Different positions on slaveholding and abolition between northeastern and southern synods was one cause.[53] Another was the Plan of Union, formed in 1801 to counter the success of the Baptists, the Methodists, and other evangelicals in the West. The plan meant Congregationalist and Presbyterian settlers could join together to form one church with a minister from either denomination. The plan was quite successful, especially in the old northwest.[54] In the end, however, the merger became intolerable to some Presbyterians. The conservative wing, including the southern, proslavery synods, abrogated the Plan of Union in 1837, driving the liberal "New School" forces to form a separate church.[55]

On the level of theology, schism and conflict were also common among the established churches. In 1819 William Ellery Channing's Baltimore sermon produced such a conflict. Seeking to define American Unitarianism and distinguish it from more orthodox views, Channing was attacked by Jedediah Morse, the conservative editor of the *Panoplist*, who claimed American liberals were really very similar to English Unitarians and were concealing their heterodoxy. Channing rebutted in a pamphlet, but matters did not end there.[56] Moses Stuart of Andover took issue with Channing, who had also touched on matters of biblical interpretation. Stuart asserted that any portion of the Bible had ultimate timeless authority whether or not, as Channing asserted, it was in agreement with the general spirit of the rest of the Scripture.[57] To this challenge, Andrews Norton, who had just become Professor of Sacred Literature at Harvard, responded, claiming Stuart's approach to biblical interpretation was loose and inconsistent.[58] In addition, Leonard Woods, a member of the Andover faculty, challenged Channing's assumption about man's potential for Christ-like goodness; and this thrust for Arminianism was countered by Henry Ware, whose appointment over Morse in 1805 to Harvard signaled the beginning of Harvard's Unitarian reformation. The so-called Wood n' Ware Controversy "extended for four years and ran to five good-sized volumes, two by Woods . . . and three by Ware."[59]

This was only one of the many theological controversies of the day in New England, agitated by currents of German historical scholarship, by the "new measures" of Protestant revivalism, and by an acceptance of a liberal version of Arminianism (the belief that man can be an active agent in his own conviction of sin and conversion to Christ because he is neither powerless nor overwhelmingly sinful).[60]

The late but inevitable disestablishment of the standing churches in New England also contributed to the sense of fragmentation and destabilization, especially for Congregational and Presbyterian ministers.[61] Ann Douglas has written powerfully about the loss in status, theological authority, and job security that came with the end of state support for the traditional churches.[62] On the other hand, there were revealing exceptions on the part of those who changed with the times. Charles Finney, mentioned earlier for his successful revivals in New York City, was one of the Congregational and Presbyterian ministers whose powers grew during the 1820s and 1830s, because of his success in developing a psychologically effective method of preaching: everything about his revivals, from their advanced publicity, to his protracted, pressured meetings, was premeditated.[63] The other prominent exception was Lyman Beecher, who first feared disestablishment, but then realized that it compelled clergy to move closer to the needs of the people and to work more vigorously to maintain their leadership.[64]

The leveling effect of revival religion also had an impact on the free-thinking attitudes of certain individual worshipers. One result built on a tendency that had existed since earliest colonial times. Some individuals began to see it as their own right and within their own intuitive powers to achieve a direct personal knowledge of God's glory and his law. If the antinomian tendency, first manifested by Anne Hutchinson, was an early manifestation of this antiritualistic and antiauthoritarian religious strain, Jacksonian democracy brought with it a nineteenth-century variant. As Tocqueville had observed, equality makes a man want to judge everything for himself: "it gives him, in all things, a taste for the tangible and the real, a contempt for tradition and for forms."[65]

John Higham describes American culture at roughly this period as "a culture with a very indistinct sense of limits, a culture characterized by a spirit of boundlessness."[66] In order to better define this sense of boundlessness, he also refers to William Ellery Channing's 1841 lecture on "The Present Age" in which Channing focuses on the prevalence of "universality," the tendency to democratize all knowledge, and "expansion," the tendency to fly into transcendental and unexplored realms and to honor no spiritual or intellectual boundaries.[67]

In addition to the well-known Transcendentalist group, the range of religious diversity and innovation in this expansive era was quite remarkable. There was the millennialism of William Miller, who believed that in 1843 the Second Coming would occur, and who gained broad appeal as a revivalist in the early 1840s, leaving a legacy of Adventist movements despite the failure of his own prediction.[68] There was Universalism, which grew out of the belief that through Christ it is God's purpose to save all mankind, and which evolved into a doctrine quite similar to Unitarianism for the rural and less educated population. More exotic, there was Mormonism, founded by Joseph Smith, Jr., a young uneducated man in Palmyra, New York. In the late 1820s Smith claimed to have found golden plates "giving an accout of the former inhabitants of this continent, and the sources from whence they sprang." He claimed that the "fullness of the everlasting Gospel was contained" on the plates and that there was as well, fastened to a breastplate, two seer stones "that God had prepared . . . for the purpose of translating the book."[69] By 1830 Smith claimed he had translated these plates into a new Bible, the Book of Mormon. Also appealing to people's appetite for the unbounded and the esoteric was Swedenborgianism, with its method of biblical exegesis and theory of correspondence, and its influence in diverse areas such as health, sex, and spiritualism. Finally, there were the Christian communities: the Shakers, founded by Mother Anna Lee, which spread millennialist communities; The Community of the Publick Universal Friend, a similar movement, founded by Jemima Wilkinson;[70] the German pietistic communities such as the "Rappites"; the Oneida community, a Christian, socialistic group founded by John Humphrey Noyes, with nonconformist views of marriage; and Hopedale, founded by Adin Ballou, a Universalist minister who believed he could bring God's kingdom to earth by establishing economically successful Christian communities.[71]

Perhaps the best picture of the multiple religious denominations and sects in America in middle of the nineteenth century can be gotten from a description of the Chardon Street Convention, sponsored by the Friends of Universal Reform and held in Boston in November 1840. The Chardon Street Convention, described in *The Dial* in 1842, was probably as close to Cane Ridge as Boston would come:

> These meetings attracted a great deal of public attention, and were spoken of in different circles in every note of hope, of sympathy, of joy, of alarm, of abhorrence and of merriment. The composition of the assembly was rich and various. The singularity and latitude of the summons drew together, from all parts of New England and also from the Middle States, men of every shade of opinion from the straitest orthodoxy to the wildest heresy, and many persons whose church was a church of one member only. A great variety of dialect and costume was noticed; a great deal of confusion, eccentricity and freak appeared, as well as of zeal and enthusiasm. If the assembly was disorderly, it was picturesque. Madmen, madwomen, men with beards, Dunkers, Muggletonians, Come-outers, Groaners, Agrarians, Seventh-day Baptists, Quakers, Abolitionists, Calvinists, Unitarians and Philosophers,—all came successively to the top, and seized their moment, if not their hour, wherein to chide, or pray, or preach, or protest. . . . If there was not parliamentary order, there was

life, and the assurance of that constitutional love of religion and religious liberty which, in all periods, characterizes the inhabitants of this part of America.[72]

The next day, *The Boston Evening Transcript* could not resist a chuckle at the participants for their love of religious liberty to the point where they rejected the idea "of so far abridging the freedom of each individual member" to elect a "presiding officer, to keep order at the meeting." A good deal of the day, the newspaper reported, was given over to this procedural issue, which lost.[73]

What effect did all this interdenominational competition have on the individual, not only those men and women on the frontier but those in New York, Boston, and New England?

In assessing this question, one factor worth keeping in mind is that for every church member who had undergone a conversion there were many "sympathizers" who rented pews and attended church regularly. A reliable estimate concerning the Presbyterian Church is that there was an eight to one ratio, so that if there were 250,000 national members in 1836, there were two million "allied population."[74] This "allied" group was the potential source of converts during revivals; but they were also the potential defectors to other churches, and their mixture of resistance to conversion yet sympathy to church life suggests that they were open to consider alternative and competing theologies so long as these did not violate their general religious outlook. Also, if they were literate, as many Americans were,[75] another relevant factor is their exposure to religious tracts, periodicals, and newspapers, where doctrines were debated and religious wars detailed. "It seems an inescapable conclusion," says Whitney R. Cross, "that a considerable proportion even of laymen read and relished the theological treatises."[76] And in addition to the religious newspapers and magazines, there was also religious fiction, which often dramatized a conflict faced by a woman between faith and skeptical rationalism, or between a form of Protestantism and Catholicism.[77] All in all, Americans would have been exposed through semons, lectures, their own reading, and, most important probably, the inevitable discussions and arguments in the workplace, the tavern, or the town square, to consider many different religious issues, and to weigh them in their own minds: What was the appropriate education for a minister? Were itinerant ministers and their "new measures" part of the showering of divine intention or instances of apostasy? And what was the right degree of reform to be adopted from the old dogmas of divine sovereignty, human powerlessness and total depravity, and free grace? Was man's soul capable of being an active agent for his own conversion? Was his nature more good than evil? Was Christ a supernatural being or a model man? These were many of the issues swirling around in the turbulent reformation of the nineteenth century.

One result of all this interdenominational struggle and heightened consciousness about religious issues was that people not uncommonly changed churches.[78] Certainly among the mobile, immigrant, frontier group, proximity was often a large determinant for church affiliation. And in New England there is evidence, for different reasons certainly, of a fair degree of change: out of thirty prominent New England spokeswomen studied by Ann Douglas, for example, about half changed churches at least once.[79] Some of these changes may not signify deep theological shifts. But sometimes the shifts were significant and reflected the swirling religious atmosphere. In the course of his life, Orestes Brownson went from Presbyterian, to Universalist, to Unitarian, to Transcendentalist, to Catholic—becoming with his conversion to Catholicism one of the most prestigious of the hundreds of thousands who converted to Catholicism in the nineteenth century.[80]

Others who struggled with religious truths simply avoided churches altogether. If they possessed sufficient independence of mind and literacy, the sectarian rivalries often produced a skeptical distance from all churches and dogmas. Lucy Smith, the mother of the Joseph Smith, Jr. who founded Mormonism, says in her memoirs, "I spent much of my time in reading the Bible and praying; but, notwithstanding my great anxiety to experience a change of heart, another matter would always interpose in all my meditations—If I remain a member of no church all religious people will say I am of the world; and if I join some one of the different denominations, all the rest will say I am in error. No church will admit that I am right, except the one with which I am associated."[81] The only truly uncorrupted position, in other words, is distance from denominations and dogma—a position we will find later in Emily Dickinson. Lucy Smith's famous son Joseph initially inherited her rejection of camp meetings. He said to his mother: "I can take my Bible, and go into the woods and learn more in two hours than you can learn at meeting in two years, if you should go all the time."[82] Yet the pressure of competing sects was evidently powerful, especially during periods of revival. Joseph lived within thirty miles of a Shaker community and twenty-five miles of a Universal Friend community, as well as having been exposed to the innumerable revivalists who gave western New York the spiritually seared appellation of the Burnt-over District.[83] Understandably, when Joseph had his first religious vision sometime in his early teens, he reported that "My object in going . . . [into the woods to pray] was to know which of all the sects was right, that I might know which to join."[84]

This nineteenth-century atmosphere of diverse and competing religious denominations is the historical background that buttressed Melville's attraction to dramatizing in *Moby-Dick* an ever-shifting array of metaphysical viewpoints. Clearly, Melville wanted to represent, within the metaphysical scheme of his work, the experience of oscillating viewpoints about the Deity; and it is likely that his interest derived not only from his own vacillations between belief and disbelief but from the religious shifts that many Americans were undergoing. Admittedly, these oscillations on the part of others were often more theologically specific and denominationally identifiable, not couched in the general theological categories of "malignity" and "benignity" used by Melville. Nevertheless, it seems reasonable to observe that, in his increasingly relativistic age, Melville was trying to reflect the prevalence of warring religious concerns about the nature of God, man, and truth. And his method, as I will demonstrate in Chapter 4, was to structure a representative analogy or allegory in which heterogeneous Matter and fluctuating Mind interacted and created for the reader the effect of oscillating metaphysical perspectives. These oscillations simulated the contemporary experience in religion as well as the loss of stable points of reference in other domains.

In Chapter 3 I will be describing Emerson's interest in the shifting moods and multivalenced perspectives that addled his ideal philosophy. The external climate of divergent religious and social enthusiasms, however, cannot be ignored as an influence on his mind and art. Mary Kupiec Cayton describes Emerson's situation as the minister of Boston's Second Church from 1829 to 1832, where he was surrounded by conflict between Unitarians and orthodox evangelicals led by Lyman Beecher, and where Emerson preached that both sides of the controversy were sacrificing a true relation to their souls and Christian morality in favor of partisan issues.[85] In a somewhat later period, when he had already left the church and become a lecturer and writer, Boston's social and religious context was even more powerfully characterized for Emerson by the variety and disarray of opinions. Although the possibility of underlying spiritual unity is never forsaken, Emerson's journal entries from the years 1838–1841 suggest his sense of cultural diversity and disarray:

> Yet see how daring is the speculation, the reading, the reforming of the time[;] see how many cotemporaneous parts prosper in Magnetism, Phrenology, Transcendentalism, Abolition, Anti Govt. Dietetics Association. . . . If now some genius should arise who could unite these!

> On rolls the old world and these fugitive colors of political opinion . . . chase each other over the wide encampments of mankind, whig, tory; pro- & anti-slavery; Catholic, Protestant. . . .

> A good deal of character in our abused age. The rights of woman, the antislavery,—temperance,—peace,—health,—and money movements; female speakers, mobs, & martyrs, the paradoxes, the antagonism of old & new, the anomalous church, the daring mysticism & the plain prose, the uneasy relations of domestics, the struggling toward better household arrangements—all these indicate life at the heart not yet justly organized at the surface.[86]

To some degree, Emerson was always able to reconcile the multiplicity of enthusiastic options of the times with his underlying idealism. But these passages do suggest—his ideal view of the origin of these leading tendencies notwithstanding—that the religious volatility of the times was a factor in shaping his interest in fluid, shifting viewpoints. Indeed, it would appear that the constant pressure of this multiplicity can not be ignored in a complete view of Emerson's subjectivity; and that while he viewed this multiplicity as an upsurge and working through of greater spirit in human history, a qualification of his view from a temporal and historical standpoint is necessary. What was going on outside him, as the above passages indicate, had a definite effect on the alternating manner in which he viewed his inner life.

As for Walt Whitman, he acknowledges that he is deliberately creating in his poems an analogical representation of the multiplicity of his age. He says in his 1876 preface to *Leaves of Grass* that his "form" had "strictly grown from" his "purports and facts" and "is the analogy of them."[87] And while clearly the social and material variety on the streets of New York is the greater influence on his form, the religious panorama of nineteenth-century life was also a factor. As George B. Hutchinson has argued, "our understanding of Whitman and of his broadest cultural significance should link the poet to the widespread religious movements of his age"—to what Hutchinson nicely describes as "the individualistic spiritual immediatism" spreading across America.[88] For if all religions (as Whitman would likely put it) were equally spiritual and American, equally true and false, then their common denominator, the Oversoul coursing through his spirit, could only be fully appreciated if one saw the historical corruptions of this spirit in the narrow, confining, disputatious denominations of the age. Their limitations, splinterings, and rivalries were the implicit argument in favor of Whitman's universal power. Only when each man was a church unto himself would the democratization of religion be complete.[89]

III The Philosophical-Psychological Context: The Changing Idea of the Self

I have been trying to suggest a way in which it is possible to see literary works in terms of a causal relation, translated by the imagination, between prominent social and religious forces in the background and the artworks themselves. As I have implied, it is also possible, to a certain extent, to demonstrate that relationship. What is required is an excavation and definition of deep-seated social perspectives and sufficient evidence about shared cultural dilemmas to claim that many individuals, literary artists included, constructed their image of the world similarly and did so because they shared, not only a problem, but a prevalent thought-form for describing it—in the case of my study, democratic diversitarianism.

Sketching in the effect of the philosophical and psychological context on literature is somewhat easier than defining the effect of urban and religious changes. Since philosophical and psychological developments involved changes in conception of inner nature, it is easier to point to literary consequences in how human nature was reconceived and literary vision reanimated.

Both Romanticism and scientific empiricism were the origin of these new, vitalized approaches. Separately and together, they led to the construction of a newly diversified and fugitive self—a self that was comprised of many sides, that continuously presented new fronts and possessed deep and elusive foundations or essences. Romantic correspondence, in the process of redefinition, opened the doorway for exploring subjective depths through the use of external symbols. Empiricism offered new evolutionary ways to conceive of human nature as well as new ways to reduce and divide the mind into parts to which particular behavior could be ascribed. In both romantic and scientific realms, the idea of a human being ultimately ordered by affinity to a higher spiritual realm was replaced by a conception of the self as transient, varying, successive, and unstable. And it was inescapable that in the effort to represent such a self, patterns of oscillation and segmentary fragmentation would be dominant.

Recalling a trip to Boston from his ministry in Bangor, Maine, Frederic Henry Hedge remembers how in 1836 the three founding members of the Transcendental Club,

> Mr. Emerson, George Ripley, and myself . . . chanced to confer together on the state of current opinion in theology and philosophy, which we agreed in thinking very unsatisfactory. Could anything be done in the way of protest and introduction of deeper and broader views? What precisely we wanted it would have been difficult for . . . us to state. What we strongly felt was dissatisfaction with the reigning sensuous philosophy, dating from Locke, on which our Unitarian theology was based. The writing of Coleridge, recently edited by Marsh, and some of Carlyle's earlier essays . . . had created a ferment in the minds of some of the young clergy of that day. There was a promise in the air of a new era of intellectual life.[90]

James Marsh, professor of philosophy and president of the University of Vermont from 1826 to 1833, had familiarized a number of bright young men with Coleridge, some through his teaching and others through his writings. Marsh was dissatisfied with the undue emphasis placed by both his own Congregational Church and the Unitarian Church on external evidence and authority. Neither the orthodox preoccupation with the authority of Scripture nor the Unitarian emphases on sensationalism and biblical scholarship answered Marsh's need for an individual, intuitive basis for belief.[91]

The Scottish Common Sense philosophy, a simplification of Lockean thought that dominated New England religion and philosophy in the first half of the nineteenth century, was the direct source of Marsh's dissatisfaction. A reaction to the corrosive skepticism of Hume, Common Sense philosophy had been a fitting adaptation of Locke for the times. As Daniel Howe has put it, it "answered the desires of an expanding, dynamic society especially well by accepting material things at face value and discouraging idle speculation."[92] Not unrelated, Common Sense philosophy was also the foundation of both Unitarian epistemology and nineteenth-century science. During this period, theologian and scientist alike believed that science was reconcilable with biblical descriptions of the creation of the earth, the origin of man, and miracles of the Old and New Testaments. They believed that "knowledge about God and knowledge about the world are of the same kind," and that "in the process of investigating one a person always makes discoveries about the other."[93] They argued that if a scientist's findings deviated from religion, something might "be wrong with his methods, motives, or data."[94]

In this cultural context Marsh published Coleridge's *Aids to Reflection* in 1829, with his long preliminary essay. As Alexander Kern has put it, Coleridge "furnished the spark which set off the intellectual reaction."[95] There had been exposure to German and other forms of transcendental thought in the translation of Madame de Staël's *De l'Allemagne*, in August Schlegel's ideas on the "classical" and the "romantic," in articles in the *North American Review*, and in Sampson Reed's *Observations on the Growth of the Mind* (1826). Yet, as Kern has put it, Marsh's book was spark put to tinder; and by 1836, when Hedge, Ripley, and Emerson began to draw people together to form their discussion and editorial group for a new journal, the desire for change was strong.

Unitarianism failed to recognize what was felt to be an accessible spiritual reality; it offered, instead, external "evidences" of God to which the rational individual assented when these arguments were presented by an ecclesiastical and scholarly elite. Coleridge, on the other hand, described a reason higher than understanding that participated in a spiritual reality embracing man and nature and carrying man to a more complete perception of life; and he emphasized a living religious faith that arose from immediate conviction, not systematic rational evidence. For Coleridge, reason, Christ, and universal spirit were one and the same unconditioned ground out of which arose both mind and world.

The Transcendentalist group around Boston was ready to grasp the new vision. The worldview of their powerful but unsatisfying fathers lacked some essential ingredient. They felt an emotional need for intensity of life and for spiritual warmth. They wanted an active spiritual relation to the world, a way into a living universe so that the heart and mind could feel a part of it. And if Coleridge's higher reason was the spiritual agency, the bridge between the mind and the world aesthetically and psychologically was the idea of correspondence.

While Coleridge's *Aids to Reflection* did not pursue the aesthetic implications of correspondence, his other writings on the imagination and symbolism did point toward a reciprocal unfolding of mind and world — the kind of literary exploration of the psyche that he hazarded himself in "Kubla Khan." With roots not only in Romanticism and Platonism, but also in American Puritanism,[96] correspondence flourished as a thought-form in America in the 1830s. The currency of terms such as analogy, identity, type, sign, symbol, and emblem[97] derived from the growing view that there was an underlying unity between the material universe and the world of spirit, and that perception of this unity was accessible to the individual through living perception or through art. That material facts are symbols of spiritual facts, that "nature is the symbol of the spirit,"[98] carried the poet-philosopher or natural theologian into a range of correspondential observations, some didactic or philosophical, some transformative or ecstatic, and some a mixture of the ecstatic and the philosophical.

Clearly a reaction against external religious authority and the sterility of Common Sense philosophy, this quest for a living correspondence between world and spirit often involved as well a wish for greater contact with emotion. Usually, as William Ellery Channing desired, it was a hope for nature or art to provide natural phenomena that correspond with unrealized feelings of "infinite love." Margaret Fuller manifests this tendency when she says, "Only by emotion do we know thee, Nature. To lean upon thy heart, and feel its pulses vibrate to our own; — that is knowledge, for that is love, the love of infinite beauty, of infinite love. Thought will never make us born again."[99] John Sullivan Dwight, writing about music, expresses the Transcendentalist view that the arts also "can convey a foretaste of moods and states of feeling yet in reserve for the soul, of loves which yet have never met an object that could call them out."[100] The type of the feelings sought here were predominantly tender ones, fringed with religious sentiment; they were feelings that carried the individual upward, out of self-concern and desire, into a realm of high sentiment and delicate affirmations.[101]

Yet, despite this spiritualizing tendency, it was inevitable that correspondence drew the more psychologically adventurous toward a revelation of psychic depths and the expression of private anguish.

Correspondence depended on subjectivity. It did not really require a belief in the circulation of the spirit through nature and man as Transcendentalists such as Emerson envisioned. Given the emphasis of Transcendentalism on self-realization, there developed, consequently, in those not preoccupied by religious sentiment, a richer, more variegated unfolding between emotion and scene. Certain literary figures in particular, reflecting the diversitarian spirit of Romanticism, could not help but realize that the means to individual vision was exactly through an ever-shifting and deepening interaction between internal depths and external scenes.

Emerson, who misses very little, had sensed the potential. His own interest was never in depth psychology, but in psychophilosophy—in the variety of philosophic viewpoints about idealism and correspondence revealed by a devotion to the variousness of human moods. Nevertheless, early in his career, he had said not only that "Nature always wears the colors of the spirit"[102] but that "Every appearance in nature corresponds to some state of the mind, and that state of the mind can only be described by presenting that natural appearance as its picture."[103] It required the fiction of Poe, Hawthorne, and Melville, however, for the objectification of psychic states to become realized as a vehicle for exploring the unconscious of the individual. One thinks of Poe's use of the physical deterioration of the House of Usher to symbolize Roderick's mental condition; or Hawthorne's use of dream-vision to symbolize Robin's rage at his Royalist uncle in "My Kinsman, Major Molineux"; or even Ahab's transference of his rage at a cruel Fate or Deity to "the abhorred white whale," which he then "pitted himself, all mutilated, against."[104]

However, once a thinker is committed to following the different feelings that nature can reveal in him, the attraction to this subjective journey can also exceed the spiritual confidence that first authorized it. This is the story Melville tells in *Pierre; or, The Ambiguities* (1852), where a young man feels divinely inspired to idealistic action, only to discover that there is no answering height, no actively concerned Deity, and that his confidence in correspondence is a delusion. Subjective idealism becomes subjective relativism, extremely rich from an artistic standpoint but philosophically terrifying. This is also the dilemma that the later Emerson explored when moments of transcendence became less frequent and the fragmentary viewpoints he experienced seemed as though they exhausted the range of human experience.

Empirical science, which was an even stronger influence at the time than romantic idealism, also led to a fragmentary view of the self. The history of psychology in the nineteenth century is, in fact, a *descendental* process: the approach to the deep forces of the mind descends from idealist concerns to an increasingly materialist analysis of its component parts. If the end product is Freud's dynamic view of the parts of the mind, the decisive revision is Darwin's linking of lower with higher life.

Early German romantic theory on the psychology of art, wishing to convey the natural and spontaneous processes of creativity, repeatedly used the concept of the unconscious. Goethe conveys this when he says, "I believe that everything which genius does as genius, eventuates unconsciously."[105] Although they did not use the word as commonly as the Germans, English romantic poets were also concerned with lower levels of the mind. Blake's early defense of instinct and attack on repression, his and Wordsworth's advocacy for the child as the father of the man, and Coleridge's assimilation of German ideas about the "unconscious activity" of the creative genius,[106] all anticipate later developments. In America, as an important part of his effort to shift "the ground of religion from church to psyche,"[107] Emerson also placed considerable emphasis on the term "unconscious." As Jeffrey Steele explains by first quoting from Octavius Frothingham, " 'Transcendentalism . . . was an assertion of the immanence of divinity in instinct, the transference of supernatural attributes to the natural constitution of mankind.' This internalization of godhead," Steele continues, "depended upon the acceptance of a new psychological language" and "the key term in this new psychological language is what Emerson calls 'the Unconscious'."[108] In short, in both European and American Romanticism, the unconscious was viewed as a wellspring for authentic action, originality, spiritual insight, and full development. To some degree the linking of higher and lower nature had begun, although the overriding emphasis so far was on the unconscious as an ocean of ideal energies, a fountainhead for the enlargement of humankind.

The abundant romantic vision of the mind, however, was to undergo a transformation after the mid-nineteenth century at the hands of the increasing power of materialism and science. Until 1850 science and religion were able to coexist to some degree in America.[109] Scientists attempted, with some sense of success, to reconcile scientific discoveries with the story of the Bible. Indirectly, what was at stake, in addition to biblical authority, was a spiritually unified view of man. John C. Burnham attempts to elucidate this gradual victory of a nonreligious science over religion in nineteenth-century America by examining the attempt to explain the mind by accounting for "phenomenon in terms of events on a lower level." Describing this tendency as the "major intellectual strategy of the nineteenth and early twentieth centuries," Burnham defines reductionism as "a relentless pursuit of the idea that knowledge of components led to knowledge of causes." By studying the reductivistic impulse, he believes it is possible to show, "in the psychological-medical realm," how "the initial concept was the soul, and the final intellectual product was dissociative phenomena."[110] He points to phrenology as "the first challenge to the unitary soul," adding that even when phrenology had died out "the pattern of thinking of people's behavior in terms of independent units based on brain divisions" persisted, leading in the late nineteenth century to trends in neuroanatomy and neurophysiology, and in the early twentieth century to instinct theory.[111]

Scientific work in evolutionary studies also began to play a role in the formation of views of the mind. Darwin's work and even pre-Darwinian evolutionary studies began to suggest the transformational continuity from lower to higher creatures in the animal kingdom. Earlier views of fixed gradations of nature in the great chain of being had placed man at the midpoint between the spiritual and the material. The individual was urged to drive a wedge between his rational and animal propensities—to follow spiritual reason and to avoid animal passion. But with the increasing recognition of mankind's lowly origins, this approach underwent a slow revision. By the 1840s, when Tennyson was composing "In Memoriam," evolutionary science was already disturbing enough for Tennyson to want to reject "the cunning casts of clay" of a reductive scientific materialism:

> Let Science prove we are [cunning casts of clay], and then
>   What matters Science unto men,
> At least to me? I would not stay.
>
> Let him, the wiser man who springs
>   Hereafter, up from childhood, shape
>   His actions like the greater ape,
> But I was *born* to other things.

Such a prospect compelled Tennyson to cry: "Arise and fly / The reeling Faun, the sensual feast; / Move upward, working out the beast, and let the ape and tiger die."[112] Yet with the advent of *The Origin of the Species* (1859), it became far more difficult to "let the ape and tiger die." Darwin himself, at great pains to indicate his respect for the central and superior position of man in the natural world, nevertheless is most explicit. This is the final sentence of *The Descent of Man* (1871):

> We must, however, acknowledge . . . that man with all his noble quali-
> ties, with sympathy which feels for the most debased, with benevolence
> which extends not only to other men but to the humblest living crea-
> tures, with his god-like intellect which has penetrated into the move-
> ments and constitution of the solar system—with all these exalted pow-
> ers—Man still bears in his bodily frame the indelible stamp of his lowly
> origins.[113]

If we adopt for a moment a telescopic view beyond the time-frame of this study, we can see that Darwin's painful concession led forty years later to Freud's view of early instinctive life as a foundation of human nature. Freud believed that either we learn to acquaint ourselves with and make an accommodation to our unconscious life or human experi-ence will always be characterized by ignorance, blindness, and neurotic suffering.[114] The influence of Darwin on the evolutionary social theories of Herbert Spencer, in particular Spencer's belief in the "survival of the fittest," is well known. In twentieth-century literature the influence of this naturalistic approach to human nature is also clearly discernible, for example, in the influence of Spencer on Jack London in *Call of the Wild* (1903), on Theodore Dreiser in *The Titan* (1914), on Ernest Hemingway's interest in the bullfight and the safari as symbolic rituals of self-realiza-tion, and in the fiction of Norman Mailer, commencing with *An American Dream* (1964). In each case, the writer's view of human nature is shaped by the idea and image of the animalism of the unconscious.[115] Yet the first and perhaps most powerful statement of this naturalistic perspective oc-curred long before in *Moby-Dick*.

Melville was always a theologian first before he was a psychologist. Reasoning in *Moby-Dick* by analogy, as would a natural theologian, Mel-ville inferred the possible nature of the Deity from the attributes of his natural creation. Yet Melville was also a naturalistic psychologist. Stirred by the myriad and contradictory modes of nature, Melville used them to gain an intuitive grasp of the diverse aspects of the mind. He worked from an intuition of the psychological correspondence of man with the mo-dalities of nature. Melville's view of man in *Moby-Dick* ranges from "sword-fish, and sharks," through every gradation of aggression and delicateness he observes in the whale, to the "gentle thoughts of the feminine air" embodied in the "snow-white wings of small, unspeckled birds."[116] And if, as comparative anatomists and embryologists were finding, the history of the embyro recapitulates the evolutionary history of the species, then Melville's view was not only accurate scientifically, but opened up a profound panorama on the multiple links of human nature to its evolutionary origins.

Leon Chai remarks somewhat gnomically that the theory of correspondence is a corollary of the *scala natura* or great chain of being.[117] He means, I assume, that creatures near man on the chain are fitting objects for correspondential intuitions. With the acceptance of the evolutionary ladder that linked man "indelibly" with lower orders of animals, there was an even more powerful inducement to approach human nature through correspondences with the animal world. As Chapter 4 will discuss, this approach led Melville to a view of human nature that included all sorts of animal parallelism. Ultimately, Melville's correspondential psychology, combined with an impressive vitalism, comprises the unifying element that holds together his dizzyingly fragmented vision of man.

In the nineteenth century, as the spiritual, unitary view of the mind splintered into various parts, scientific analysis replaced holistic intuition. The words "mind" and "self" began to be used interchangeably with "soul" or "spirit."[118] Steadily, also, reductive analyses, with recourse to lower levels of mental life, were felt to offer the best explanations of the mind's activity. Whether it was the multiple faculty organs of phrenology, the diversity of basic drives in instinct theory, or the analogy to animals, human psychology had undergone a near total inversion. The primary determining forces of life to which the conscious individual had to give attention were now those elements of lower nature that were anathema to an earlier worldview. In many respects, Melville makes this transition far earlier than most while retaining the metaphysical overview because of his inability to fully believe or disbelieve. Emerson, more steady in his faith in unity despite his recognition of fragmentation, does not truly enter the new view of depth psychology although he understands it.[119] Emerson's greatness, as we shall see in the next chapter, is to be found in his courageous submission to subjective flux and to the problem of identity that arises from fragmentary consciousness.

PART TWO

The Manyness of Things

3

Shooting the Gulf:
Emerson's Sense of Experience

I

In moving from cultural context to the study of an individual writer, there is a danger, on the one hand, that cultural generalizations will be applied without adequate exploration of the writer's uniqueness and, on the other hand, that the writer's uniqueness will become so particularized that similarities with a general cultural pattern will be impossible to see. The reducing of a writer to a cultural pattern is the excess that a literary study most needs to avoid, while the pitfall most likely to endanger a work of cultural history is growing too concerned with literary detail. In this study, which is primarily a work of literary analysis, it is important to avoid reducing a writer's viewpoint in order to bring it into harmony with his or her cultural context. There is also another methodological problem. Having planned to include chapters about cultural forces that shape the literary text, how can one avoid drawing the context to suit the text? How can one avoid selecting the details of the context to dovetail with the details of the work in question, so that the fit is neat and the study is tight? In other words, how can one avoid predetermination? There must always be deductive planning; books must be organized from top down as well as built with an edifice of fact and perception from bottom up.

My approach has been to study the individual writer, not excluding cultural background, but emphasizing the theme of fragmentation in the writer's text. Then I have examined the pattern of fragmentation in a particular cultural domain. And, finally, only after this pattern has been defined, have I returned to the writer one more time, to understand his or her particularity of vision in light of encircling cultural tendencies. At this point, we can see the congruences, but we can also see the differences, the things that are probably best accounted for by the writer's individuality—by his or her psychology and imagination. These similarities between writer and context may even contain subtle differences and the differences subtle similarities, but it is important to remember that we are looking at ideas and literary works arising from either the New York or New England cultural environment. Similarities or differences, when they exist, are not apt to be absolute but often more variations on a common theme.

In the case of Ralph Waldo Emerson, his primary similarity to those around him is his dissatisfaction with Unitarianism and his recourse to a recovery of feeling and to romantic idealism. A major difference between Emerson and most of his Boston romantic peers is that his idealism was shaped by another influence—rationalism and its empirical method. Empiricism ultimately resulted in the development of a psychological realism that pointed him inward to his subjectivity rather than outward to the study of nature. Emerson was not entirely alone in this fusion of idealism with the rationalist tendencies of Unitarianism and scientific empiricism. The work of several other Transcendentalist ministers and humanists also manifested this combination. In the case of Theodore Parker, it led to biblical research in the tradition of German "higher criticism";[1] in the case of Henry David Thoreau, it led to the study of nature. In Emerson's case, it led to psychological research. This was not research into unconscious depths but a self-conscious and detached study of his subjectivity. Finally, in addition to the synthesis of a "warm" idealism with an empirical interest in the flux of the mind, there is a third constituent of Emerson's sense of experience, one that perhaps can only be explained biographically and psychologically. I refer to Emerson's emphasis on life as transition, his doctrine of letting go of all forms of security, and yielding hour by hour to transformations of mood and viewpoint. To use a metaphor from the world of Lewis and Clark, Emerson was willing to "shoot the gulf."

Seeking answers to problems of identity and vocation, Emerson's solution was, as I have indicated, an individual response to the general complaint about the impersonality of Unitarianism. Specifically, it was to envision a fluid, creative, divine spirit that "does not build up nature around us, but puts it forth through us, as the life of the tree puts forth new branches."[2] This version of romantic idealism involved a spontaneous intuition of divine energy and an active god-like role for man as "the creator in the finite" (CW, 1:38). Emerson's descriptions, moreover, of an "influx of spirit" (CW, 1:45) and an "instantaneous in-streaming causing power" (CW, 1:43) are highly suggestive of a psychological relief he found from the lassitude and self-doubt about which he often complained[3] and which was typical, on a philosophical plane, of the impasse described by Hedge, Ripley, and Marsh. In addition to closing the gap between the soul and the "Not-Me" that a "corpse-cold" Unitarianism was unable to address, it is possible that Emerson's characterization of an in-rushing spirit may well convey the filling of the void created by the absence of a father in his development.[4] We can note, for instance, that he explicitly equates reason and spirit with a father at one point in Nature: "That which, intellectually considered, we call Reason, considered in relation to nature, we call Spirit. . . . And man in all ages and countries, embodies it in his language, as the FATHER" (CW, 1:19).

This entry "from within or behind" of a light that "shines through us upon things" (CW, 2:161) came to Emerson with emotional depth upon his engagement and marriage to Ellen Tucker in 1828–29. Surprisingly, he was even able to carry it through the period of mourning after her death in 1831. Gay Wilson Allen has claimed that Ellen "thawed his emotions and expanded his sympathies."[5] And Robert Milder has extended this insight, claiming that the emotional thawing led to a "heart knowledge of religion that separated Emerson from the Unitarian gospel" of rationalism and gradual moral transformation.[6] Consequently, "affection" played an important role in Emerson's view of religious regeneration and ecstatic perception, just as it did for Brownson, Fuller, and Channing (CW, 2:114). Whether these were the "holiest affections" (CW, 1:44) in the tradition of Jonathan Edwards, the reverberations of the "common" or universal heart Emerson described in "The Over-Soul" (CW, 2:160, 170), or the intense feelings of love for his wife (JMN, 3:248–49), "affection" figured significantly thereafter in Emerson's notion of spirit.[7]

Let me defer for a moment my discussion of Emerson's rationalism and touch briefly on what I have described already as the third aspect of Emerson's sense of experience—his preoccupation with temporality. In teaching "the infinitude of the private man" (JMN, 7:324), Emerson embraced the paradox of the eternal spirit being identical with the flux of processional consciousness. He never did justice to this problem philosophically.[8] His interest lay in temporality, in the transience of mood and viewpoint, regardless how subtle or self-contradictory. When one compares Emerson's affinity for change, for example, with Orestes Brownson's (whose ideas changed more than any of his contemporaries[9]) what is apparent is that Emerson's interest in change was not on the level of abstract idea or dogma but involved immediate subjective experience. Emerson was committed to a progressive, dynamic view of nature and man as they were manifested in the fluidity of human consciousness. And the origins of this unique aspect of his mind were highly individualized, originating psychologically and biographically more than from his reading or from the rapidly changing "spirit of the times" to which he often referred. To account for this, one has to consider, first, the many losses of intimate family members Emerson suffered by the time he was thirtynine—a father, two brothers, a young wife, and a child. Add to this his serious concern about his own health in the late 1820s and early 1830s. And then there is his renunciation of his career in the ministry, which left him open to an uncertain future, without professional or intellectual security. Finally, there is his aspiration in the mid-1830s to become a poet—someone, he envisioned, who watched the metamorphosis of mind and nature, with a passionate devotion to perception as the fountainhead of beauty and truth. If the reforming "spirit of the times" was also an influence, as no doubt it was, as often as not it echoed the internal transformations he was undergoing. For these reasons, I would argue, the origin of his openness to psychic change was to an important extent anachronistic and private, the result of personal history.

The other factor in Emerson's sense of experience is his rationalism, manifested in his attraction to empiricism and skepticism. His rationalism—suggesting in part the influence of the rationalism of his Harvard and Unitarian training and in part the leaning of his temperament—assumed a highly unusual profile when fused with his transcendental idealism. David Robinson captures in superb detail the arc of Emerson's maturing enthusiasm about empiricism at the time of his visit in 1833 to the Paris Museum of History, especially to the live exhibit of the Garden of Plants.[10] The story is one of his admiration for "the most current system of botanical and zoological classification;"[11] a growing awareness that the design of nature included a flux or dynamism of forms that revealed the symmetrical laws of the universe and the unifying mind of its Creator;[12]

a flirtation with becoming a naturalist; and then the conclusion that classification as an end is "superficial" and "tedious" (*EL*, 1:70) and that
"true classification" is concerned with spiritual "tendency":

> The true classification will not present itself to us in a catalogue of a
> · hundred classes, but as an idea of which the flying wasp & the grazing
> ox are developments. Natural History is to be studied not with any pre-
> tention that its theory is attained, that its classification is permanent, but
> merely as full of tendency. (*JMN*, 4:290)

Throughout his life Emerson remained imbued with a view of nature that
we think of as "romantic science."[13] Rising from an empirical classification of natural facts, it moves to a perception of the symmetry of nature
and the parallel symmetry of the mind of the observer, until, finally, it
arrives at a perception of the Unity that is the mind of God and the scientist's privileged participation in that Mind.

This unified view of organic and mental life was to engage Emerson
in a lifelong plan of writing a work about the parallelism of natural history and consciousness. His series of lectures in 1870–71, "The Natural
History of Intellect," was his belated effort in that direction. And the
reason for his inability to realize his ambition earlier takes us to the other
facet of Emerson's rationalism—his skepticism.

A little background is necessary. The product of Emerson's romantic
idealism and scientific classification was his doctrine of correspondence
that he developed fully in *Nature* in 1836. In Paris the doctrine is already
observable in his famous statement about becoming a naturalist: "Not a
form so grotesque, so savage, nor so beautiful but is an expression of
some property inherent in man the observer—an occult relation between
the very scorpions and man. I feel the centipede in me—cayman, carp,
eagle, & fox. I am moved by strange sympathies, I say continually, 'I will
be a naturalist' " (*JMN*, 4:199–200). But the problem that ultimately presented itself from the doctrine of correspondence and for which a dose of
"skepticism" was needed was not this protoevolutionary psychological
intuition Emerson articulated in Paris in 1833—this he never did quite
pursue. It was the result of his commitment to study the reciprocal relations between mind and matter that he fully articulated as a philosophy
of truth and beauty in *Nature*. The unending correspondence of mind and
matter is, on the one hand, the focus of Emerson's celebration of plenitude. Yet the diversitarian impulse to affirm the fecundity of the divine

spirit in man, as it circulated through every permutation of mood and circumstance, also became an inescapable commitment to follow the reciprocal relations of subject and object when they led into despair as well as into exaltation. The problem Emerson faced, then, was segmentary fragmentation, the splintering of vision into multiple viewpoints, each with its symmetry of external fact to support its worldview. And as he passed through this merry-go-round, propelled by the diversitarian impulse (and with external variety answering to each internal stop on his route), he needed detachment to face his situation fully and honestly. And it is for this that he needed models of skepticism, which he found in his reading of David Hume and Michel de Montaigne. Emerson obtained confirmation of the chaos that results from extreme subjectivism in Hume, who claimed that man's ideas "are nothing but a bundle or collection of different perceptions, which succeed each other with inconceivable rapidity, and are in perpetual flux and movement."[14] As John Michael has observed, in Hume "Emerson was forced to confront a threat to the identity he was trying to found," and to "see what the personal dangers of skepticism really are."[15] But if there was dread, there was also the admiration Emerson felt for Hume's honesty—honesty that the psychologist in Emerson would need. From Montaigne, the other great skeptical influence, Emerson learned a detachment from the tyranny of mood and the need to acquire a sturdy intellectual grace. Unlike the nihilism of Hume, Montaigne's skepticism exemplified finding "a middle ground . . . between extremes of unbelief and credulity,"[16] of suspending judgment in the face of contradictory viewpoints or moods. The "value of the skeptic is the resistance to premature conclusions," says Emerson as an outgrowth of his reading in Montaigne (*JMN*, 9:295).

Together Hume and Montaigne gave Emerson what he needed to pursue his project of Unity while remaining true to the psychological realism that science required—the Humean courage to explore the variety of the self and the stability of Montaigne to occupy the middle ground where faith in unity could wait for propitious moments.

Personal history, temperament, reading, and cultural and intellectual forces—these, then, make up the complex web of influences that shape the sense of experience I am about to explore.

II

The fragmentary sense of self that Emerson diligently describes alongside the unitary sense of self he regularly espouses are both crucial aspects of his sense of experience. Emerson's objective as a writer was to bring the spiritual man and the "axis of vision" into harmony with the secular man and "the axis of things."[17] He found man "disunited with himself" (*CW*, 1:43)—divorced from the universal spirit within him, his psyche obstructed from its essential source.[18] Without a clear spiritual channel, man's view of the world lay in ruins: the world of things was without spiritual transparency and the world of internal consciousness lacked a "sliding scale" that "ranks all sensations and states of mind" (*CW*, 3:42). Moods, opinions, and events confronted man in disjointed succession, their multiplicity posing a threat to a coherent or continuous selfhood. At the top of his own "sliding scale" of being, Emerson might see the encompassing design, the deified Whole, but often he was troubled by a sense of disjunction and disarray. Hume, we might say, loomed in the background.

In addition to his sense of the self in disarray, Emerson also described a "gulf" or fissure between subjective truths. Oscillating from one state of being or viewpoint to another, Emerson calls attention to a chasm of nothingness between shifting modes of selfhood. Temporal man, he implies, confronts a gulf when he is in transit from truth to truth. Emerson's recognition of the vacuum between points of truth has various "modern" implications, in particular his relation to the history and tenets of existentialism and, more recently, to the problem of unstable meaning emphasized by deconstructionism.

In "The American Scholar," the Divinity School Address, and many of his 1841 essays, Emerson emphasized man's ability to unite the spiritual with the secular aspects of his existence. Drawing on the optimism of a period of intense self-realization, Emerson gave expression to a powerful belief in man's ability to achieve spiritual self-reliance. Men did not need to be farmers or scholars: they could be "Man on the farm" or "Man Thinking" (*CW*, 1:53). Yet as Emerson's journal indicates, even during this predominantly optimistic period of writing and lecturing, he recognized that man possesses noteworthy psychological limitations. In an 1838 entry, Emerson diagnoses the human situation in terms of man's confinement in partial, fragmentary points of view despite the presence of a universal spirit within him:

Succession, division, parts, particles,—this is the condition, this the tragedy of man. All things cohere & unite. Man studies the parts, strives to tear the part from its connexion, to magnify it, & make it a whole. He sides with the part against other parts; & fights for parts, fights for lies, & his whole mind becomes an *inflamed part*, an amputated member, a wound, an offense. Meantime within him is the Soul of the Whole, the Wise Silence, the Universal Beauty to which every part & particle is equally related. (*JMN*, 7:105–6)

In *Essays: Second Series* (1844), Emerson's perspective continues to include a pungent awareness of human limitation and partiality. Emerson sees men caught up in the passions and partisanship of the moment, although he does indicate that this excessiveness has a purpose: it is nature's way of insuring expression, action, efficacy. In his second essay titled "Nature," Emerson says,

> No man is quite sane; each has a vein of folly in his composition, a slight determination of blood to the head, to make sure of holding him hard to some one point which nature had taken to heart. Great causes are never tried on their merits; but the cause is reduced to particulars to suit the size of the partisans, and the contention is ever hottest on minor matters. (*CW*, 3:108–9)

Emerson's view of man caught up in partisanship is an expression of what F. I. Carpenter has categorized as the Yankee, rational, and realist side of his nature.[19] In reading Emerson's journals, one observes, moreover, that his realism manifests itself often when he is looking *outward* from Concord at society—at religious institutions, reform groups, politicians, Boston society, and New York masses. His idealism, on the other hand, seems to emerge strongly when he is looking *inward*—at man's relation to the world of spirit and nature, at philosophy and literature, and at his own spiritual-imaginative development. Yet the pervasive nature of Emerson's bipolar vision means that this separation, while illustrative for the scholar, never really occurs. Emerson's idealism invades his social thought; his realism is turned on his private life and inner world;[20] and, at times, the interactive conjunction of these two tendencies is so swift as to bring about the threat of incoherence. In "Nominalist and Realist" in the second series, Emerson says,

> We must reconcile the contradictions as we can, but their discord and their concord introduce wild absurdities into our thinking and speech. No sentence will hold the whole truth, and the only way in which we can be just, is by giving ourselves the lie. . . . All the universe over, there

is but one thing, this old Two-Face, creator-creature, mind-matter, right-wrong, of which any proposition may be affirmed or denied. (*CW*, 3:143–44)

An increased realism, in particular an increased *psychological* realism, emerges in Emerson's writings after 1841.[21] Emerson's ultimate goal of establishing unity between men's outward lives and inward spirit never changed. His objective as a writer remained that of bringing the spiritual man and "the axis of vision" into harmony with the secular man and "the axis of things" (*CW*, 1:43). Yet he labored with increasing deliberateness in the 1840s on the problem of the fluctuating and incoherent sense of self—on what Hume described as men's ideas succeeding "each other with inconceivable rapidity . . . in perpetual flux and movement." B. L. Packer has put this problem somewhat similarly in *Emerson's Fall* (1982) as she describes "one giant question" that remained unanswered for Emerson:

Are the ruined, blank eyes of man capable of "self-healing" by the effort of will *or* imagination? Or are they passively subject to the endless alternations, the "fits of easy transmission & reflexion," that give to our organs of perception a nature first opaque, then transparent, then opaque, then transparent, and so on to eternity?[22]

My view is that Emerson's response to this Humean dilemma was somewhat like that of a modern psychologist studying repetitive aspects of emotional life. He adopted an empirical approach, carefully scrutinizing the influence of moods and pushing himself to construct generalizations about their pattern of recurrence. These patterns or configurations ultimately became the subject or part of the subject of several of his major essays. He had thought or written about aspects of these patterns earlier, but in the 1840s his concern with the potentially segmented nature of the self led to more focused attention. In "Compensation"—an essay from his first series that reflects his psychological interests—he explores the polarity of psychic life: he sees the mind as a shuttle of emotional actions and reactions. In "Experience," "Nominalist and Realist," and "Montaigne," he explores a second pattern: the mind as a "succession" or "rotation" (*CW*, 3:142) of moods and viewpoints, the mind as "parti-colored wheel" (*CW*, 3:34). And in "Nature," and again in "Experience" and "Montaigne," a third pattern is defined—the schism between dream and realization, between the intimation or brief achievement of an "ideal" experience and the disappointing actuality that succeeds it. In each of these essays, segmentary fragmentation is at the core of the problem.

In what sense was Emerson's view of man "psychological"? First, it is psychological in quite a different sense than Hawthorne's or Melville's. Hawthorne is interested in motivation and abnormality. The recurrence of dreams and symbols in his fiction suggests his sense of a repressed unconscious life. Melville's sense of psychic life, at least in *Moby-Dick*, is colored by the primitive forces of the natural world. Emerson, on the other hand, is not interested in depth psychology, or in the etiology of personality types and problems. He is wedded to a universal sense of man, and interested in how consciousness colors the flux of self and experience. His sense of man is phenomenological. In addition, Emerson is interested in the way the pattern of human moods generates a problematical sense of self, and in how shifting moods create different perspectives on idealism and correspondence as a philosophy of life. Emerson's approach to the problems of the human psyche can best be described as *psychophilosophical*.

Emerson's tendency, then, was to view fluctuations of viewpoint as shifts in consciousness rather than changes in the external world. He did not discount the force of the outer world but, as a result of his belief in the doctrine of correspondence, perceived it and the mind as interrelated; and as a result of his philosophic idealism,[23] Emerson believed that mind, not world, was the origin of the fluctuations men experienced. Even dramatic societal events, or tragic personal events, must pass through the medium of consciousness before their significance can be decided. In his journal, rather playfully, he considers the fluidity of "Opinion":

> Fluxional quantities. Fluxions, I believe, treat of flowing numbers, as, for example, the path through space of a point on the rim of a cartwheel. Flowing or varying. Most of my values are very variable. My estimate of America which sometimes runs very low, sometimes to ideal prophetic proportions. My estimate of my own mental means & resources is all or nothing, in happy hours, life looking infinitely rich; & sterile at others. My value of my club is as elastic as steam or gunpowder, so great now, so little anon. Literature looks now all-sufficient, but in high & happy conversation, it shrinks away to poor experimenting. (*JMN*, 15:166; see also *JMN*, 9:66)

Emerson was an explorer of the flux of individual consciousness. In nineteenth-century American literature, only Melville, as we shall see, represents a more radical exploration of the relativism of human perception and the epistemological questions that the oscillation of human viewpoint precipitates. Melville's major work emphasizes religious and philosophical uncertainty: the elusiveness of final truth and the need to live in uncertainty are essential to each of his quest narratives. Emerson, in apparent contrast, gathers his forces again and again to assert a consistency of vision, a unity within multiplicity, despite the doubts and difficulties he acknowledges. But as sensitive readers of his essays discover, it is in Emerson's efforts to capture the living experience of his doubts that the integrity of his intellect and artistry is manifested.

In Emerson's abrupt departures into the hortative to assure us of the "influx of God" or the "unity of Being," the reader encounters a mode of argument admittedly different from empiricism. The realization that there are two sorts of truth in Emerson's essays, one sort growing out of direct (albeit psychological) experience and one out of a priori conviction, has unquestionably devalued Emerson's worth for many modern readers. Yet they must realize that his faith meant that passages such as the one that follows were not as inconsistent to Emerson as they are to us today: "If I have described life as a flux of moods, I must now add, that there is that in us which changes not, and which ranks all sensations and states of mind" (CW, 3:42). Emerson's insertion of statements of belief in passages committed to description of experience reflects a deviation on the part of a sincere religious nature. When he seems to depart from reason, Emerson actually is being true to a higher reason. Contemporary readers also need to realize that while Emerson's a priori belief insulated him from a nihilism that moderns are inclined to admire, his belief also freed and emboldened him to experiment. Part of the basis for his great elasticity of mind and feeling is the trust and faith he possesses in a morally coherent universe.[24]

Charles Eliot Norton was correct in his centenary speech when he observed that Emerson's "faith was superior to any apparent exception to his doctrine; all of them could be brought into accordance with it."[25] Nevertheless, while the moral unity of Emerson's worldview derives from Thomas Reid's Moral Sense philosophy and the eighteenth-century model of a perfect moral universe, his absolute commitment to subjectivity and individual experience places him among those nineteenth-century thinkers who speak most meaningfully to our century.

III

The most sweeping statement about Emerson's view of the nature of experience is the most useful as a jumping-off point: life is consciousness.[26] Only when the individual's circle of consciousness encompasses external "facts" do these "facts" become a significant part of reality, a part of experience. The other major aspect of Emerson's concept of experience is its flux: experience involves a flow of consciousness and is therefore endlessly in transition, endlessly in metamorphosis. Other than the fact of transition, little remains the same about it: "Power ceases in the instant of repose," Emerson says in "Self-Reliance." "It resides in the moment of transition from a past to a new state, in the shooting of the gulf, in the darting to an aim. This one fact the world hates; that the soul *becomes*; for, that forever degrades the past" (*CW*, 2:40).

The two foregoing generalizations—that immediate individual experience is the medium by which the world is known and that consciousness is a ceaseless stream—are the double doorway into Emerson's sense of experience; and they lead us to his ideal of innovation. Emerson insisted on severance with the past in varying ways. Although his insight about transition is a profound and consistent one, he varied the contexts to which he applied it and the degree of urgency with which he urged abandonment of any fixed position in favor of remaining on the cresting wave of the present. If one takes Emerson's doctrine literally, as it is expressed above in "Self-Reliance," it describes a quest for power that is *never* achieved, because achievement—the attainment of an aim—is the end, not the beginning of power; power and authenticity are found in transition. But taken more loosely as an artistic and philosophic approach urging openness to new truths at all times, as a recognition that truth evolves, it is a powerful doctrine of alertness to the flux of life—a doctrine rooted in a phenomenological sense of existence and in the artistic and intellectual courage to record it. Valor in man, says Emerson, consists in "his preferring truth to his past apprehension of truth; and his alert acceptance of it from whatever quarter; the intrepid conviction that his laws, his relations to society, his christianity, his world, may at any time be superseded and decease" (*CW*, 2:183). Although stated here by Emerson in largely external terms, a world in such upheaval strongly implies revolutions within. Indeed, according to Emerson, yielding to internal metamorphosis makes the valorous man the enemy not only of received tradition or fixed institutions but of his own prior accomplishments: "The wild fertility of nature is felt in comparing our rigid names and reputations with our fluid consciousness" (*CW*, 2:81). Even yesterday's ideas can seem conservative in the face of today's mood: "But lest I should mislead any when I . . . obey my whims, let me remind the reader that I am only an experimenter. . . . No facts are to me sacred; none are profane; I simply experiment, an endless seeker, with no Past at my back" (*CW*, 2:188).

At his front, Emerson assumed transition led ultimately to ascension—to access to spiritual power. For this reason, each of the essays to be touched on in the following sections—"Compensation," "Experience," "Nature," "Nominalist and Realist," "Montaigne; or the Skeptic," and "Illusions"—has its moment of reaffirmation of a spiritual unity that transcends the fluctuating and fragmentary description of man it presents. But for the scholar interested in Emerson's protomodern tendencies, it is his description of the segmenting process, the means and not the ends, that bears emphasis. Emerson's careful exposition of the mind's polarity, the rotation or succession of moods, and the schism between dream and realization reveals that patterns of transition can involve transitions that still other transitions will revise; that is, temporarily, transitions can be lateral and unascending; they can even be descending. There will always be the influx of spiritual power—such is Emerson's credo, his living faith—but in the meantime, in the intervening phase that can involve large periods of time, a problematical sense of self emerges on the verge of the modern. Emerson may reveal his view of this transitional phase, when he says in "Self-Reliance," "Inasmuch as the soul is present, there will be power not confident but agent" (*CW*, 2:40). By "confident," he probably means "crystallized"; and I take him to mean in this sentence that in transition the soul may not always manifest its power but is nevertheless always an agency toward its power.

This emphasis on the transitive aspects of existence has led Richard Poirier in *The Renewal of Literature* (1987) to propose an Emersonian "tradition." This Emersonian line arises, says Poirier, from a rejection of the view of literature as a stable statement about reality, human values, and cultural wisdom. This tradition favors instead an embrace of the "bareness" of American culture, the same social bareness that Henry James and other writers lamented. According to Poirier, the Emersonian finds in cultural thinness the motivation for incessant innovation. Through literature, Emersonians want to recover the "naturalness, authenticity, and simplicity" of "the naked and true self" and to do this by combating culture's ossifying tendencies in language.[27] Within Emerson's rejection of cultural stability, Poirier sees Emerson winding up disparaging even "the power of words, regardless of how explicitly" Emerson "wishes to insist that words and actions are compatible." "The preamble of thought, the transition through which it passes from the unconscious to the conscious, is action," says Poirier quoting from "The American Scholar";[28] and if action is located "in the movement toward but never *in* a result,"[29] then Poirier reasons with Emerson that words, concepts, fixed ideas of the self as well as fixed ideas of authors and texts are all inauthentic—all products of waning power. Full power occurs in the moment leading up to, and possibly including, expression, but never in its emulation. On the issue of whether power occurs in the crystallization of language as idea and thought or only in the "preamble of thought," Poirier seems to prefer the preverbal, precognitive view. He makes the point, for example, that an individual trope in itself can always be accused of being a fixed verbal solution; and adds that it is "never any particular trope that matters, but rather the act of troping."[30] In the Emersonian approach to reading, therefore, Poirier sees Emerson recommending "the reading of life or of art" not as "a search for morally stabilizing moments or summary, but for infusions and diffusions of energy, for that constant redistribution of forces called troping, including the troping of the self."[31]

Yet beyond the contestation of culture's rigidifying tendencies and the expression of the self through figures of speech, Poirier's definition of the literary self is disappointingly shadowy. And it is this near-total definition of the self and experience around transition without acknowledging another polarity to experience that I want to distinguish from my own position. "The self in Emerson," Poirier says, "is not an entity, not even a function; it is an intimation of presence, and it comes upon us out of the very act by which the self tries to elude definition."[32] While Poirier includes William James in his Emersonian line and borrows James' terms the "transitive" and the "substantive" to describe the "stream of thought,"[33] Poirier's use of transition as the basis for an approach to literature and reading veers sharply into the transitive realm.[34] For the sake of his rhetorical strategy, Poirier seems to ignore the pragmatic reality that the transitive and substantive aspects of thought and language are inescapably complementary. Moreover, by characterizing Emerson as seeking creative power, not a transcendental spiritual unity, Poirier has perhaps made it too easy to emphasize Emerson's skeptical side.

In the foregoing effort to describe patterns of oscillation and instability in Emerson's view of experience—indeed in my treatment of
oscillation and instability throughout this book—I have included the substantive as well as the transitive aspects of Emerson's thought on transition. While, as Poirier argues through Emerson, cultural confidence
about stable constructs may be the primary enemy of creative power, and
while a philosophy of transition may lie at the heart of a program for the
renewal of literature, transition alone cannot be the foundation of existential or literary authenticity. As Emerson says in "Montaigne," balanc-
ing both the transitive and substantive poles of experience, "We are
golden averages, volitant stabilities, compensated or periodic errours,
houses founded on the sea" (*CW*, 4:91).

IV

The first pattern to be examined will be the polar movements of the
mind described in "Compensation." Commentators have generally focused on the "moralistic and consolatory" aspects of this essay,[35] and
have ignored its delineation of the polarities of psychological life. As
Harry Hayden Clark has remarked, "the preceding Age of Franklin and
Paine had gone to extremes in emphasizing the Argument from Design
in the outward cosmos at the expense of psychological Inwardness; he
[Emerson] transcended the emphasis of the preceding Age of Reason by
including it in a larger synthesis involving the outward *and* the inward."[36]
Integral to understanding this depiction of an inward psychological polarity in man is an understanding of the influence in "Compensation" of
the romantic principle of polarity. To overlook the romantic influence is
to overlook the essay's naturalistic vision of man and nature and to see
only the ghostly mechanistic notion of reward and punishment.

The rhythmic undulation of the wave, the complementary relationship of subject and object, positivity and negativity in electromagnetism,
and the Newtonian law of action-reaction are all phenomena subsumed
by romantic philosophers under the term "polarity." In each of these
cases, a variation of the universal truth is demonstrated that things are
dual and have two realities without which they cannot be adequately
comprehended or accounted for. The paragraph that opens the body of
"Compensation" is a list of such phenomena:

> Polarity . . . we meet in every part of nature; in darkness and light; in
> heat and cold; in the ebb and flow of waters; in male and female; in the
> inspiration and expiration of plants and animals . . . in the centrifugal
> and centripetal gravity; in electricity, galvanism, and chemical affinity.
> Superinduce magnetism at one end of a needle; the opposite magnetism
> takes place at the other end. If the south attracts, the north repels. To
> empty here, you must condense there. An inevitable dualism bisects na-
> ture, so that each thing is a half, and suggests another thing to make it
> whole. (*CW*, 2:57)

Emerson's idea of polarity was derived from German romantic philosophers and through his contact with Frederic Henry Hedge.[37] Thomas
McFarland has shown the pervasiveness of the notion of polarity in romantic thought and its fullest realization in Germany: "Under the name
'Polarität,' and, conceived on the analogy of the positive and negative
poles of magnetism, it dominated the whole spectrum of German scientific speculation called *Naturphilosophie*."[38] McFarland presents a compelling picture of a "Romantic community of thought" of which Emerson
was clearly a member.[39]

Emerson's depiction of human psychology in "Compensation" takes
its character from one of the major influences on romantic polar thought:
Newton's third law of motion.[40] For every action (or strong emotion)
there is an equal and opposed reaction. Undulation and polarity, moreover, are manifestations of the law of nature and are also linked with the
laws of spirit: "That great principle of Undulation in nature, that shows
itself in the inspiring and expiring of the breath; in desire and satiety; in
the ebb and flow of the sea, in day and night, in heat and cold, and . . . is
known to us under the name of Polarity—these 'fits of easy transmission
and reflection,' as Newton called them, are the law of nature because they
are the law of spirit" (*CW*, 1:61). Polarity reflects the universal spirit from
which the world emanates, both in naturalistic terms and in the moral
terms that produce the operations of a cosmic system of compensation.
Though we might protest that naturalistic undulation and a system of
rewards and punishments are two different principles,[41] Emerson, in his
characteristic fashion, presents them as two sides of one reality. In one of
the key sentences in "Compensation," he fuses the phenomenon of sub-
sidence after excess with the tax for pleasure, implying thereby that the
naturalistic and moralistic interlock. Emerson says that in response to
excess of joy or fancy, "it would seem, there is always this vindictive

circumstance stealing in at unawares, even into the wild poesy in which the human fancy attempted to make bold holiday, and to shake itself free of the old laws,—this back-stroke, this kick of the gun, certifying that the law is fatal; that in Nature, nothing can be given, all things are sold" (*CW*, 2:63). Even after surges of affirmation, in other words, there is the reaction, the counterthrust, equal in force and conservative in direction. Action and reaction are one psychic event; one cannot occur without the other.

Emerson's explanation of the internal reaction to all action is not that it is merely an equal and opposite tendency, but that it is the corrective reaction of the whole soul to the partial action of the will. Throughout Emerson's work, a tension exists between individuality and universality, between the realization of the individual self and the obedience of the self to higher law. In "Compensation," he says that the moral universal aspect cannot be escaped. "What we call retribution, is the universal necessity by which the whole appears wherever a part appears" (*CW*, 2:60). Yet men are forever trying to return to selfish ends. While the soul strives to "work through all things" in a spiritual direction, "the particular man" always has partial aims: "to be somebody; to set up for himself; to truck and higgle for a private good" (*CW*, 2:61). "The ingenuity of man," says Emerson, "has always been dedicated to the solution of one problem,—how to detach the sensual sweet, the sensual strong, the sensual bright, &c. from the moral sweet, the moral deep, the moral fair; that is, again, to contrive to cut clean off this upper surface so thin as to leave it bottomless; to get a *one end*, without an *other end*" (*CW*, 2:61). Yet any attempt "to act partially, to sunder, to appropriate" is hopeless; "the parted water re-unites behind our hand" (*CW*, 2:61).

A broader vision of experience as oscillation should not be lost on us within Emerson's nineteenth-century antimonies of the sensual and the spiritual, the partial and the whole. Nor should his recommendation. Emerson is saying that the danger does not lie in the dualism but in man's attempt to escape from the dualism of nature. If men attempt to deny the see-saw motion of life, if they believe they can detach the "mermaid's head" from the "dragon's tail" (*CW*, 2:62), then disequilibrium and fragmentation occur. If, however, men submit to the reversals, the humbling alterations, the contradictory assertions to which psychic life gives rise, then they will slowly find flexible footing amidst the antitheses of their inner life. Polarities will not vanish but a reduction in their swing will occur; and with greater stability, a greater centrality of vision will follow.

"There is a deeper fact in the soul than compensation," says Emerson, "to wit, its own nature. The soul is not a compensation, but a life. The soul is" (*CW*, 2:70).

Emerson's sense of experience as oscillation and fragmentation was not confined to his sense of polarity. While it was his habit in a given essay to throw his whole being into a particular perspective, once outside that essay he knew that perspective would have to be combined with others. Consequently, references to the doctrine of compensation diminish in Emerson's writings after the 1830s. While polarity continues to prove useful as a means of understanding certain aspects of politics and history (see *CW*, 3:124; *W*, 6:253–57), it too never again assumes the universality that the German romantic philosophers persuaded him to give it in "Compensation." Presumably, Emerson realized from his greater involvement with the multiplicity of psychic and societal life that the myriad data of existence do not fall into neatly paired opposites. If Schelling, on one hand, sought a "principle that connects inorganic and organic nature," on the other, he said in the same work, "I hate nothing more than the mindless attempt to destroy the multiplicity of natural causes by means of invented [*erdichtete*] identities."[42] Or perhaps Emerson had read in Bacon that "the human understanding is of its own nature prone to suppose the existence of more order and regularity in the world than it finds. And though there be many things in nature which are singular and unmatched, yet it devises for them parallels and conjugates and relatives which do not exist."[43] Whatever the reason, whether due to his own experience or his reading, Emerson seems to have decided about compensation that "this is a fragment of me" (*CW*, 3:47) and gone on to other perspectives.[44]

V

One of those other perspectives on segmentation in psychic life is the notion of a multiplicity of moods and events that successively color man's view of life, and the formlessness and inconsistency in the perception of reality that result. Emerson's antidoctrinal doctrine of openness to new truths encouraged receptiveness to all facets of life and the rejection of dogma and system; but, as critics have observed, it also worked against logical and descriptive consolidation. Or so they have maintained. For it is now possible to recognize the "existential" soundness of Emerson's notion that man cannot get his mind around the whole of life at one time, that it comes to him in fragments, and that cognitive systems or attempts at consistency will only, as H. D. Gray articulates for Emerson, result in "stifling truth by forcing it into set and definite terms."[45] That Emerson was grappling with a set of philosophic themes about man and direct experience, only later to receive focused attention, we can see now with the benefit of hindsight. Later I will consider Emerson's relation to existentialism, but first some elaboration is in order about the second pattern or configuration of consciousness Emerson defined: the view of man as a rotation or succession of lenses on life.

Usually, Emerson described this pattern of rotating viewpoints in fairly abstract terms, using "mood" as a shorthand term to help signify the subjective flux of emotions and ideas: "There is the power of moods, each setting at nought all but its own tissue of facts and beliefs" (*W*, 4:175). "Our moods do not believe in each other. . . . I am God in nature; I am a weed by the wall" (*CW*, 2:182). "I am always insincere, as always knowing there are other moods" (*CW*, 3:145). This kind of statement, which Emerson often picked from his journal entries and used in his essays, conveys his sense of truth as incomplete and partial, although each hour may briefly persuade him of its wholeness. Men want consistency and permanence, but find that time involves them in "the necessity of a succession of moods or objects" (*CW*, 3:32), each of which claims their consciousness. Stanley Cavell goes so far as to say that Emerson attempts "to formulate a kind of epistemology of moods" in which moods are as constitutive of our worldviews as sensory experiences are of objects around us. "Sense-experience is to objects," Cavell says, "what moods are to the world."[46] In "Experience" Emerson asserts that this transitory and slippery nature of things is "the most unhandsome part of our condition." In some of the gloomiest passages in all his writings, he speaks of life as a "dream" that "delivers us" to other dreams, and complains that even suffering and loss fail to make life sharp and real (*CW*, 3:29–30).

But while Emerson can be gloomy about life "amid surfaces," he can also greet the flux of moods with gusto, asserting, for instance, that "the true art of life is to skate well on them" (*CW*, 3:35). As O. W. Firkins observes in a Melvillian image, Emerson "had a marvelous knack of keeping his footing upon mobile surfaces, as sailors walk steadily on a heaving deck."[47] Emerson's penchant for dramatic presentation of his epistemological dilemma is not far from Melville's either. "We cannot write the order of the variable winds," Emerson says in "Illusions." "How can we penetrate the law of our shifting moods and susceptibility?" (W, 6:321). Or, "With such volatile elements to work in, 'tis no wonder if our estimates are loose and floating. We must work and affirm, but we have no guess at the value of what we say and do" (W, 6:320). Some of the implicit themes here that call for explicit statement are the tyranny of mood and the relativity of viewpoint, the disorientation between the various planes of existence, the unending need for adaptiveness, and the mystery about man as a creature of ever-unfolding meaning.

One kind of response in Emerson to the enigma of man as a succession of moods is to approach him realistically. Temperament, he saw, limited the number of moods each man actually experienced. If "life is a train of moods like a string of beads," then "temperament is the iron wire on which the beads are strung"; and most individuals possess only a limited number (CW, 3:30). "Our friends early appear to us as representatives of certain ideas, which they never pass or exceed" (CW, 3:33), he says. But Emerson was not altogether prepared to sacrifice the belief in an underlying universality in each man. Briefly he gives the monistic impulse its sway: in a leap of what I would call "bifocal" vision (a leap from foreground to background) he asserts in "Nominalist and Realist" that although men's moods limit what they perceive at any one time, through the rotation of many moods they discover the possibility of an immense breadth of life (see CW, 3:144). The doctrine of correspondence explains how the succession of perspectives, while ostensibly creating a fragmentary experience, actually reveals the universal interrelatedness between man and world:

> Really, all things and persons are related to us, but according to our nature, they act on us not at once, but in succession, and we are made aware of their presence one at a time. All persons, all things which we have known, are here present, and many more than we see; the world is full. (CW, 3:142)

Universality, then, is not impossible for fragmentary man. The more men can give themselves to their inner nature, the better their chances of comprehending the sweep of human viewpoint: the better they can understand the conservative and the reformer, the nihilist and the believer. In "Montaigne" Emerson says that the alterations of "beliefs and unbeliefs appear to be structural," that is, psychologically inescapable. The sooner therefore "man attains the poise and vivacity which allow the whole machinery to play," the sooner "he will not need extreme examples, but will rapidly alternate all opinions in his own life" (*W*, 4:175). The entire spectrum of responses to existence will then be accessible to him. One dividend, obviously, is knowledge of the world. But another is the realization that while the Transcendentalist ethic of self-trust and spontaneity is necessary to get the ball of self-discovery rolling, detachment is, ultimately, the way. Emerson speaks in "Montaigne" of a "wise skepticism," describing it as a state in which one knows that "there is no practical question on which any thing more than an approximate solution can be had" (*W*, 4:157). It is the detachment of the wise skeptic that makes possible the ability to step back from the absoluteness of mood just enough to grasp one's inner pattern (see *W*, 4:176). Regarding the "rotation of states of mind," Emerson says, "I suppose it suggests its own remedy, namely, in the record of larger periods" (*W*, 4:176). Packer characterizes Emerson's recommendation somewhat differently, in terms of a slight "elevation of thought" from enthusiasms. But the key element, I would argue, is not "a little height of thought" (although Emerson does say this in "Self-Reliance" [*CW*, 2:34]), but distance, detachment in whatever direction. Packer herself does justice to this nicely at another moment when she says that the ironic attitude Emerson recommends in "Montaigne" is "predicated upon self-awareness, that slight dislocation of our own centers from the Center of Life that allows us to speak *knowingly* of our enthusiasms."[48]

VI

Emerson's effort to describe "the parti-colored wheel" of moods in man took him fairly close to the texture of immediate experience. In his treatment of a third pattern of consciousness—the schism between the dream and its limited realization—he comes closer still to describing daily life and those precognitive qualities of psychological experience that later "existential" philosophers took up with great interest. "In every house, in the heart of each maiden and of each boy, in the soul of the soaring saint," Emerson says, "this chasm is found,—between the largest promise of ideal power, and the shabby experience" (*W*, 4:184–85). And while he declares categorically that "this parallelism of great and little . . . never react on each other, nor discover the smallest tendency to converge" (*W*, 4:179), he attempts on several occasions to describe this elusive convergence, resorting like a novelist to pithy dramatic illustration. What Emerson implies in his treatment of the gap between the ideal and the real is that estrangement from reality—disunity—is as inseparable a part of human experience as unity or affirmative "tendency" (*CW*, 3:42).[49]

In "Experience," Emerson describes how elusive fullness of being can be, and how it is complemented, more often than not, by feelings of lack or the disappearance of being. "Every ship is a romantic object, except that we sail in," he says. "Embark, and the romance quits our vessel, and hangs on every other sail in the horizon." The same elusiveness occurs in men's desire for meaningfulness in their lives: "Men seem to have learned of the horizon the art of perpetual retreating and reference. 'Yonder uplands are rich pasturage, and my neighbor has fertile meadow, but my field,' says the querulous farmer, 'only holds the world together' " (*CW*, 3:28). Wherever the individual intrudes himself, bringing with him the "colored and distorting lenses which we are" (*CW*, 3:43), estrangement comes with him. Nothingness is not an ontological category for Emerson; only Being is primary; but on a secondary or phenomenal level, self-consciousness and alienation are unavoidable. Emerson says this most explicitly in "Experience" where he provides a nineteenth-century, romantic updating of postlapsarian man: "It is very unhappy, but too late to be helped, the discovery we have made, that we exist. That discovery is called the Fall of Man" (*CW*, 3:43).

In Emerson's second essay titled "Nature" (1844), he develops more extensively the notion of man as a terrain of unfulfilled expectation. "There is throughout nature something mocking, something that leads us on and on, but arrives nowhere," he says. "Every end is prospective of some other end, which is also temporary" (*CW*, 3:110). He continues:

> There is in woods and waters a certain enticement and flattery, together with a failure to yield a present satisfaction. This disappointment is felt in every landscape . . . the poet finds himself not near enough to his object. The pine-tree, the river, the bank of flowers before him, does not seem to be nature. Nature is still elsewhere. This or this is but outskirt and far-off reflection and echo of the triumph that has passed by, and is now at its glancing splendor and heyday, perchance in the neighboring fields, or, if you stand in the field, then in the adjacent woods. . . . But who can go where they are, or lay his hand or plant his foot thereon? Off they fall from the round world forever and ever. (*CW*, 3:111–12)

Nature allures but never fully satisfies. The complete reality is always else-where. Consequently, individuals are compelled to live "a referred exis-tence, an absence, never a presence and satisfaction" (*CW*, 3:112). Begin-ning with his first *Nature*, where he spoke of man as "disunited with himself," Emerson's work manifests not only the idealist affirmation but the depiction of man's separation from himself and nature in all its vex-atiousness. And "it is the same among the men and women, as among the silent trees." The lover loses the "wildest charm of his maiden in her acceptance of him" (*CW*, 3:112). Even the full force of a work of art or literature cannot be experienced twice: "each will bear an emphasis of attention once, which it cannot retain, though we fain would continue to be pleased in that manner" (*CW*, 3:33). Nature, lovers, art—each falls short of our fullest expectation. Because we bring our inner disunity with us, "an absence" as well as a "presence and satisfaction" pervade our experience.

VII

The adventurous image of "shooting the gulf" held a special attrac-tion for Emerson. He used it in "Self-Reliance" to convey a sense of the unending flow of existence and the necessity of accepting the uncertainty of transition. His assertion there, that to attain the full potential of exis-tence one must live in flux, bears requoting: "Power ceases in the instant of repose; it resides in the moment of transition from a past to a new state, in the shooting of the gulf, in the darting to an aim" (*CW*, 2:40). "Shooting the gulf" also appears in "Montaigne," where Emerson has in mind the unknown of death: "So, at least, I live within compass, keep myself ready for action, and can shoot the gulf at last with decency" (*W*, 4:167). And it appears also in the 1841 address "The Method of Nature," where, wanting to awaken man's heroic potential, Emerson says, "Here art thou with whom so long the universe travailed in labor; darest thou think meanly of thyself whom the stalwart Fate brought forth to unite his ragged sides, to shoot the gulf,—to reconcile the irreconcilable?" (*CW*, 1:129).

In all three cases "gulf" signifies a chasm into which or across which the individual must bravely travel. The bold and creative forces of the human spirit compel him. In "Self-Reliance," moreover, it is implied that shooting the gulf involves the devaluation of established "truth." One enters a void between a past and a future state of being, an interstice where man has the potential—is "agent"—to a higher state of being; but he is in the meantime the victim of uncertainty and nothingness.

In Emerson's sense of experience as polarity, rotation, and schism between dream and realization, we have seen how unstable is his sense of truth. I have placed the phrase "shooting the gulf" in my chapter title to emphasize his sense of the gulf between different states of being and the need for intellectual courage to traverse them. Each of the various patterns of consciousness that Emerson delineates has two or more modalities and no single state of being ever attains the ultimate status it briefly imagines it possesses; its "validity" is always unseated by another state. In transition, relativism and uncertainty prevail.

Emerson responded to the problem of multiplicity and disjunction in a variety of ways. One response was as a philosopher or more accurately, as a *psychophilosopher*.[50] In this role, he sought to describe and examine the effect on perception of the fluctuations of the mind. How "truth" was refracted through the shifting lens of the individual psyche absorbed and fascinated Emerson. This pursuit led him not only to a description of the relativism of human perception but to an acknowledgment of the sense of illusoriness that multiplicity produces when its alternations became intense and encompassing. In large part because of his sense of the devaluation of any particular truth, the description of the epistemological problem became for him the substantive truth he sought to define. As Charles Feidelson, Jr., has put it, for Emerson the "*how* of knowledge—the process, the method, the form—is identical with the stuff of knowledge."[51]

Emerson also responded emotionally and artistically to the uneasiness and incompleteness that a discontinuous sense of reality produced. He dealt with the overwhelming and disjunctive nature of the mind's multiplicity by describing it, seemingly, in terms fairly close to the stripe of his own feelings and experience. He personalized the description of the problem and sought release from its incubus by considering it from various perspectives—from the subjective in "Experience," from the abstract and lyrical in "Nature," from the bifocal in "Nominalist and Realist," and from the skeptical in "Montaigne." Unlike the Emerson who emerges in the journals of the 1840s, where he is nearly always the detached intellectual observer, the professional thinker, the manner in which he returns repeatedly in his essays to certain themes of disjunction suggests more artistic obsession than is generally associated with him. Certainly, his essays, or at least those discussed here, represent a remarkable combination of objectivity and internality—qualities whose fusion is found only in the mature artist, on familiar terms with the darker sources of his subject.

Finally, much of Emerson's response to the fluctuations of experience was tactical. How does one deal with the unstable and beguiling shifts of consciousness? How does one keep one's footing? Emerson's answer seems to have been that the best defense against the vexing metamorphoses of consciousness is a familiarity with its patterns. Polarity, rotation, and the schism between dream and realization were, we have seen, patterns of subjectivity that could not be readily transcended but might be stabilized through acceptance and familiarity. If Emerson could at least delineate the common patterns, the individual could acquaint himself with the unique states of being or points of view that make up his private vision. Emerson hoped to provide a means by which the individual might detach himself a little from the tyranny of his internal unfolding. Finally, he hoped to impart to men the realization that all life was within them— all values, all attitudes, all selves—and that each person, thereby, had the potential to weigh and assess all viewpoints.

In his essay on Plato, whom he sees as the epitome of the "balanced soul" (*W*, 4:55), Emerson's view of the "gulf" or transition from one point of being to another is that it produces a fertile intellectual opportunity, not a nullifying breach. Maintaining that "our strength is transitional, alternating," Emerson goes on to illustrate its bipolarity in terms of "the seashore, sea seen from shore, shore seen from sea; . . . our enlarged powers at the approach and at the departure of a friend; the experience of poetic creativeness, which is not found in staying at home, nor yet in travelling, but in transitions from one to the other, which must therefore be adroitly managed to present as much transitional surface as possible" (*W*, 4:55–56). The emphasis on "transitional surface," which must be "adroitly managed" to preserve as much of it as possible, represents a somewhat different view of transition from what we have emphasized. It points the thinker toward the opportunity to possess within himself two points of view at one time and to use their contiguity to assess their relative strengths and weaknesses. The prerequisite is the "balanced soul."

VIII

Before turning to the final concern of this essay, Emerson's relation to existentialism, I want to address the implications of this gulf in man with respect to deconstructionism. Although Poirier distinguishes his view of Emerson from deconstructionism, his extreme reading of Emerson's view of transition comes quite close, it seems to me, to pulling Emerson into the deconstructionist camp. However, before giving Poirier his opportunity to differentiate Emerson from de Man, I want to engage the question of Emerson's similarities to deconstruction more directly, using terms drawn from my own discussion.

Does the rupture of meaning between different moods or opinions carry over from Emerson's attitude about firsthand experience to literature? A proponent might recall the line, "we must reconcile the contradictions as we can, but their discord and their concord introduce wild absurdities into our thinking and speech" (*CW*, 3:143). If discontinuities exist between states of being, then in all likelihood they exist also between the writer's thoughts and the assigned meaning of the words the writer uses to convey those thoughts and images. In a telling journal entry of 1836, Emerson says that a "fact . . . is the terminus of a past thought . . . a means now to new sallies of the imagination" (*JMN*, 5:177).[52] The moment the spirit becomes concretely wedded to material fact, or the moment that fluid consciousness assumes verbal form, that moment is also a "terminus," a burial of fluid spirit in fixed form, which encourages new imaginings to begin.

Emerson's involvement with subjectivity and his recognition of varying degrees of discontinuity—some propitious, some disturbing, to meaning—implies his awareness of the margin of "disrelation of language and world."[53] One does feel, at least with regard to "Experience," that deconstructionism could valuably approach this essay in terms of (to quote Geoffrey Hartman) "what we all feel about figurative language, its excess over any assigned meaning" or that the "word carries with it a certain absence or indeterminacy of meaning."[54] The trope about the unending stair at the beginning of "Experience" is an example of a nightmarish metaphor whose haunting "story" extends beyond the discourse that follows.[55] But if the limitation of representational discourse is the primary notion of deconstructionism and the indeterminate play of surface meaning is merely the area of aesthetic interest it is left with (and so must make a virtue of), then Emerson does not embody a theoretical or practical advance guard on the deconstructionist movement. In Emerson a principle of abundance of meaning is at the core of his poetics, not a radical fissure between signifier and signified. As Feidelson suggests, he points toward an endless web of correspondence.[56] Still, delinquent verbal meaning is a corollary of this viewpoint. While the present finds verbal form only as it becomes the past, the stream of consciousness overflows in multiform directions that the writer cannot control within the limits of a finite work.

While "Emerson may sometimes sound deconstructionist himself," Poirier's differentiation of Emerson from deconstruction is somewhat different. Although he concedes similarities, he emphasizes, ultimately, the element of will and action in Emerson's view of "troping." He says that while deconstructionists like Paul de Man "want to show, repeatedly, how words in a text release themselves from the active control of any presumptive human presence," Emerson insists that "this very same temporariness is instigated and perpetuated by the human will." "The turning or troping of words is," Poirier explains, "in itself an act of power over meaning already in place."[57] It is a "sign not of human subservience" but of human agency and creative power.[58]

A question that is more important historically (although its emotional distance from the present may blind some to this fact) is the issue of Emerson's relationship to existentialism, that European philosophical movement that has sought, since its origins in Kierkegaard, to shed ties with objective systems and objective notions of essence and to center itself instead on the immediate and concrete aspects of individual experience. In the introduction to his well-known collection of existentialist writings, Walter Kaufmann says that the rejection of schools of thought, the sense of the inadequacy of fixed bodies of belief or systems, and an impatience with traditional philosophy as "superficial, academic, and remote from life" is "the heart of existentialism." He adds that while existentialism is a "timeless sensibility" discernible "here and there in the past," it is "only in recent times that it has hardened into a sustained protest and preoccupation."[59] Discussion of the general nature of existentialism is often conducted in terms of common themes. These recurrent themes, beside those Kaufmann mentions, are an emphasis on life as it is empirically known, an interest in extreme states of emotion, the intentional nature of consciousness, freedom and choice, the limits of reason, nothingness, and the concern with achieving an authentic philosophy. Reviewing this list of themes with Emerson in mind makes one aware of the lines of development between him and existential philosophers of the twentieth century.

There have been a few scholarly articles that have placed Emerson beside religious existentialists and found areas of similarity. Harold

Fromm in "Emerson and Kierkegaard" and Paul Lauter in "Emerson through Tillich" have noted the commonality between Emerson's approach to philosophical truth and Kierkegaard's emphasis on "subjectivity" and Tillich's on *Innerlichkeit* or inwardness.[60] Certainly, Emerson's great influence on Nietzsche[61] —who in turn influenced Jaspers, Heidegger, and Sartre[62] —constitutes an argument for his place in the history of philosophy that leads to modern existentialism. Yet if we accept Alasdair MacIntyre's assertion that "some kind of metaphysical rationalism [idealism] is almost always the background for existentialism" and that the work of modern existentialists involves a reaction against this tradition,[63] then Emerson's adherence to philosophical idealism from beginning to end[64] is a strong argument against considering him an early existentialist. Emerson believed in the existence of a divine intelligence in spirit and in the necessary existence of higher spiritual "ideas" for the natural world to exist; and this belief links him indissolubly with the history of idealist philosophy, despite his rejection (like Kierkegaard's) of objective systems.[65]

On the other hand, there are several themes to which Emerson's work does give expression and to which modern existentialists are attracted generally. Briefly, these are: (1) truth is subjective and grounded in direct individual experience; (2) man's grasp on life in any given moment is limited; (3) lack of being, estrangement, or alienation is part of the texture of experience; and (4) the demand for consistency and systems of logic lead away from truth rather than toward it. Emerson's ideas also seem consonant with Husserl's phenomenological notion that the objective world has existence only as consciousness is directed to it by human intention.[66]

In the end, however, Emerson's differences with existentialism mean that he is neither an early proponent nor an immediate forebear such as Kierkegaard, Nietzsche, or Husserl. Emerson's cosmic optimism while the existentialists were to be preoccupied with failure, anxiety, dread, and death; Emerson's emphasis on submission to spiritual truth while the existentialists were to emphasize freedom and choice; and Emerson's belief that idea precedes matter while the existentialists were to break with German idealism, each involves a strong argument against calling him a direct forerunner of existential philosophy.

Emerson's importance in the history of existential thought is the degree to which he asserts the authority of personal experience, for in doing so he both anticipates and helps pave the way for the more radical departures yet to come. In addition, an awareness of the "advanced" aspects of his thought makes possible an appreciation of its amazing arc. Although he reached boldly toward the twentieth century, Emerson kept one foot in the past. Although he grappled with relativity and disjunction, he also sustained a belief in the One. Instead of diminishing him or suggesting incoherence, Emerson's bipolar vision reaching from deism to existentialism represents a most extraordinary development.

4

Multiplicity and Uncertainty
in Melville's *Moby-Dick*

I The Wonder-World of the Imagination

In Herman Melville's *Moby-Dick* we shall see a different kind of segmentary fragmentation from Emerson's, one that arises from the heterogeneity of the physical world as well as from a multiplicity of states of
mind. In Melville's *Moby-Dick*, in fact, matter and mind sometimes assume
a parallel movement, a common modality, that is felt in the work to represent or at least to suggest a higher metaphysical power. This higher
metaphysical power, if it exists, moves natural events and manifests,
within the limitations of what can be known, a range of essential characteristics. Segmentary fragmentation in *Moby-Dick*, therefore, in addition
to multiple interactions of mind and matter, compels us to embark on an
inquiry into multiple ideas about God—ideas that the characters are
moved to by the same forces that move natural events themselves.

Let us begin where most critics end, summarizing the meanings that
Ahab, Ishmael, and Queequeg generate. We can then approach the cetology material, which is central to the theme of fragmentation, with the
significance of *Moby-Dick's* main character having already been defined.

As a result of his greater openness to the fluid natural world, his
antiheroic tendencies, and his intimate friendship with the pagan Queequeg, Ishmael as a character and narrator suggests revisions of Ahab's
absolutist, metaphysical anger. If Ishmael is vexed also by the problem of
evil, he is nevertheless freer of fixed categories of thought and closer to

what Blake, Coleridge, and Wordsworth considered the truer self, the imagination. In other words, Ishmael's achievement is to be found in the nature of his consciousness, which has accepted its own terms of being and knowing. His freedom from fixed value and viewpoint and his release from the tyranny of the will carry him into a deepened area of inwardness, a realm of being free of the circumstantial. They carry him to a place described in the first chapter as "the wonder-world"[1] of the imagination. This inward freedom, with its "wild conceits" and preoccupation with a "grand hooded phantom," is the doorway through which Melville retells the young whaleman's story from the vantage point of Ishmael, the romantic tragic artist.

We never do see the nature of the consciousness Ishmael achieves revealed in the plot; we never see Ishmael the neophyte whaleman integrate his organic mentality with the Ahabian impulse toward heroic assertion. It is only revealed in the retrospective narration. Nevertheless, Ishmael's survival suggests he has gone beyond Ahab's diabolical impasse and found a more fruitful relation to life—if only through art. Where Ahab embodies the power of will, fixed meaning, and purposeful rage, Ishmael seems to point to an organic and meliorative set of values that emerge from the processes of the mind: values of natural instinct, spontaneity, detachment, flow, flexibility, unheroicness—what Robert Caserio calls an "agency of passivity,"[2] values whose powers of renewal and vision the heroic can never safely eschew.[3]

Ishmael's shift is from an inward and outward sense of conflict to a recognition of the similitude of man and natural world. And his relationship with Queequeg is clearly the basis of his transformation. As early as "A Bosom Friend" (ch. 10), Ishmael confesses that the "wolfish world" has driven him into a psychological corner and that his new savage friend produces a "melting" in him that relieves him of conflict: "No more my splintered heart and maddened hand were turned against the wolfish world. This soothing savage had redeemed it" (10:51). And it is this pattern on Ishmael's part, of finding release and openness to life through his trust and intimacy with the pagan harpooner, which is at the heart of the psychological deliverance that Queequeg effects. The wolfishness of society and the sharkishness of nature do not vanish with a change of viewpoint. Yet a change of viewpoint affects Ishmael's ideas about these forces; and such a shift from an inwardly and outwardly conflicted struggle to an un-Ahabian impulse toward integration is central to the transformation Ishmael undergoes.

Queequeg lives immersed in the totality of existence, in the sharkish-ness and the gentleness of natural things, and he enacts all parts "care-lessly and unthinkingly" (47:214) with a noble indifference to his fate. Therefore, as the coffin engraved with the figures from Queequeg's tat-tooed body rises to the surface in the epilogue, it is the savage health of Ishmael's generous friend that saves Ishmael—combined with the "cun-ning spring" (epilogue:573) of fate. Queequeg's legacy is the recognition of the similitudes of mind and world. Man and nature are animated by the same forces—including Ahabian tornadoes that destroy!

In the cetology chapters, to which we now turn, the exploration of the nature of the whale grows out of this insight into the shared ground of man and nature. Without this commonality as an underlying premise, the primitive depths and manifold meanings of the whale would not be accessible to the romantic artist.

II Fragmentation and Epistemological Disarray in the Cetology Chapters

In the cetology chapters of *Moby-Dick*, the theme of the segmentary fragmentation of life receives its most explicit literary and philosophical development. In the span of whaling chapters extending from Chapter 55 to 105, although Ishmael is still seemingly the narrator, the philosoph-ical interests and lines of development exceed our idea of Ishmael's char-acter. They take him beyond the role as narrator of Ahab's tragedy and his own story, and involve him in other imperatives and priorities, phil-osophically related to but not rooted in the story. Melville moves from story to encyclopedic exposition, with the whale continuing to serve as the subject, "the common denominator," as J. A. Ward puts it, both "ob-ject of quest" and "object of exposition."[4] Yet when examined closely neither the aesthetic effect nor the philosophical import is intended to create an impression of unity. On the contrary, the aesthetic and philo-sophic goal of the cetology material is to convey a sense of epistemologi-cal fragmentation and disarray. In addition, Melville wants to dramatize a suprahuman perspective about the manifold interactions of mind and matter. He wants to present a clashing and boundless ocean of material forms and conscious meanings at the center of life.

Melville accomplishes his goal of talking about mind and matter by introducing into his treatise on the whale an unwieldy and heterogeneous mass of subject matter and by organizing and studying this subject matter in terms of multiple theories of knowledge and types of erudition. Some of these approaches to knowledge, such as the empirical and the symbolic, are reconcilable: the symbolist needs a foundation in factual reality. But most other approaches are mutually exclusive. In any case, all are in turn unsatisfying and incomplete; and they are intended to speak of an epistemological disarray in the face of complex and discordant planes of experience. "I wonder, Flask, whether the world is anchored anywhere; if she is, she swings with an uncommon long cable" (121:511), says Stubb to his mate as they tie down the anchor. And it is precisely the artistic equivalent, in terms of form and content, of this kinaesthetic sensation of a "world of mind"[5] swinging from a long cable, without any points of reference or unified theory of knowledge, that Melville is seeking to communicate.

In order to understand this disharmonious, fragmentary experience of reality, we need to look first at the discontinuous approaches to knowledge that are adopted in the study of the whale and see how the problem of knowledge emerges as a major concern beside the quest theme. Then we need to examine the heterogeneity of the material, in order to indicate how it contributes to a vision of a discordant and multitudinous world, and then to understand the function of this immense diversity of material in terms of the story.[6] The cetology material has been approached somewhat similarly by Edgar A. Dryden. He describes Ishmael's method as "a Joycean 'joco-serious' one." And he conceives of Ishmael's identity and world as imagined ones.[7] The difference between Dryden's view and my own, which will become apparent as I cover some of the cetological ground he treats, is that he sees Ishmael's orientation as entirely literary and the world he creates as a verbal construct based on prior verbal constructs.[8] On the other hand, I see Ishmael marshaling constructs to take the measure of realities "out there," realities that he wishes us to conceive as multitudinous and diverse, bristling with energy and manifesting surprising forms and detail. He may not be able to penetrate to the first cause of this world, but Ishmael's imaginative rendering of it is intended to evoke material and spiritual realities beyond those heretofore described.

In cetology, a motif of hectic, often circular appropriation and repudiation of different epistemologies and their working methods emerges. This motif does not exactly overshadow the substantive process of investigation into the nature of the whale. Yet Ishmael's recurring pattern of embrace and rejection of different ways of knowing reality does seem to allude to a broad cultural phenomenon existing in nineteenth-century Europe and America—the tension between rational and intuitive methods of obtaining knowledge, with the natural sciences and the empirical biblical scholars on one side, and the idealist philosophers and romantic poets on the other. Cetology dramatizes the prevailing sense of philosophical and cultural opposition between science and religion, reason and poetry, empirical observation and transcendental intuition, and between firsthand experience and knowledge derived less directly through cultural transmission, especially books. At the end of this chapter, we will return to the effect of this cultural context, looking specifically at how pre-Darwinian evolutionary ideas provide an underpinning for Melville's imagination.

As part of Melville's plan for Ishmael to be carried away in the cause of knowing the whale,[9] he has him bring to bear on the inquiry a farcical mass of pseudoerudition and specialization. The whale, as Howard P. Vincent observes, is considered from nearly every conceivable angle of formalized knowledge.[10] This satirical use of specialized areas of knowledge as an organizing principle is fairly evident in the sociological treatment in "Fast-Fish and Loose-Fish" (ch. 89), the phrenological treatment in "The Prairie" (ch. 79), and the legendary treatment in "The Honor and Glory of Whaling" (ch. 82). Less evident and requiring further discussion, however, is how Melville brings into high relief the theme of incomplete and sometimes contending modes of knowledge and how they are played off against each other in the comic vein. In the first sequence of cetology chapters (55–57), Ishmael conducts an encyclopedic survey into the portrait of the whale in the visual arts, and in the process many different ways to knowledge—through analytic science, through living intuition, through poetic vision—are isolated and discussed. Typically, his scorn is most keen for "the scientific Frederick Cuvier, brother to the famous Baron," who may never have seen a living whale, though he wrote a natural history about it, including illustrations of the sperm whale. Ishmael indignantly discusses the problem of scientific drawings. He says they have been taken from stranded—that is, beached—whales and "are about as correct as a drawing of a wrecked ship, with broken back, would correctly represent the noble animal itself in all its undashed pride of hull and spars" (55:262–63). Analytic science, in other words, loses the living truth; scrutinizing the whale out of his natural medium deprives him of his animated vitality.

What, then, of firsthand observation as a basis for obtaining the true view of the whale—the vantage easily accessible to the seaman–truth-seeker? At first, Ishmael seems to favor this approach, saying, "The living whale, in his full majesty and significance, is only to be seen at sea in unfathomable waters"; but then he adds that "afloat the vast bulk of him is out of sight, like a launched line-of-battle ship." Now, apparently, while one may observe the living majesty of the whale and gain poetic insight from contemplating him, a definable totality eludes the rational intellect. The truth remains submerged in unfathomable waters of mind and world. Ishmael also adds that "out of that element it is a thing eternally impossible for mortal man to hoist" the whale "so as to preserve all his mighty swells and undulations." The pure object of consciousness, in other words, cannot be extrapolated from the medium of its existence.

In the spirit of rational analysis, some may also suppose that "from the naked skeleton of the stranded whale, accurate hints may be derived touching his true form." But Ishmael assures us that "though Jeremy Bentham's skeleton . . . correctly conveys the idea of a burly-browed utilitarian old gentleman," the whale's skeleton "gives very little idea of his general shape." He asserts that "the mere skeleton of the whale bears the same relation to the fully . . . padded animal as the insect does to the chrysalis that so roundingly envelopes it" (55:263).

The first of a series of occasions then occurs in which Ishmael asserts the limitations of the mind. For all the preceding reasons, Ishmael remarks, "any way you may look at it, you must needs conclude that the great Leviathan is that one creature in the world which must remain unpainted to the last" (55:264). Neither analytic science nor contemplative intuition will provide a complete view of his reality. (Later, in the middle of the cetological material, after putting the empirical and documentary methods of science to serviceable use in studying the whale, Ishmael cries out in frustration once again at all the strange motions of the creature he cannot comprehend: "Dissect him how I may . . . I but go skin deep; I know him not, and never will" [86:379].) But just as his initial criticism of empiricism does not prevent him from taking it up as a serviceable method, his experience of whaling as a potentially annihilative endeavor does not prevent him from heroically declaring, "the only mode in which you can derive even a tolerable idea of his living contour, is by going a whaling yourself" (55:264). And while he is quick to add that "by so doing, you run no small risk of being eternally stove" in, Ishmael clearly places little stock in a cautious pursuit of truth. Caution, as "The Lee Shore" asserts, can be just as killing as courage. Thus, toward the end of the cetological material, in Chapter 103, Ishmael still punishingly straddles the paradoxical view of quest as, at once, imperative and annihilative.[11] Although as a survivor he knows the consequences of Ahab's quest, he recommends the living hunt a final time and decries the systematic scientism he has alternatively adopted:

> How vain and foolish . . . for timid untravelled man to try to comprehend aright this wondrous whale, by merely poring over his dead attenuated skelton. . . . No. Only in the heart of the quickest perils; only when within the eddyings of his angry flukes; only on the profound unbounded sea, can the fully invested whale be truly and livingly found out. (103:453–54)

This same paradoxical view shapes Ishmael's judgment of certain paintings of whaling. The ability of a French painter to capture the action of a whaling scene "wonderfully good and true" inclines Ishmael to believe that the man "was either practically conversant with his subject, or else marvellously tutored by some experienced whaleman" (56:266). But it is in the painting by a whaleman of the scene of his own amputation that Ishmael's ideas of revelation and amputation, of meaning and death, come together:

> On Tower-hill, as you go down to the London docks, you may have seen a crippled beggar . . . holding a painted board before him, representing the tragic scene in which he lost his leg. There are three whales and three boats; and one of the boats (presumed to contain the missing leg in all its original integrity) is being crunched by the jaws of the foremost whale. Any time these ten years, they tell me, has that man held up that picture, and exhibited that stump to an incredulous world. But the time of his justification has now come. His three whales are as good whales as were ever published in Wapping, at any rate; and his stump as unquestionable a stump as any you will find in the western clearings. But, though for ever mounted on that stump, never a stump-speech does the poor whaleman make; but, with downcast eyes, stands ruefully contemplating his own amputation. (57:269)

Speechless with horror, the crippled beggar personifies the heroic ethic and problematic aesthetic out of which *Moby-Dick* rises. The difference, of course, is that Ahab fights back, Ishmael talks back, while the whaleman is reduced to a cipher.

In this unit of chapters surveying the artistic representation of the whale, a final type of knowledge is introduced that recurs throughout the cetological sections. It is poetic vision, vision achieved by going to pseudo-rational extremes, so that madness becomes method and the hectic obsession with detail becomes a pretext for going beyond rationality and fact to the realm of transparent vision. Other, more reliable forms of poetic knowledge, through simile, analogy, metaphor, and symbol, are used in the cetological material; but this most extreme mode of being carried away by the inner movement of the mind is, in a sense, a polar representative of all the poetic forms of apprehension in *Moby-Dick*; and, as the most extreme example, it serves to underscore most clearly the antithesis between poetry and discursive reason.

Still not finished with his survey of "whales variously represented," Ishmael moves from the crippled beggar to skrimshander, the whaleman's art of carving sketches of the trade on whale teeth or bone. Claiming that this art arises from the "wonderful patience of industry" typical of savage cultures (and whaling ships!), Ishmael is able to make his point about the need for a cannibal, amoral savagery in achieving an art that deals with annihilation and that wrests its vitality, so to speak, from the teeth of the difficulty. "Your true whale-hunter is as much a savage as an Iroquois," he says. "I myself am a savage, owning no allegiance but to the King of the Cannibals; and ready at any moment to rebel against him" (57:270).

A penultimate shift then occurs: Dürer's woodcuts (Ishmael has just called Dürer "that fine old German savage") stimulate a train of associations about whales carved in South Sea war-wood and placed on American whalers' forecastles, about brass whales used as door knockers, about sheet iron whales used as weathercocks on old-fashioned church spires. The line of associations grows increasingly mundane. Then from real though trivial examples of whale art, Ishmael's associations move to the image of the whale read into the world:

> In bony, ribby regions of the earth, where at the base of high broken cliffs masses of rock lie strewn in fantastic groupings upon the plain, you will often discover images as of the petrified forms of the Leviathan partly merged in grass, which of a windy day breaks against them in a surf of green surges.
>
> Then, again, in mountainous countries where the traveller is continually girdled by amphitheatrical heights; here and there from some

lucky point of view you will catch passing glimpses of the profiles of whales defined along the undulating ridges.

What follows is increasing self-absorption and autointoxication, an irresponsible whimsy taking over the flow of thought:

> But you must be a thorough whaleman, to see these sights; and not only that, but if you wish to return to such a sight again, you must be sure and take the exact intersecting latitude and longitude of your first standpoint, else—so chance-like are such observations of the hills—your precise, previous stand-point would require a laborious re-discovery; like the Solomon islands, which still remain incognita, though once highruffed Mendanna trod them and old Figueroa chronicled them. (57:270–71)

Northrop Frye says about the satiric-intellectual prose tradition that influenced the cetology material that "at its most concentrated . . . [it] presents us with a vision of the world in terms of a single intellectual pattern";[12] and the fact that ideas or images are in the saddle here, riding man, instead of the reverse, is underscored still more strongly as the *idée fixe* begins to "lift" and "expand" the sphere of vision:

> Nor when expandingly lifted by your subject, can you fail to trace out great whales in the starry heavens, and boats in pursuit of them; as when long filled with thoughts of war the Eastern nations saw armies locked in battle among the clouds. Thus at the North have I chased Leviathan round and round the Pole with the revolutions of the bright points that first defined him to me. And beneath the effulgent Antarctic skies I have boarded the Argo-Navis, and joined the chase against the starry Cetus far beyond the utmost stretch of Hydrus and the Flying-Fish. (57:271)

What occurs here, in essence, is a transition to a steadily less referential form of poetic statement—a transition from a romantic to a symbolist poetics.[13] Hence, in the chapter's closing lines the impulse of the imagination largely sheds its correspondence with the external world, except as an expression or symbol for inner, visionary aspiration. Ishmael concludes: "With a frigate's anchors for my bridle-bitts and fasces of harpoons for spurs, would I could mount that whale and leap the topmost skies, to see whether the fabled heavens with all their countless tents really lie encamped beyond by mortal sight!'' (57:271). The poet's mind, evolving through symbols steadily less related to the external world, dreams of mounting the figure of the whale and riding or being conveyed by it over the last barrier of the dualistic world.

Yet it is important to note that Ishmael expresses a wish and that he cannot leap with poetry into an eternal sphere. This passage, perhaps, can be most valuably viewed as a delineation of the limits of poetic vision in *Moby-Dick*, in contrast, say, with *Paradise Lost*, its predecessor in the epic, where the fabled heavens are actualized, Monarch and all. In *Moby-Dick*, symbolism will yet assume a major role as a way to knowledge; but it will be a symbolism rising solidly and consistently out of a bedrock of physical fact in the chapters that study the whale's anatomy. It will not be the complete transcendental departure longed for here. This impulse to nullify the solid, recalcitrant, inscrutable world, moreover, is comprehensible in its context. For as the encyclopedic survey of the pictorial arts comes to a close without a definite image of the whale's form or even a reliable method of ascertaining it, the frustrated impulse to ''leap the topmost skies'' is understandable.

The romantic pattern of going to an extreme in order to enter a realm of poetic inspiration is seen also in ''The Fountain'' (ch. 85), and to some extent in ''The Blanket'' (ch. 68).[14] ''For, d'ye see, rainbows do not visit the clear air; they only irradiate vapor'' (85:374), Ishmael explains in ''The Fountain,'' where the pseudoscientific issue about what rises from the whale's spout is resolved in favor of the vapor theory and the vaporous controversy becomes, satirically, a road to ''wisdom.''

''The Fountain'' comes near the end of the long and important chain of anatomical chapters that examine the whale's head, eyes, battering ram, tun, forehead, and brains. In contrast to the metaphysical implications that arise from the documentary complexities of those chapters, the anatomical problem raised by ''The Fountain'' about whether the whale spouts water or vapor is insignificant and suggests the attenuated sense of proportion that afflicts Ishmael when a line of inquiry has gone on too long.

Prior to the onset of visionary confidence, many of the themes and patterns of Chapters 55–57 recur. Indeed, one has the sense of an internal structure of Melville's imagination repeating itself, and of him enjoying, from an ironic vantage, the antics of a scientific inquiry swept up in the flow of an equally doubtful subjectivity.

The same epistemological problem of the living object being unapproachable in rational terms returns:

> as for this whale spout, you might almost stand in it, and yet be undecided as to what it is precisely.
> The central body of it is hidden in the snowy sparkling mist enveloping it; and how can you certainly tell whether any water falls from it, when, always, when you are close enough to a whale to get a close view of his spout, he is in a prodigious commotion, the water cascading all around him. (85:373)

Also, as in the chapters surveying the history of the whale in art, the danger of knowledge (in this case, of even empirical inquiry) is present:

> Nor is it at all prudent for the hunter to be over curious touching the precise nature of the whale spout. It will not do for him to be peering into it, and putting his face in it. . . . For even when coming into slight contact with the outer, vapory shreds of the jet, which will often happen, your skin will feverishly smart, from the acridness of the thing so touching it. . . . Another thing; I have heard it said, and I do not much doubt it, that if the jet is fairly spouted into your eyes, it will blind you. The wisest thing the investigator can do then, it seems to me, is to let this deadly spout alone.

Also, there is the same onset of self-intoxicated whimsy, which in "The Fountain" is heightened by the wonderful suggestion that all this reasoning about vapor is, in effect, big talk about nothing: "Still, we can hypothesize, even if we cannot prove and establish. My hypothesis is this: that the spout is nothing but mist" (85:373). There follows the same "expandingly lifted" tone and scope about the subject, the same fanciful self-absorption with which Ishmael reviewed the whales in the starry heavens. Here, he says he is impelled to believe that vapor is only mist because of

> considerations touching the great inherent dignity and sublimity of the Sperm Whale; I account him no common, shallow being, inasmuch as it is an undisputed fact that he is never found on soundings, or near shores; all other whales sometimes are. He is both ponderous and profound. And I am convinced that from the heads of all ponderous profound beings, such as Plato, Pyrrho, the Devil, Jupiter, Dante, and so on,

there always goes up certain semi-visible steam, while in the act of thinking deep thoughts. . . .

And how nobly it raises our conceit of the mighty, misty monster, to behold him solemnly sailing through a calm tropical sea; his vast, mild head overhung by a canopy of vapor, engendered by his incommunicable contemplations, and that vapor—as you will sometimes see it—glorified by a rainbow, as if Heaven itself had put its seal upon his thoughts.

And then, finally, once indefatigable inquiry has passed through whimsy and expansiveness, access to the "Muse" begins. Moreover, the value of the method shines through colorfully: divine inspiration comes only to those who are able to be carried away in the search for truth, for only then does method dissolve into a medium of transparent vision:

For, d'ye see, rainbows do not visit the clear air; they only irradiate vapor. And so, through all the thick mists of the dim doubts in my mind, divine intuitions now and then shoot, enkindling my fog with a heavenly ray. And for this I thank God; for all have doubts; many deny; but doubts or denials, few along with them, have intuitions. Doubts of all things earthly, and intuitions of some things heavenly; this combination makes neither believer nor infidel, but makes a man who regards them both with equal eye. (85:373–74)

Is there again a false sweetness, a delusory sense of poetic flight and religious confidence? To a limited degree there is, especially in the phrase giving thanks to God. This optimism, however, does not dominate the passage. Inasmuch as Ishmael claims intuition of only *some* things heavenly, and inasmuch as this is counterbalanced by "doubts of all things earthly," the passage, on the whole, finds an equilibrium between the extremes from which it rises.

My purpose thus far has been to bring into view the multiple avenues of knowledge that the cetology material highlights and, in so doing, to illustrate the sense of epistemological fragmentation that Melville wished to underscore. Chapters 55–57 and later cetological chapters have discussed and characterized different types of knowledge: empirical study, contemplative intuition, intuition in the living act, secondhand knowledge, and imaginative vision, this last being a prototype of the whole spectrum of possible poetic responses to reality but, most especially, of the symbolist approach. Ishmael's pattern of embracing different ways to knowledge and of then discarding them as they prove unsatisfactory is intended to sharpen the overall impression of the intellectual resourcefulness and the ultimate infeasibility of the narrator's enterprise. It is also intended to suggest the mind's incapacity before the boundless dynamism of nature and, perhaps more particularly, the fact that "systems of analysis deal in categories, and categories are static, while nature—that to which the categories are applied—is always in process."[15] In turning now to consider the heterogeneity of the material in the "cetological center,"[16] it is worth noting that multiple viewpoints continue to emerge. They do not, however, consist of references to types of knowledge orchestrated for satiric or philosophic effect; they are instead *incipient views of reality* that rise directly from the physical dimensions of the subject matter at hand.

This is perhaps the moment, also, to return to Edgar Dryden's approach to the cetology material and to further distinguish it from my own. As I indicated earlier, Dryden emphasizes the dependence of Ishmael the storyteller on other books on whaling rather than on firsthand experience. "The creative act begins," Dryden says of an Ishmael who swims through libraries, "not with the material to be shaped but with an exploration of previous verbal plans for creation."[17] Although Dryden does expand his conception of Ishmael's imaginative activity from literary reconstruction to imaginative construction, Dryden is also clear about the limits of Ishmael's creativity. He observes that the foundations of Ishmael's "construct are verbal fictions, since the material ones are unspeakable because unknowable." Ishmael's system "refers to nothing outside itself."[18] Regarding the various anatomical parts that Ishmael describes in search of the whale's hidden significance, Dryden again asserts rigid epistemological limits: "Ishmael's view of the whale as a hieroglyph . . . points to man's attempt to make everything an object of consciousness, and, at the same time, suggests that he must necessarily fail because material objects are 'dead, blind wall[s]' of silence. They resist the transforming powers of the phonetic alphabet and may be represented only by enigmatic figures."[19] As will become quickly apparent in the following section, I see Ishmael trying to confront material reality with a symbolist's approach and succeeding, to the extent of his achieving *fragmentary* revelations, incomplete but nonetheless illuminating. My conception of Ishmael as a romantic artist involves his effort not only to penetrate to the supernatural core of reality but to represent the surface with its textured variety and multitudinous forms. By striving for summary generalization and bypassing textual detail, Dryden overstates Ishmael's goals, omitting Melville's commitment to descriptive presentation and mimetic assimilation of surprising and unexpected aspects of reality, beyond any prior verbal constructs.[20] That the natural and imaginative vitality of *Moby-Dick* cannot be entirely squared with an intertextual view of literature like Dryden's will be even more evident, if it is not yet, as I move into Melville's treatment of the heterogeneity of the materials of whaling.[21]

In order to consider the heterogeneity of the cetological material, its function and significance, I plan to focus on one sequence of chapters — that which follows the survey of art history. These chapters comprise a unit in that they contain a sequence of steps in the processing of the whale and use Stubb's whale (killed in ch. 61) as a demonstration model.[22] It is important to keep always in mind the varied ground these chapters cover. Too often, for lucidity's sake, writers describe this material as being about whales and whaling, overlooking the immense diversity one encounters in this central section.

They deal with the *Pequod*'s sailing into a sea-meadow of brit and with the emergence of a giant squid; with a description of the coilings of the line in the whaleboat; with the sighting, pursuit, and killing of a whale. They explain the changing of places in the whaleboat so that the lance may be darted by the officer, not the harpooner, and how the harpoon rests in a "crotch." They describe a comic scene between Stubb and the cook and how the dead whale's carcass is devoured by sharks. They contain a gastronomic survey of the whale as a fish. They encompass the massacre of the sharks feeding on the whale carcass, the cutting and raising of the blubber, an analysis of whether the blubber is the whale's skin, a meditation on the "vulturism" on earth. They include a gam with the *Jeroboam* and Captain Mayhew's story about Gabriel and, finally, the manner in which a sailor on deck, by means of a rope, steadies a harpooner balanced on the rotating whale carcass during the cutting-in.

Is there any uniformity to be observed in these chapters? In terms of manner of presentation, subject matter, and theme, there are small pockets of homogeneity. "The Line" (ch. 60), "The Dart" (ch. 62), and "The Crotch" (ch. 63), for example, each describes, in considerable detail, a particular item of whaling gear; each is presented as Ishmael's firsthand demonstration; and two of the three end similarly, by means of poetic analogy or simile. In Chapters 64–66—"Stubb's Supper," "The Whale as a Dish," and "The Shark Massacre"—the subject matter of sharks and the "sharkishness" in man as well as nature comprises another small area of similarity. Thematic coherence also emerges from the statements in "Brit" (ch. 58) that "dreaded creatures glide under water, unapparent for the most part" and that the "horrors of the half known life" (58:274) exist in the mind as well; for the next chapter actualizes these claims in the horrible giant squid arising from the sea. But the narrative movement in these fourteen chapters provides scarcely any sense of progressive unity. Only the chapter about "speaking" to the *Jeroboam* (ch. 71) bears directly on Ahab's vengeance. Ahab's other appearances in "Stubb's Supper" (ch. 64) and "The Sphynx" (ch. 70) are more reminders of the tone of his presence than additions to the plot.

On the whole, these chapters create a sense neither of uniformity of material nor of thematic coherence. Within the circumscribing universe of a whaling voyage, there could not be more diversity of subject matter, more microcosmic attention to factual detail, more variety of expositional situation and literary mode, more novelty of macrocosmic reference. Also, at one with this diversity is the impression of the untiring conscientiousness, the comic busyness, of the narrator trying to do justice to his superabundant, hydra-headed vision of life. Ishmael alludes to these arduous demands as he explains an aspect of the cutting-in that he overlooked at the proper time:

> In the tumultuous business of cutting-in and attending to a whale, there is much running backwards and forwards among the crew. Now hands are wanted here, and then again hands are wanted there. There is no staying in any one place; for at one and the same time everything has to be done everywhere. *It is much the same with him who endeavors the description of the scene.* (72:319; italics mine).

The impression this unit of chapters makes, then, with its abbreviated sequences, its abrupt shifts in venue, proximity, and mode of presentation, with its sense of multitudinous variety and relative absence of concerted narrative action, is of a plenum of life and of an equally animated and inexhaustible versatility of mind. If there is unity, it is unity of only the highest, most general sort. The theme of the dangerousness of life is a unifying element; so is the mutual abundance of mind and world, yoked together even when antagonistic, by an immanent energy, an interrelated and multifaceted vitality, which animates everything and which the whale both symbolizes and embodies.

Of Melville's heterogeneous aesthetic two effects can be isolated. One is the implication that not only at the center of the work but, in a sense, at the center of man's life on Earth, there is a generative sea of existence, a reservoir of limitless phenomena, whose inexhaustible forms and meanings exceed the limited truth of any particular life or mind. This superabundant, suprahuman perspective is consonant with the timeless scale of events implied by the five-thousand-year-old sea that closes over the *Pequod* at the end. But this effect is only secondary. With regard to the narrative and dramatic sections of *Moby-Dick*, the function of the unbridled diversity of cetology is to present authentication of the many and sometimes fluid viewpoints of the main characters, and to do so from a standpoint at some remove from the subjective intensities of the story. In this way, the manifold nature of reality and the problematical indeterminacy of the final nature of things are reinforced and further extended without undue reliance on the philosophical intensities of the characters. Ishmael's terror at atheistical voids, his transient visions of benignity, Ahab's conviction of an inscrutable malice as well as other permutations of truth unimagined by the characters—all these emerge from the teeming variety of the subject matter, and sustain and heighten our participation in the final mystery of things.

There are many examples of how material, extrinsic to the characters, clearly suggests the same noumenal intuitions as the characters themselves have expressed. Melville validates Ishmael's feeling of a spiritual emptiness or demonism at the heart of reality as set forth in "The Whiteness of the Whale." Utilizing a verbal shorthand by which metaphysical connotations can be economically attached to physical events, Melville deliberately recalls the meanings of Moby Dick's albino hue as he describes a placid sea as a "vacant sea" (61:282) or the whale's skeleton as an "utter blank" (103:453). But in addition to these often casual verbal allusions to Ishmael's insight, there are other moments that depend far more on the physical properties of the subject matter to symbolize metaphysical truths, moments when the superimposition of verbal cues is only supplemental and the objective qualities of the material contain the symbolic germ. One of these events occurs in the chapter describing the *Pequod*'s encounter with the *Albatross*, a whaler homeward bound after four years at sea. The *Albatross*—rather like the "white-lead chapter" about the color white (42:194)—was always the white ship its name implies; but it is now whitened from wear also: "All down her sides, this spectral appearance was traced with long channels of reddened rust, while all her spars and her rigging were like the thick branches of trees furred over with hoar-frost." As Ahab inquires about Moby Dick, the "strange captain, leaning over the pallid bulwarks" (52:236–37), gives no reply; in the act of answering, his megaphone falls in the sea. The moral and physical exhaustion of the *Albatross* and her crew strikes the same note of silent terror as does the whiteness of the whale. They convey the same noumenal void, the same ultimate horror, at the core of reality.

But the most effective authentication of the demonic powers implied by Moby Dick's whiteness occurs in the emergence of the giant squid. Here again Melville's physical symbolism is heightened by a verbal shorthand. When first sighted, the squid is mistaken for Moby Dick and familiar imagistic phrases are employed from Chapter 1 (where Moby Dick is referred to as a "grand hooded phantom, like a snow hill in the air"): "In the distance, a great white mass lazily rose, and . . . gleamed . . . like a snow-slide, new slid from the hills." Upon taking to their boats, however, the crew finds that the monster, though wondrous and terrible, is not Moby Dick:

> A vast pulpy mass . . . lay floating on the water, innumerable long arms radiating from its centre, and curling and twisting like a nest of anacondas, as if blindly to clutch at any hapless object within reach. No perceptible face or front did it have; no conceivable token of either sensation or instinct; but undulated there on the billows, an unearthly, formless, chance-like apparition of life. (59:276)

Faceless, sensationless, formless, chance-like—these abstract qualities, rising from the physical impression of the squid and helping to crystallize its symbolic import, refer both backward and forward in the book. Backward, they recall the intuition of a demonic and possibly godless and accidental universe from "The Whiteness of the Whale"; and ahead, they lead to "The Battering Ram," "The Prairie," and "The Nut," where the whale's faceless and sensationless head becomes a symbol for the "dread powers" (79:346) of a Deity whose "face shall not be seen" (86:379).

We have been speaking about the corroboration of Ishmael's views provided by the cetological matter in *Moby-Dick*; yet clearly the specter of a faceless and insensate creature correlates with Ahab's view of God as well. What, then, are the cetological validations of Ahab's belief in an "outrageous strength," an "inscrutable malice," behind the "mask" of the physical world? (36:164). These occur primarily in the systematic study of the whale, where features such as the whale's forehead signify the brutal power that Ahab conceives in the cosmos. By means of a whole range of literary techniques,[23] Melville is able, especially with regard to the whale, to persuade us that natural facts may be symbols of spiritual facts. Indeed, in the case of the whale's brow, so close is the correspondence between its physical properties and Ahab's spiritual conception of the Deity—faceless, insensate, outrageously brutal (76:336–37)—that the reader himself might be persuaded by the same transcendental logic that convinces Ahab. In the "battering ram" of the whale's forehead, "that wall, shoved near" (36:164), Ahab virtually locates the Deity in the physical world.

In "The Tail," the same terrible, annihilative powers are found as in the whale's forehead; here, however, an impression of delicate beauty as well as dread force emerges: "infantileness of ease undulates through a Titanism of power" (86:376). But if the motions of the whale's tail suggest a highly differentiated level of organization, "The Nut" casts a different light on the whale's cranial development and the Deity behind it. There is not much brain to be found, about "ten inches in length and as many in depth" (80:348). On the other hand, the whale's optics convey still other hypotheses as to his braininess and differentiation. Because the location of a whale's eyes are like that of a man's ears, "the whale . . . must see one distinct picture on this side, and another distinct picture on that side" (74:330); it may even be that the whale is forced to reason or act upon "divided and diametrically opposite powers of vision" at one and the same time. Gentleness may exist within him along with antagonism, much as if "a man were able simultaneously to go through the demonstrations of two distinct problems in Euclid" (74:331). And as this state would explain the "extraordinary vacillations of movement" and the "helpless perplexity of volition" of a whale surrounded by his hunters, it would also contain implications about the possible predicament of a Deity who might be caught between clashing powers of vision, one benign, the other malevolent, so that they tend to cancel each other out or to reduce Him to helplessness.

Finally, there are authentications in the whale's anatomy of Ishmael's experience of benignity in man and nature. Behind the whale's forehead and for one-third the length of his body lies the "immense honeycomb of oil," the upper part of which, called the case, contains "the highly-prized spermaceti" (77:339–40). Just as the whale's destructiveness toward his hunters has been the basis for inferring a possible cosmic malice, so here the profit from the oil to the crew and the benefits to mankind must underscore a possible cosmic beneficence. But most persuasive here is the cleansing effect the sperm oil has on Ishmael emotionally when he is squeezing case (94:415–16). The oil becomes the very medium of Ishmael's transformation; it provides, as Leslie A. Fiedler points out, a "counter-baptism" to Ahab's baptism of fire.[24] Indeed, the sperm oil becomes an objective correlative for all the emotive and poetic richness Ishmael discovers.

In sum, then, from the hue, forehead, tail, brains, eyes, and case of the whale, the cetological center provides data of an empirical sort about the whale, information which, in most instances, also suggests symbolic possibilities about the character of God. This quasi-scientific commitment to presenting objective information about the whale provides, as a result, a kaleidoscopic richness of natural fact and symbolic connotation, much of which corroborates Ishmael's and Ahab's transcendental intuitions. But besides underscoring the primacy of certain metaphysical viewpoints belonging to the main characters, these chapters often provide additional combinations and permutations of the primal forces of the natural world, as was noted in "The Tail" and in the discussion of the whale's optics.

Which of these chapters best illuminates the ultimate truth? Which analysis of the primal elements of nature coincides most closely with the work's view of God, nature, and man? Strictly speaking, no chapter offers greater insight than any other; no one provides discoveries that rise above the rest. Some chapters may seem subtler and more closely allied with the dualistic complexion of reality that pervades the work; but there is no implication that an overwhelming finality is arrived at from a particular anatomical precinct.

The nature of the whale and its spiritual dimensions are fully revealed neither by the analytic mind nor by the symbolist imagination. On the contrary, the underlying comic pattern and tone suggest that the whale is greater than the sum of its parts,[25] greater than science or the powers of intuition to penetrate to a first cause. Also, as the terrifying impact of Ishmael's experience on the *Pequod* brings him to want to dissect the symbol and source of his terror, the chapters on the whale's anatomy are often presented in the spirit of demonstrations into the root forces and mysteries of life. As often as not, they are efforts to document the radical danger he has known, rather than to press further into the unknown. They do not portray Ishmael's progressive intellectual development nor a resolution of his fears.

Melville does not try to tally the different emergent viewpoints spread through the midsection of *Moby-Dick*. He cannot. Instead, he allows the panorama of the cetological material to speak for itself—to suggest through its discontinuities and fragmentary intensities a reality that is never finished unfolding, a reality of process, diversity, contrariety, and plenitude.

In *The Salt-Sea Mastodon* (1973), Robert Zoellner tries to show that the cetological chapters are intended to detail a progressive history of Ishmael's discoveries about himself and nature.[26] In my view, this approach muscles the text into a pattern of linear meaningfulness that is not there and that is out of step with the prevailing spirit of diversity and abundance. Also, Zoellner locates Ishmael's observations in the cetological chapters in the story-time of the *Pequod*'s voyage, further contributing to his fallacious thesis that the things Ishmael describes change him. Seeing is *not* becoming in *Moby-Dick*, certainly not in any permanent and progressive manner. Outward reality is multifarious; mood and point of view are shifting, transient, and, in response to outward diversity, multidirectional. It is probably significant that Zoellner puts so little stress on the meditation in "The Gilder" (114:492), which speaks of the cyclical nature of human development and philosophy.

III Fragmentation and Meaning in the Final Chase

The aesthetic and philosophic goals of *Moby-Dick*'s midsection, then, are to represent a multitudinous world and convey epistemological fragmentation and disarray. By introducing an unwieldy mass of subject matter about the whale and by scrutinizing it from diverse perspectives, Melville is able to "dramatize" manifold interactions of mind and world. He is able to indicate incomplete and contending modes of knowledge at the same time as he provides validation of Ahab's, Ishmael's, and other intuitions about the primal nature of the world and its Maker. And amidst profusion and contrariety of viewpoint, he is also able to underscore the indeterminate nature of ultimate truth.

While the midsection of *Moby-Dick* is largely exposition, the three chapters of the final chase comprise a narrative whose torpedolike action leaves no room for discursive analysis. Lacking the opportunity to digress on the whale's behavior or the character of the God whom he embodies, the final chapters nevertheless carry forward from the midsection the themes of epistemological and deific segmentation already developed there. Within certain limitations, they imply a more precise idea of the nature of the whale. Blending themes of multiplicity with themes of moral coherence, the final chapters require us to refine what may have already been formulated and to reach for a final larger understanding.

Before proceeding, however, let us consider an example of how the final chapters are deliberately intended to sustain themes from the "cetological center." One of Ishmael's quandaries as both neophyte whaleman and retrospective narrator is whether the White Whale is simply a naturalistic whale or whether he is a creature of supernatural properties, an agent or emblem of the Deity. The final chapters keep this question alive by subtly suggesting the latter possibility. They describe Moby Dick not as a finite, observable figure, but nearly always as an elusive presence in motion: his being seems to overflow the mold of his physical form. He is described as darting into motion with an "ungraduated, instantaneous swiftness" (135:569) as though normal changes of position do not explain his movements. Adjectives describing him are modified with carefully selected adverbs, playing up the mystical quality of sensuous impressions: the circles Moby Dick swims around Ahab are described as "planetarily swift" and "revolvingly appalling" (133:551). The nouns used emphasize motion: "swiftness," "celerity," "velocity" (133:548, 549, 552). Three properties are implied by such language: that Moby Dick is at times irreducible to a static perception; that he sometimes acts abruptly, instantaneously, as if outside sequential time; and that he has at moments a planetary, a cosmic, quality. These phrases enforce his function as a symbol, an objective correlative, for the problem of knowledge already delineated in the work: it is impossible to grasp him. More specifically, they promote the feeling that Moby Dick may be a creature of supernatural origin whose numinous reality is almost palpable within the blur of his awesome activity.[27]

Moby Dick's behavior in "The Chase—First Day" typifies the two-sided pattern of his actions throughout the final chase. As the *Pequod*'s boats enter the whale's circle of serenity, gaiety and a mood of celebration permeate all things, animate and inanimate, as though they reflect and give expression to Moby Dick's deep mood of tranquillity. The very details described by the narrator convey the idea of the whale's confluence with his aqueous medium and the Dionysian joy his immersion in the natural world produces. Ultimately, this gilded moment joining whale and world, nature and observer, is consummated by the rising arc of a visionary passage in which the whale's "gentle joyousness" (133:548) is said to surpass even the pleasures of the Olympian gods.

Yet the events that follow the description of the White Whale in this state of mildness reassert Ahab's view of him as violently destructive. "The wrenched hideousness" of Moby Dick's jaw has been withheld from sight beneath the "serene tranquillities of the tropical sea" (133:548) — whether deliberately or inadvertently is not clear. But when he raises himself, sounds, and reappears, he metamorphoses into a murderous beast intent on destroying Ahab's boat.

Why does a spell of poetic evocation overtake the narration as the whaleboats first approach Moby Dick? Why is he described in such mild and deifying terms that one critic is prompted to describe the scene as a "noumenal epiphany" in which Moby Dick "manifests himself"?[28] The answer is multifaceted. One aspect of the answer is that Melville is trying to convey through this spell of poetic vision the wonder of the men as they finally approach the object of so much rumored divinity and find him serene. Another is that Melville is trying to dramatize for the questing consciousness of Ishmael, the storyteller, the mythopoeic ecstasy of arriving at the central symbol of the work — the White Whale himself. Richard H. Brodhead has written illuminatingly about Melville's "exploiting the differences of imaginative potential of disparate genres of fiction." He observes that Melville thinks of reality as "a range of possibilities, each of which requires a specific sort of human perception for its realization."[29] This encounter with the peaceful side of the White Whale's nature on the first day of the hunt is an instance of just such an exploitation of a "genre" — in this case of the protosymbolist's relation to reality where the distinction breaks down between subject and object, observer and observed. Bairnard Cowan, in his study of the crisis of allegory in *Moby-Dick*, has suggested that a few special scenes such as "The Grand Armada," "The Castaway," and "A Squeeze of the Hand" involve "attempts at going beyond allegory" and "forming a dialectical movement between mediated and unmediated vision."[30] One of the countermovements to the allegorical attempt "to figure the whale in fixed terms or images on the page"[31] is the use of a direct encounter of a character with the whale that "leads the chain of signification outward toward the reader and presents the transcendent connections" of the whale "as faithfully as possible."[32] Having used the appropriate literary mode to capture the pith and marrow of the crew's moment of revelation, Melville is also then in a position to depict fully the abrupt contrast between this assent to a benign vision of existence and the violent actualities on the other side of the moment.

That there is detachment in this segment (133:548–49) is evident from the paragraph that calls attention to the whale's strange power to entice. As a retrospective narrator who is both in and out of the scene, Ishmael not only rhapsodizes from the perspective of the primitive whaleman about the "enticing calm" of Moby Dick, but also forewarns (having survived the events he is describing) about the deceitfulness and wrath within Moby Dick's "quietude":

> the whale shed off enticings. No wonder there had been some among the hunters who namelessly transported and allured by all this serenity, had ventured to assail it; but had fatally found that quietude but the vesture of tornadoes. Yet calm, enticing calm, oh, whale! thou glidest on, to all who for the first time eye thee, no matter how many in that same way thou may'st have bejuggled and destroyed before. (133:548)

Several explanations suggest themselves for the shift in Moby Dick's behavior from serenity to malice in "The Chase—First Day." Coordinate with the fragmented lines of speculation that the characters and narration have generated, these explanations run the same segmentary gamut from Moby Dick being a naturalistic creature, benign, malicious, indifferent, or dualistic in nature, to his being a creature of spiritual dimensions belonging to an angelic, a demonic, an indifferent, or a bipolar principle of the cosmos. Finally, there is Paul Brodtkorb's view that Moby Dick is "numinous and mute,"[33] and that nothing conclusive can be said about him.

In the dark view of Moby Dick, in its naturalistic as well as metaphysical variety, his serenity as the whaleboats approach can be seen as a deception, with his evil reality hidden beneath the surface and the glittering "mask" of sense impressions exercising a superficial enticement. In the optimistic view, Moby Dick may be seen as benign, without propensity for malice or capacity for forethought; whatever aggression he exhibits may be explained as having been forced upon him by men. In the bipolar view of him (as indifferent and malicious by turns), Moby Dick, swimming peacefully on the first day of the chase, may not see his approaching hunters; or else he is at peace with the watery world and indifferent to humankind. But when he reacts, he sounds and emerges as a transformed creature intent upon destroying his destroyers.

In light of Moby Dick's behavior in the chase that ensues, rejection of certain of these hypotheses and validation of others are possible up to a point. And since I want to go past categorization of the fragmentation of Ishmael's vision to how *Moby-Dick* assesses the nature of each hypothesis, I shall continue to analyze the implication about each viewpoint that can be derived from the remaining narration.

In the final chapters, Melville dispenses with Ishmael's risible tragicomic delivery, wanting instead a third-person voice, whose relative impersonality gives evenness of focus and tone to the narration of the tragic denouement. Yet while the narrator of the final three chapters is more or less neutral and omniscient, narrative qualifications crop up at salient points as to what is directly knowable about Moby Dick's motives and what is only speculative. For instance, in the passage describing the whaleboats' approach on the first day of the chase, Moby Dick is said to be *"seemingly* unsuspecting" (133:548; italics mine) of the hunters, in order to leave open the alternate possibility that he is not as innocent as he appears. In a similar vein is the passage describing Moby Dick's last-minute shift in his angle of attack on Ahab's boat, so that the "malicious intelligence ascribed to him" is preceded by the qualifying phrase, "But *as if* perceiving this stratagem" (133:549; italics mine). Such passages are obviously intended to reinforce Ahab's view of Moby Dick as intelligent and malicious. The other view, reinforced several times in the three-day chase with an "as if" phrase, is that Moby Dick is indifferent to his hunters, his "general stolidity" at one with the rest of the natural world.[34]

As for the question of the origin of the narrative viewpoint, formalistic distinctions[35] produce more problems here than they solve. The information supplied in the epilogue, that Ishmael was Ahab's bowsman on the third day, establishes a firsthand view of the action for Ishmael; it supplies the basis, should a critic wish, to find in the narration of that day the values of Ishmael's consciousness. Yet we speak only of the last day. It would also appear to be a necessary inference that Ishmael, who has always been a member of Starbuck's crew, was not among the hunters on the two preceding days. In obedience to Ahab's wish, "all the boats but Starbuck's were dropped" (133:547). Thus, the ecstatic passage describing the approach to the whale does not—formally speaking—derive from a first-person viewpoint. The narration speaks of the generic "hunter" rather than the identifying "I." Ishmael, therefore, must be said to narrate the three-day chase from within only the loosest convention of a first-person retrospective viewpoint, a convention from within which Melville feels free to imagine the locus of Ahab's final days, establishing the desired tragic tone and even abdicating Ishmael's viewpoint alto-gether—except when themes from the preceding sections of the work require Ishmael's selective intrusions. Neither a "witness narrator"[36] within the action nor an "omniscient narrator" outside, Melville's nar-rative persona fulfills the requirements of the tragedy and yet is able to impart the philosophical elaborations consistent with earlier portions of the work.

Of the various segmented views of Moby Dick's nature listed above, the naturalistic, Rousseauistic view of him suggested by his unanticipated tranquillity on the first day is, indeed, enticing. He has been hunted per-sistently in the weeks preceding his encounter with the *Pequod*. Both the *Delight* and the *Rachel* have lowered for him; a lance remains in his back. His experience of persecution, therefore, complemented by his unex-pected gentleness, would seem to suggest an alternative hypothesis to Ahab's view of his intelligent malignity: that he is benign and a victim of evil men against whom he is forced into mortal combat. This view, how-ever, when considered in light of Moby Dick's behavior in the three days of battle, proves unsupportable.

The point in question is whether Moby Dick exhibits malice and fore-thought in the course of the struggle, whether he seems to possess the instinct and volition to execute destructive designs. Zoellner, with his penchant for embracing minority views, has argued against this position. Concerning Moby Dick's rising under Ahab's boat on the first day, he has asserted that "despite Ishmael's anthropomorphic stress on the 'devilish' and 'crafty' movements of the whale, everything he does is well within the response-capacity of any highly-developed animal." And with regard to the whale's assault on all three boats at once on the second day, he says:

> If Melville—or Ishmael—were intent upon demonstrating intelligence or malignity in the White Whale, this handling of the event-continuum represents another missed opportunity. Moby Dick does not *choose* a sin-gle boat, does not *decide* upon an adversary, does not *follow* any apparent plan of action. Rather, he engages, like the veritable animal he is, in unfocused "appalling battle" randomly prosecuted "on every side."[37]

A look at the passage in question, however, suggests that it is intended to make dramatically vivid Moby Dick's menacing fury; and the fact that his hunters succeed in temporarily eluding him does not significantly di-minish the effect of this impression:

As if to strike a quick terror into them, by this time being the first assailant himself, Moby Dick had turned, and was now coming for the three crews. Ahab's boat was central; and cheering his men, he told them he would take the whale head-and-head,—that is, pull straight up to his forehead. . . . But ere that close limit was gained, and while yet all three boats were plain as the ship's three masts to his eye; the White Whale churning himself into furious speed, almost in an instant as it were, rushing among the boats with open jaws, and a lashing tail, offered appalling battle on every side; and heedless of the irons darted at him from every boat, seemed only intent on annihilating each separate plank of which those boats were made. But skillfully manoeuvred, incessantly wheeling like trained chargers in the field; the boats for a while eluded him; though, at times, but by a plank's breadth. (134:558)

Moby Dick's assault on all three boats—as though he were one of Homer's heroes pressing into the thick of battle—connotes threefold fury rather than a fraction of the amount required to destroy one foe. But be that as it may, more to the point is the fact that Zoellner's denial of Moby Dick's observably destructive intentions really does not acknowledge the bald facts of the struggle: that on all three days Moby Dick initiates the hostilities; that on the first and second days, at some point during the battle, he rises under Ahab's boat; and that, for whatever reason, he singles out the whaleship as a viable foe and proceeds, as we had been told was possible in "The Affidavit," to charge, stave in, and utterly sink it. Narrator's interpretative embellishments aside, these are the facts of the case. One might argue, it is true, that the fishery, in the larger view, created this destructiveness, and that Ahab merely incites it to the point of demoniacal fury; nevertheless, the fact remains that, whatever the preconditions, Moby Dick's behavior during the three days of the chase demonstrates a sustained malice and a capacity for sustained execution of that malice. If there was not in him a predisposition to these attributes, his behavior would not have assumed such pronounced form.

What, then, of the pessimistic view, disseminated by rumor, amplified by superstition, and brought into dire focus by Ahab, that Moby Dick is designing and destructive, not a "dumb thing"—as Starbuck would have it—madly singled out by Ahab, but a creature of "inscrutable malice," full of reason behind its "unreasoning mask" (36:164)? Although the facts listed in the previous paragraph support this view, another set of observations about Moby Dick's behavior contradicts them. For Moby Dick's practice, after each day of battle, is to swim away from his foes, so that it is they, all night, who must pursue him. Even on the third day, after the first encounter, he swims away; and always he swims in the same direction. His course to leeward, in addition, also argues against any designing intent, for the *Pequod* can readily pursue him by sailing " 'full before the wind' " (133:553), whereas if he had swum to windward—into the wind—direct pursuit would have been impossible. Also, while he swims rapidly, he swims steadily, "at a traveller's methodic pace" (134:560), as though the *Pequod* were not of final importance to him but only, as the narration speculates, "a stage in his leeward voyage" (135:568). Moby Dick's nocturnal leeward progress, therefore, would seem at least to balance off the possibility of his total malevolence, and to speak persuasively of his final disinterest in human enemies. Newton Arvin articulates this view of Moby Dick best when he says, "Demoniac as he can be when hunted and harpooned, he himself seems rather to evade than to seek these meetings." He deals out "ruin only when provoked by his pursuers."[38]

Elsewhere in the work, other bipolar positions are articulated. In "The Line" we are told that the calms of life are without any ultimate benignity: "the profound calm which only apparently precedes and prophesies of the storm, is perhaps more awful than the storm itself; for, indeed, the calm is but the wrapper and envelope of the storm; and contains it in itself" (60:281). "The Gilder," on the other hand, asserts a bipolarity that is intrinsically double: "Would to God these blessed calms would last. But the mingled, mingling threads of life are woven by warp and woof: calms crossed by storms, a storm for every calm" (114:492). There is even the still more affirmative position of "The Grand Armada," which reverses the view of the calms as a mere "envelope" or "vesture" of storms. Ishmael the narrator claims that storms of his inner nature are merely peripheral phenomena:

> amid the tornadoed Atlantic of my being, do I myself still for ever centrally disport in mute calm; and while ponderous planets of unwaning woe revolve round me, deep down and deep inland there I still bathe me in eternal mildness of joy. (87:389)

In the end, however, the most difficult question may not concern the reality of evil in Moby Dick but the elusive reality of good. Although the status and relative proportions of "calms" and "storms" may vary in passages such as those above, the retrospective nature of the novel leaves little room for equivocation about the presence of destructive forces in the natural world. Danger, death, amputation, storm, predation, even the all-but-total shipwrecking of the human universe, are the *donnée* of the work, insofar as the experience of Ishmael the whaleman informs the consciousness of Ishmael the narrator. Far less easily resolved is the status of good.

Another motif related to that of "calms" and "storms" is Ishmael's view, consonant with Ahab's, that all beauty and mildness in nature are enticements that bejuggle, then destroy. In Ishmael's description of the tranquil surface of the sea in mild weather, the sense of beauty and harmony he experiences always, in the end, proves superficial and delusive; invariably, the true reality beneath is remorseless, aggressive. In "The Mast-Head," it is a token of the youthful attitude being satirized that the young sailor, lulled by mild, sunny days, confuses "every dimly-discovered, uprising fin of some undiscernible form" with the "embodiment of those elusive thoughts that only people the soul," while those forms are really the fins of sharks (35:159). In "The Gilder," there are "the times of dreamy quietude, when beholding the tranquil beauty and brilliancy of the ocean's skin, one forgets the tiger heart that pants beneath it" (114:991). In "Brit," regarding the "subtleness of the sea," "its most dreaded creatures glide under water, unapparent for the most part, and treacherously hidden beneath the loveliest hints of azure" (58:274). Even in the ecstatic moments, rowing out on the first day of the chase (when the language of "The Grand Armada" recurs in the description of Moby Dick's "gentle joyousness"), there occurs yet another transcendental temptation that subsequent events undercut.

As suggested before, while Ishmael survives the *Pequod*'s destruction, and while the symbolism of Queequeg's coffin rising to save Ishmael connotes his attainment of a more benign psychological relation to life than Ahab's, the work does not present a stable apprehension of that reality in Ishmael's re-creation of his experience. Emblems of something positive, the calm mild days at sea are not an illusion; they exist and form an intrinsic part of the pattern of experience. But exactly what they signify about the cosmic scheme, or nature's ultimate particle, or the human mind is something that Melville seems unable fully to resolve. Are these calms evidence, as Ishmael's expansive tendencies would have it, of an equivalent, separate "good" pervading man and nature, one that offsets the reality of "evil" and offers the basis of a strong affirmation? Probably not. Are they, as Ahab is inclined to believe, a hiatus in the assaults and challenges flung at man, but with no ultimate significance? Or are they, as Ishmael's psychological advance would seem to suggest, two poles of one inseparable reality, perhaps not equal in force or extent, but nevertheless intrinsically double, combinable, and the basis for human growth, creativity, and spiritual development, even if that development is inescapably tragic?

This differentiation between a monism of evil and a bipolar reality is never provided. At the heart of the problem may be the volatile and suggestive nature of the mind as Melville saw and experienced it. Always desperate for an affirmation with which to protect itself from overwhelming pessimism, man's mind is also unable to avoid exaggerating the basis of belief. Pertinent here is Melville's comment to Hawthorne on the danger of transcendental moments when "men insist upon the universal application of a temporary feeling or opinion."[39] But so is Hawthorne's observation that Melville "will never rest until he gets hold of a definite belief."[40]

The peculiar problem of grasping a verifiable good is also alluded to in "The Symphony" in the passage that develops the sharp "contrast" between the strong, physical, instinctive, and "masculine" promptings of life, represented by the "mighty" fish rushing "far down in the bottomless blue," and the gentle, dreamy, immaterial, and "feminine" aspects of life, represented by the flight of small birds "hither, and thither, on high" (132:542). These characterizations of the modalities of nature imply that *in man* as life rises from its primal, instinctive depths into consciousness, and as it becomes spiritually and intellectually refined, it also becomes more various, more capricious, and—turning Plato on his head—less true. The inescapable truth, which Ishmael describes as the "truth with malice in it" (41:184), lies in the primal depths, where Ahab finds his angry power.

This ambivalence about a monistic or bipolar view of Moby Dick and nature generally reflects the same ambivalence in Melville's attitude toward Ahab. On the one hand, Ahab is celebrated as an exceptional individual, a hero whose adherence to his perception of the total malice of life is the source of both his greatness and his destruction. On the other hand, in chapters such as "Moby Dick" (41:184–86) and "The Chart" (44:201–2), Ahab is portrayed as a disordered and impious person, whose rejection of a moral good (rising from the heart and linking all men) condemns him to wickedness and error. This ambivalence of attitude, straddling Ahab's rightness as a hero and wrongness as a man,

Melville tries to subsume under the idea borrowed from Coleridge (writing about *Hamlet*)[41] that "all mortal greatness is but disease" (16:74). But Melville's effort does not obscure his own indecisiveness about the proper relation to the malice of nature on the part of the exceptional man.

This ambivalence of attitude is sustained to the end. In the closing pages, the work praises Ahab as an exceptional individual willing to sink to hell to steal "a living part of heaven" (135:572), while at the same time it passes judgment on him as a man. In order to illustrate that judgment—in the popular wisdom, that *a man reaps what he sows*—Ahab is shown at the end to encounter in objective conditions the same demonic reality that has exemplified his inner life. As a result of Ahab's rigid adherence to one idea of himself and the world, his moral reality is shown to become his circumstantial reality, his character, his fate. In one instance, his head becomes the center of the "direful zone" (133:551) around which the enraged whale swims, causing us to reflect on Ahab's role in eliciting such appalling malice from the forces of nature. In another, the sharks, on the third day, seem to follow Ahab's boat: the oars grow smaller and smaller, as though his destructive purpose can no longer be supported. A final instance is found in the deliberate use of Calvinist language to describe Moby Dick as he charges the *Pequod*—in the "predestinating head" and the "retribution, swift vengeance, eternal malice" seen "in his whole aspect" (135:571). This language is not intended to suggest a last-minute embrace of Calvinist doctrine on the narrator's part; rather it dramatizes, better than any other language can, the terrifying aspect of the scene. Only the Calvinist visage of God's wrath can sufficiently evoke the retributive malice that the *Pequod*'s crew sees swimming toward it. This malice and will to revenge have been the animating truths of Ahab's world, and it is logical that the destruction of his world should bear the visage of the condemning God he has repudiated.

IV   Underpinnings: The Evolutionary Context

What are the cultural forces, exercising from within Melville's imagination, a shaping power over his conception and realization of *Moby-Dick*? If naturalism and Christianity can be described as the two most important poles of his mind in the creation of *Moby-Dick*,[42] then evolutionary thought and Calvinism can be considered two primary cultural influences. The shaping power of Calvinism on Melville's mind and art has been treated extensively by T. Walter Herbert, Jr.[43] The cultural context that most needs elucidation here, in order to more fully understand the significance and the formulation of the cetology material in *Moby-Dick*, is the evolutionary climate of the 1840s and the new relation of man to natural creatures implied by the evolutionary hypothesis and compellingly formulated by a popular evolutionary theorist of the period, Robert Chambers. On the surface, the evolutionary context may appear less central than others. But I hope to be able to demonstrate its importance and, at the same time, to continue my illustration of how certain philosophical and psychological ideas contributed to the way certain writers envisioned their material.

Melville's relations to science and religion were complex, both in themselves and as a result of the polar tension between them. His interest in science, especially in the challenge it posed to religious beliefs, was counterbalanced by his hostility to its deadening methods of classification and dissection. Similarly, his antagonism to religious authoritarianism was offset by his wish to retain a coherent worldview with a spiritual mythos and a legitimation of high perception.[44] And so if his freethinking side, hostile to religion, embraced the scientific challenge to received religious dogma, his philosophical and literary side satirized science as a limited and pompous activity.

Melville grasped the potential for lively expression of his ambivalent attitudes in an encyclopedic treatise on the wonders and terrors of the whale. He saw in an exhaustive method using different epistemologies and their working methods a form for communicating the philosophic conflict and disarray at the center of the midcentury crisis of belief. Empirical observation and transcendental intuition, reason and poetry, direct experience and secondhand truth, faith and doubt are all enacted as viable points of view by Melville, as he works through a range of ambivalent cultural attitudes about ways to knowledge, science, and truth.

Like many aware and literate laymen in the 1840s, Melville was exposed to the debate over evolutionary evidence in newspapers, public lectures, sermons, and journals. He also appears to have read, or at least to have been conversant with, several important scientific works of the period. He was familiar with Charles Lyell's *Principles of Geology* (1830–33). We know this from comparison of passages in the chapter in *Mardi* (1849) about the Isle of Fossils (ch. 131) with the details of Lyell's ideas.[45] In "Babbalanja Regales the Company with Some Sandwiches," Babbalanja presents Lyell's fossiliferous strata—albeit humorously transformed into "sandwiches"—with a degree of correctness and detail that leads an expert on Melville's use of geology to describe his knowledge as "amazingly accurate." Either he read Lyell or other books about Lyell's theory, and had his sources spread out before him as he wrote.[46] Melville's reading of Charles Darwin's *Voyage of the Beagle* (1839) is also likely. Not only was it available to him during his months on the U.S. Frigate *United States* in 1843,[47] but in 1847 Melville bought a copy of it in a New York bookstore.[48] Furthermore, similarities of "descriptive technique, diction, and phraseology"[49] between Darwin's chapter on the Galapagos and passages in Melville's "The Encantadas" (1854) also suggest that Melville may have read at least part of Darwin's early work and was exposed to Darwin's emerging ideas concerning variations of species on different island environments. Melville even parodied Darwin's numerical table of unique species on the Galapagos with a humorous one of his own, counting men, ant-eaters, lizards, snakes, spiders, salamanders, and devils.[50]

From his reading in Darwin, Melville may have gotten a sense of natural variety, of extinct species whose fossil remains spoke of aeons of natural history, and possibly of the competitive struggle for existence.[51] From his reading in geology Melville got a "sense of vastness, timelessness, and deeper significance"[52] to complement his metaphysical proclivities. When he describes his effort to classify the whale as groping "down into the bottom of the sea . . . to have one's hands among the unspeakable foundations, ribs, and very pelvis of the world" (32:136), the imagery derives from geology, archeology, and paleontology. In fact, each of the three elements that were combined by Darwin in *Origin of Species* (1859) to present his theory of evolution—vast aeons of time, the evolution of one creature into another, and the competition between creatures to survive—is presented in some form in *Moby-Dick*. In "The Fossil Whale" (ch. 104) there is a repeated evocation of the scores of millions of years of natural history needed for the transformational thesis; and there is, in that chapter as well, a reference to the development of higher organisms out of lower and the need to prove this by what Melville calls "connecting, or at any rate intercepted links" (104:456). Also, throughout *Moby-Dick* there is a perception of an inter- and intraspecies struggle for existence—what Melville describes as the "universal cannibalism of the sea; all whose creatures prey upon each other" (58:274). This is not to imply that Melville believed in evolution in 1850.[53] Unlike the period in which he wrote *Clarel* (1876), Melville wrote *Moby-Dick* at a time when evidence of evolution was building but not necessarily persuasive, in particular how and why species evolved. Melville's view of the origins of the natural world, therefore, as was the case for certain major scientists, was beset with contradiction. He could still refer to Bishop James Ussher's dating of the creation of Adam "sixty round centuries ago" (7:37) at one point in *Moby-Dick* and speak of "this antemosaic, unsourced existence" of the whale "before all time" (104:457) in the next, hoping that a claim that "time began with man" would help him bridge the difficulty.[54] As James Robert Corey concludes in his study of evolution in *Moby-Dick*, Melville "reveals himself as a man shifting frequently from the old, Genesis view of creation to the new, evolutionary view, but there is little consistency and no discernible pattern to his attitude."[55]

Probably the most influential evolutionary work for Melville was neither Lyell's nor Darwin's. In 1844 Robert Chambers published anonymously *Vestiges of the Natural History of Creation*,[56] a work written for a lay audience, which presented a view of the evolution of the heavenly bodies, the earth, and all its natural creatures, including man. Based on the nebular hypothesis of Laplace, the fossiliferous strata of Lyell, work in comparative embryology, and some tall tales, Chambers, a brilliant amateur, presented the most coherent and vigorous argument to date as to why God's special creation of each creature was "a very mean view of the Creative Power"[57] and why, more consistent with the fossil record, was a belief that "the whole creation . . . depended upon one law or decree of the Almighty,"[58] which was then manifested in "natural laws which are expressions of his will."[59] Emphasizing the unity of all natural life and the progressive gradations of changes in the fossil record from complex to simple the deeper one dug, Chambers "mobilized" the great chain of being, rendering what had been a static order into a fluid one.[60] The most flawed aspect of his theories was his notion of how one species changed into another, higher species. To variation and competitive struggle Chambers relegated a secondary role, whose purpose was "keeping the forms of life in proper balance," so that the lower, more prolific species did not overrun the higher.[61] For the mechanism of change, Chambers' naturalistic theory fell back on a divine first cause. He argued that it was part of God's plan that at certain far-flung intervals species would give birth to higher species. "Whether the whole of any species," says Chambers, "was at once translated forward, or only a few parents were employed to give birth to the new type, must remain undetermined."[62] He based this belief on the theory of recapitulation, which arose out of evidence in comparative embryology that more elaborate embryonic development was always founded on preceding natural forms. Since embryos of complex creatures pass through the stages of lower life because their "ancestors *did actually have these forms*,"[63] Chambers assumed species achieved a higher development when a "higher generative law"[64] lifted them a stage beyond their parents. The evidence that not only the general form but the brain itself of mammals in their embryonic stages passes through "forms analogous to those which belong to fishes, birds, and reptiles" had been discussed by Lyell as early as 1830.[65] In 1842–44 Louis Agassiz also published evidence for the doctrine of recapitulation and then repeated it in a popular forum in his Lowell Lectures of 1848.[66]

Chambers' notion, therefore, of the embryo serving as the vehicle for a step up the evolutionary ladder was not an unreasonable inference. All that was needed, he seems to have thought, was an extra few weeks in the womb at the right environmental moment.[67] And it is not difficult to see how such a view could have been highly attractive to Romantics such as Emerson, who already saw a "correspondence" between man and lower forms. In a journal entry of 1849, Emerson's preexisting belief that consciousness finds emblematic connections between all external things seems deepened by the theory of recapitulation:

> *Representative*. It is my belief that every animal in our scale of creatures leans upward on man, & man leans downward on it; that lynx, dog, tapir, lion, lizard, camel, & crocodile, all find their perfection in him; all add a support & some essential contribution to him. He is the grand lion, he the grand lynx, he the grand worm; the fish of fishes, and bird of birds, so that if one of these (creatures) tribes were struck out of being he would lose some one property of his nature. And I have no doubt that to each of these creatures Man appears as of (his) its own kind; to a lion, man appears the archlion; to a stork, the archstork.[68]

Emerson read *Vestiges* by 1845 and eagerly recommended it to others.[69] He thought its pious ascription of a divine plan by a Judeo-Christian "almighty" was tiresome, but otherwise he was excited by its naturalistic thesis. "Everything in this Vestiges of Creation is good," he says in his journals, "except the theology, which is civil, timid, & dull."[70] Chambers' claim that we are "bound up . . . by an identity in the character of our mental organization with the lower animals"[71] would probably have resonated in the mind of Herman Melville as well, and played a part in his tendency to draw direct and metaphorical "parallels" between the physical and mental capacities of men and whales.[72]

We lack evidence that Melville owned a copy of *Vestiges*. However, the probability that he did read it is high, given his association with the Evert Duycknick circle in New York, his practice of spending time in New York reading rooms, the accessibility of both Duycknick's and his father-in-law's libraries, and the tremendous stir caused by *Vestiges*. "The intellectual circle with which he associated," comments one scholar, "would hardly have ignored such a widely read and controversial item."[73]

Vestiges' espousal of the "theory of transmutation of species" drew attacks from the scientific community for ignoring contrary evidence and for its belief in spontaneous generation. It drew attacks also from the pulpit for its frontal assault on creationism.[74] In addition, the mystery of its author's identity further heightened attention.[75] Paving the way for a more sophisticated response to *Origin of the Species* in 1859, the book saw four editions in the first seven months, and ultimately sold 24,000 copies.[76] There were three American editions, the first put out by Wiley and Putnam, Melville's first publishers, in 1845.[77]

But this was not the only connection between Melville and Chambers. Chambers and his brother, William, were the tremendously successful publishers of *Chambers's Edinburgh Journal*, a three half-pence weekly magazine for the literate workingman that in the 1840s sold over seventy thousand copies a week,[78] and had in 1846 and 1847 included summaries of *Typee* (1846) and *Omoo* (1847) and several pages about their author.[79] Melville read these articles and it is likely that he read other issues as well in which he might have encountered references to the activities or writings of Lyell and Darwin. Although generally cautious on scientific issues,[80] the more speculative views of Robert Chambers even occasionally seeped through the *Journal*, as in this article published in March 1846:

> It is extremely curious to observe in animals ways and doings like those of human beings. It is a department of natural history which has never been honored with any systematic study: perhaps it is thought too trifling for grave philosophers. I must profess, however, that I *feel* there is some value in this inquiry, as tending to give us sympathies with the lower animals.[81]

But even if Melville did not read *Vestiges*, it is clear that its influence and, more specifically, that the influence of the theory of recapitulation were in the air in 1850 and played a part in supporting Melville's ultimate motive of determining human and divine nature through the behavior of natural creatures, in particular the sperm whale. Although primarily concerned with the spiritual facts that the whale's nature symbolized, Melville reaped fundamental perceptions about human nature as well from the creatures of the sea, taking his warrant from the fact that whale and man were both highly developed mammals.

Melville's point of departure was always his theological perspective that both man and nature reveal enigmatic metaphysical aspects of the Deity. The world of *Moby-Dick* is "pauselessly active in uncounted modes" (107:467), Ishmael tells us. A basic state of nature somewhat akin to the primary colors, these modes—violent, tranquil, maternal, rapacious— seem to correspond to elemental states of mind in man and to reflect the manifold modalities of the Deity. The "submarine bridal-chambers and nurseries" of mammalian life in "The Grand Armada" (87:389) is a mode of nature—life-giving, maternal, erotic. The unbridled rapacity of sharks "wallowing in the sullen, black waters and turning over on their backs as they scooped out huge globular pieces" of the whale are a mode of nature (64:293). The aggressive ferocity of the attacking sperm whale is a mode of nature, as is its gentle peacefulness at other moments. The most explicit sense of the similitude between the human mind and the creatures of nature is in the depiction of the "masculine sea" and "feminine air" in the opening of "The Symphony," where the modalities of the sea embody the modalities of both man and immanent Deity:

> Hither, and thither, on high, glided the snow-white wings of small, unspeckled birds; these were the gentle thoughts of the feminine air; but to and fro in the deeps, far down in the bottomless blue, rushed mighty leviathans, sword-fish, and sharks; and these were the strong, troubled, murderous thinkings of the masculine sea. (132:542)

The belief that "the brain of every tribe of animal appears to pass, during its development, in succession through the types of all those below it,"[82] would have enabled Melville to proceed confidently in his exploration of the human mind through the modes of nature. "The Grand Armada," for instance, seems a page out of twentieth-century sociobiology, as it describes the location of the cows and calves "in that enchanted calm" at the center of a vast herd of sperm whales (87:387–89). And Stubb's cruel treatment of Fleece after they watch the voracious sharks is another (64:293–97). In the first the domestic side of the human mammal is being linked with the herding patterns of mammals lower on the evolutionary chain; and in the second the shark nature in man is being linked with the sharks in the sea.

This intimately confident approach to the natural world, as though all its modalities and mysteries existed as well within the human mind, is one of the major sources of the coherence of the world of *Moby-Dick*.[83] Melville's vision of the fragmentary nature of life psychologically, morally, religiously, and philosophically is underpinned by a view of man grounded in the vital forces and history of nature. His recourse to a correspondential psychology rises out of the evolutionary climate of the late 1840s, in particular the influence of the theory of recapitulation. If, as one scholar has argued and I have subscribed to here, naturalism and Christianity are the "two poles"[84] of Melville's thinking, it is also necessary to add Romanticism to this list, especially its symbolic method, which was able to adapt the theory of recapitulation to a powerful correspondential psychology that linked man and natural creatures.[85]

We must remember also, however, that the impersonal modes of nature were not the only categories of life for Melville. There were also the fractured, fluctuating subjectivities of men that render the world a globe around which we journey "in tormented chase of that demon phantom that, some time or other, swims before all human hearts" (52:237). And let us also note, in conclusion, that for readers as well as for the *Pequod*'s captain and crew, the journey never ends. The chase retains its significance; the "phantom," its elusiveness. Story becomes retelling; reading, rereading; and we go on endlessly "over this round globe" (52:237) in quest of more ample visions of existence.

PART THREE

Isolatos

5

Personalism and Fragmentation in Whitman's *Leaves of Grass* (1855–1860)

I

When the reformer and literary man Thomas Wentworth Higginson saw Walt Whitman in Boston, he said that "the personal impression made on me . . . was not so much of manliness as of Boweriness."[1] The association with New York City's working-class Bowery—"the mark of the beery crowd," as Larzer Ziff interprets Higginson's comment[2]—is corroborated by the description of Whitman provided by another curious Boston Brahmin, Bronson Alcott, who came to Brooklyn in 1856 with Henry David Thoreau to meet the author of *Leaves of Grass*. Alcott describes Whitman as "broad-shouldered, rouge-fleshed, Bacchus-browed, bearded . . . and rank." A "red flannel undershirt, open-breasted," exposed Whitman's "brawny neck"; a "striped calico jacket over this, the collar Byroneal, with coarse cloth overalls buttoned to it; cowhide boots; a heavy round-about . . . and a slouch hat" completed the costume.[3] That Whitman would have attracted attention on the Bowery in such a flamboyant get-up is likely; but given the working-class, off-beat effect, he probably would not have been subject to the hostility saved for outsiders and authority figures. Besides Whitman's addiction to Brooklyn ferries and Broadway omnibuses, he also loved the Bowery Theater. Acknowledging the emotional excitement that sitting with the working-class audience aroused in him, Whitman describes the Bowery Theater "pack'd from ceiling to pit with its audience mainly of alert, well dress'd, full-blooded young and middle-aged men, the best average of American-born mechanics," and confesses that "the whole crowded auditorium, and what seeth'd in it, and flush'd from its faces and eyes" was "as much a part of the show as any." He recalls also, after 1840, "the rankness in the crowd"—the "types of sectional New York . . . the young shipbuilders, cartmen, butchers, firemen" and their "slang, wit, occasional shirt sleeves, and picturesque freedom of looks and manners."[4] Further revealing his familiarity with Bowery taverns and political meeting halls, as well as his proclivity for moving between middle-class and lower-class friends,[5] Whitman, in a stroke of mischievous hospitality, took Ralph Waldo Emerson to "a noisy fire-engine society" after Emerson had him for dinner at a New York hotel in late 1855. The new Fireman's Hall, a social club for firemen on Mercer Street, was intended to convey to Emerson,[6] no doubt, that *"these* are the materials of a true democratic poetry."

Not incorrectly, Whitman's poetry is understood as a response to the segmentary fragmentation of both New York City and the nation at large at midcentury. It is Whitman's effort to envision a poetic unity that embraces a multiplicity of different people, neighborhoods, classes, regions, political interests, landscapes. Visionary homogeneity rises out of social description like a glowing mist that transcends harsh divisions. Yet below this vatic and cultural embodiment of human or national oneness, on an existential level, Whitman's poetry, more basically, is a response to being one of the many, a man of the streets, of the working crowd, in the offices and taverns and restaurants of the city, where, despite pockets of congeniality, the general texture of experience is colored by estrangement and a shifting fragmentariness. The preindustrial city of Whitman's youth had given way to massive transformations in socioeconomic relations and population, with great unfamiliar hordes, "atomized and automatized,"[7] filling the streets. Irving Howe has these changes in mind in *The American Newness* when he says that "Whitman still aspires to satisfy Emerson's prescription that the American poet evoke the new democratic man . . . ; but he does not locate 'the Central Man' at the center. Anticipating the strategies, or losses, of later American writers, he locates that urgent figment in the crevices of a world changing too quickly for him, or anyone else, fully to grasp."[8] Although Howe touches on the right elements, I might restate his formulation by saying that Whitman finds man in the crevices and at the edges of a changing society, and that he tries to locate him at a *spiritual* center in order to compensate for social dislocation and marginalization.

We need to realize, in any case, that Whitman's poetry, beneath its ethos of responding to segmentation in many domains, is also grappling with the underlying problem of isolation, of Howe's "urgent figment" who has lost his sense of connectedness to society. Responding to this problem of atomistic fragmentation becomes a rudimentary challenge for Whitman; and his solution is an approach he calls "Personalism." Personalism is a powerful psychological approach to identity that tries to deepen and intensify those aspects of the self that can answer alienation by connecting the individual with the deep forces of existence. This chapter is organized around four variants of Personalism in Whitman's poetry between 1855 and 1860: *mystic/mythic* Personalism, in which he tries to merge optically with other fragments; *homosexual* Personalism, in which he tries to escape his isolation by merging with other lonely "atoms"; *tragic* Personalism, in which he accepts loss of love as being as inevitable as death; and *fragmentary* Personalism, in which he comes to terms with the condition of man as a fragment in a contingent universe.

II

Putting aside the question of whether Whitman glosses over harsh social divisions and unpleasant individualism, let us now begin to consider Whitman's poetic response to segmentary and atomistic fragmentation, beginning with his presentation of his own literary origins. Whitman wrote, he says, from

> a feeling or ambition to articulate and faithfully express in literary or poetic form, and uncompromisingly, my own physical, emotional, moral, intellectual, and aesthetic Personality, in the midst of, and tallying, the momentous spirit and facts of its immediate days, and of current America—and to exploit that Personality, identified with place and date, in a far more candid and comprehensive sense than any hitherto poem or book. (*Prose*, 2:714)

The variety of the self's responses to experience, the diversity and imprint of city and nation, an inclusive and "tallying" approach to society, and a candid treatment—these are the elements out of which Whitman says he made his poetry. And ranging over his retrospective statement of purpose is the power of individual Personality. Stripped of excessive language,

Whitman's statement describes an "ambition to . . . express . . . my . . . Personality . . . tallying . . . the . . . spirit and facts . . . of current America . . . and to exploit that Personality . . . in a . . . candid and comprehensive sense." Personality is the foundation and filter for presenting America and for embodying the spirit of the times in poetic form.

Whitman's involvement with "Personality" grows, as I indicated, out of his ideas about "Personalism." As with most of Whitman's cultural and poetic ideas, his explanation of Personalism later in his career is a formulation of what was operative in his poetry from the beginning. Intense, prideful individuality is Whitman's definition. In opposition to the principle of the democratic mass with its leveling tendency, Whitman has in mind another principle that emphasizes uniqueness of identity: "individuality, the pride and centripetal isolation of a human being in himself—identity—personalism" (*Prose*, 2:391). Whitman also defines Personalism with more specific attributes. Personalism "favors" religion: "only in the perfect uncontamination and solitariness of individuality may the spirituality of religion positively come forth" (*Prose*, 2:398). And Personalism involves "the thought and fact of sexuality, as an element in character" (*Prose*, 2:728). Personalism, in other words, apppears to be a somewhat hazily conceived intensification of those deeper needs or aspects of the self that can connect the individual with the richness of society and the larger universe. Finally, Personalism involves a visionary or messianic potential: it is "something that calls ever more to be . . . adopted as the substratum for the best that belongs to us, . . . including the new esthetic of our future" (*Prose*, 2:396). The four different "Personalisms" or intensifications of particular substrata of the self defined in this chapter are doorways into four different aspects of human experience and original poetic lenses.

III

Riding on top of a Broadway omnibus alongside the driver, Walt Whitman was in heaven. "How many hours, forenoons and afternoons—how many exhilarating night-times I have had—perhaps June or July, in cooler air—riding the whole length of Broadway, listening to some yarn," he says in *Specimen Days*. "The critics will laugh heartily," he adds, "but the influence of those Broadway omnibus jaunts and drivers . . . undoubtedly enter'd into the gestation of 'Leaves of Grass' " (*Prose*, 1:18–

19). Sometimes he rode up and down Broadway from morning until night.[9] The shifting panorama of Manhattan's major thoroughfare was all around him, and at his shoulder, at the reins, was a virile driver, filling Whitman's need for working-class male contact.

Yet once Whitman was down on the ground, walking the streets, he was one of the many and he knew the solitary, lonely condition of the individual in a large metropolis. Whitman ultimately succeeded in transmuting his yearning intensity into a new kind of poetry that expressed a love for all, but as one critic observes, this sort of general love stems from a deep personal loneliness.[10]

So that this metropolitan loneliness is seen as an objective factor related to the material configuration of the City's grid and the concentration of people, let me quote another writer's description of urban alienation. Lydia Maria Child, after she had spent eight months in New York, says:

> It is sad walking in the city. The streets shut out the sky, even as commerce comes between the soul and heaven. The busy throng, passing and repassing, fetter freedom, while they offer no sympathy. The loneliness of the soul is deeper, and far more restless, than in the solitude of the mighty forest. . . . For eight weary months, I have met in the crowded streets but two faces I had ever seen before. . . . Through what woful, what frightful masks, does the human soul look forth, leering, peeping, and defying, in this thoroughfare of nations.[11]

From one of his later prefaces, we learn Whitman tapped this loneliness both in an effort to treat it as a phenomenon of modern life and to contrive a way to answer his own need for attention and emotional sustenance:

> I would make a full confession. I also sent of "Leaves of Grass" to arouse and set flowing in men's and women's hearts, young and old, endless streams of living, pulsating love and friendship, directly from them to myself, now and ever. To this terrible, irrepressible yearning, (surely more or less down underneath in most human souls) — this never-satisfied appetite for sympathy, and this boundless offering of sympathy . . . I have given in that book, undisguisedly, declaredly, the openest expression. (*Prose*, 2:471n)

An important aspect of this "never-satisfied appetite for sympathy" was, of course, a sexual dimension. "Do you know what it is as you pass

to be loved by strangers? / Do you know the talk of those turning eyeballs?" (*LG*, p. 153, ll. 92–93), the poet asks in "Song of the Open Road."
And in a "Calamus" poem, mixing street-level realism with lonely fantasy, he addresses the

> Passing stranger! you do not know how longingly I look upon you,
> You must be he I was seeking, or she I was seeking, (it comes to me as
>   of a dream,)
> I have somewhere surely lived a life of joy with you,
> All is recall'd as we flit by each other, fluid, affectionate, chaste,
>   matured.   ("To a Stranger," *LG*, p. 127, ll. 1–4)

In this experience of street yearning—Robert K. Martin, probably
correctly, describes this as a "kind of cruising"[12]—we find the psychic root
of the aesthetic of Walt Whitman's poetry. Other processional scenes—
"the interminable rows of . . . houses . . . the ships at the wharves, / . . .
the processions in the streets . . . the bright windows with goods in them"
("City of Orgies," *LG*, p. 126, ll. 3–4)—provide parallel phenomena to
the procession of lovers' faces in the street. But emotional and sexual
longing is the key element—or, more accurately, is one-half the key element. For the other half is the convergence of this overwhelming longing
of the atomistic self with the equally overwhelming variety of city life.[13]
If Whitman's inner life brimmed with intensity, so did the multitudinous-
ness, the segmentary fragmentation, of the urban environment around
him—the "feverish, electric crowds" of appealing men and women on
the sidewalks and the chaos of clattering carriages in the street (*Prose*,
2:371).

We can assume, as a matter of common sense, that little hope existed
for Whitman in finding a sexual or emotional solution to the incompleteness he felt as one of the many. The vast population of a large city would
have made a mockery of his desire to possess all the men and women
who crossed his vision. As the "Calamus" poems (1860) evidenced eventually, sexual longing, when directly pursued, led Whitman into deeper
loneliness or pathetic illusions. Rather than periodic sexual merger with
lovers, the longing for psychological wholeness could only be found in
optical and imaginative merger with the material procession of city life.[14]
It could only be accomplished by identifying his being with the myriad
realities reported by his senses and put into language by his poetic
method, whose descriptions he says "satisfy my senses . . . and give me,

through such senses and appetites, and through my esthetic conscience, a continued exaltation and absolute fulfillment."[15] Conceptually, the answer lay in the unity that the self could bring to the diversity of American life through an inclusive poetic form, and aesthetically his means were the thought-form of correspondence and his own notion of poetic "ensemble."

An ensemble approach to material culture—providing always a collocation of many facts to form a picture, a human context, or a representative list—enabled Whitman to do justice to the multiplicity of phenomena around him. The thoroughness of presentation implied by an inclusive, ensemble approach—detail by detail, line by line—enabled the poet to find the prolonged opportunity to release the thick emotion within him. An "ensemble" approach to environment could prevent urban multiplicity from sinking into sheer fragmentation; it could do this because at the center of the "many" was the "one," the poet who could provide radii of emotional or symbolic relations to each and every object he touched.[16]

Donald Pease's delineation of Whitman's creation of a "crowd identity" is particularly illuminating of the poet's visionary motive to translate frustrated desire into a poetic satisfaction. In the correspondence between inner and outer, the poet not only seeks the unity I have emphasized; according to Pease, he also locates a "private reserve of other selves in the heterogeneous impulses within" himself.[17] The external crowd "incarnates" these inner potential selves, linking the individual "to all possible embodiments he might have assumed equally well" and alleviating incompleteness and social separation. "In assuming all the possible forms he might," says Pease, "the individual both completes himself, hence knows perfect liberty, and experiences himself completed by everything else, hence knows democratic equality."[18] The relation between the external world and the poet's inner life is that of "realized desire," in which the external world is acknowledged as "a revelation of his inner life."[19] Instead of providing the reader reflective space or solitude, Whitman's poetry draws the reader into "a crowd identity." It establishes a vitalizing democratizing space, through whose aesthetic "mass action" the reader is moved toward encounters with his or her regenerated self and future.[20]

An inclusive "ensemble" approach to the many external facts of experience, supplemented by a fusion akin to what Pease has characterized as "crowd identity," were, then, Whitman's leading ideas for poetic description; and the correspondences that ensued between the poet and the facts of the material world provided Whitman with the means to intimately connect his being with nation and nature. With his "omnivorous lines" (*LG*, p. 77, l. 1084) naming and describing, touching and vicariously entering the lives of men and women in myriad regions and events, Whitman found a way to escape his own existential reality. He entered what Michael Moon describes as "fluidity," a mode of consciousness ungrounded in the "solids" and "boundaries" of his culture, a place where indeterminate and limitless possibilities could flourish.[21] Whitman even found a hope that, if he was a great poet, his country would absorb him "as affectionately as he has absorbed it" (*LG*, p. 729), and his lonely needs would be answered.

IV

With the third edition of *Leaves of Grass* (1860), Whitman began the practice in his first lines of announcing the twin principles of the individual and the democratic mass and of implying that his poetry is able to straddle, if not reconcile, the conflicts that others such as Tocqueville saw between them:

> One's-Self I sing, a simple separate person,
> Yet utter the word Democratic, the word En-Masse.
> (*LG*, p. 1, ll. 1–2)

In later years, in *Democratic Vistas* (1871) and his prefaces of 1876 and 1888, Whitman would analyze both the parallel and polar aspects of the relationship of these two principles. His perspective, moreover, is so clear and consistent that it suggests itself as a basis for understanding his poetry as an evaluation of both the positive and negative aspects of democratic merger and intensive individuality.

One of Whitman's goals as political thinker and poet is the cultivation and celebration of democracy through the lives of working men and women not alienated from their families, their passion for each other, and their trades. His twin principle, however, as we already suggested, is that of individualism or, as we saw Whitman calls it to convey a "substratum" for his visionary tendencies, "Personalism." Clearly, the stance Whitman takes in *Leaves of Grass* is that Personalism is reconcilable with the principle of the democratic average. It may require gymnastic poetic genius to relate one's identity to the spectrum of American society; but, as Whitman's poems attest, it can be accomplished. In his later prose, Whitman clarifies his position, to the point of implying that a political and cultural theorist is not exposing an aristocratic bias if he recognizes that great individuals and leaders will always be somewhat at odds with the mass in democracy. Even if these individuals believe that their followers have the potential to duplicate their greatness, these leaders must still point the way alone. Consequently, in *Democratic Vistas*, Whitman says that joined to democracy there is

> another principle, equally unyielding, closely tracking the first, indispensable to it, opposite (as the sexes are opposite,) and whose existence, confronting and ever modifying the other, [is] often clashing, paradoxical. . . . This second principle is individuality, the pride and centripetal isolation of a human being in himself. . . . It forms . . . the compensating balance-wheel of the successful working machinery of aggregate America. (*Prose*, 2:391–92)

Whitman is speaking here in terms of political and cultural needs, but his recommendations are identical for the self-culture of the individualistic thinker or poet. The implications for the development of the complete individual, therefore, are that he must combine both tendencies, "clashing" and "paradoxical" though they may be. He must take the imprint from the physical world around him and "democratically" sympathize with, identify with, everything; and he must also be a solitary and distinct identity whose unique nature and place in time and space produce a unique consciousness. Says Whitman, "the full man wisely gathers, culls, absorbs; but if, engaged disproportionately in that, he slights or overlays the precious idiocrasy (*sic*) and special nativity and intention that he is" and "the man's self, the main thing, is a failure, however wide his general cultivation" (*Prose*, 2:394). Not only the poet's commonly shared humanity and experience, but his unique struggles and anomalies of selfhood can and should be brought to bear on his interpretation of human experience and on his role as a leader. Sometimes that selfhood needs to be pursued roughly, determinedly, refusing to be cowed by external pressure: "Provision for a little healthy rudeness, savage virtue, justification of what one has in one's self, whatever it is, is demanded." In the homogeneous environment of democracy, "negative qualities, even deficiencies, would be a relief" (*Prose*, 2:394).

Hence, if there is too much nullification of selfhood, too much absorption in the body of the world, then "the main thing," the profound
synthesis of self and world, will not occur. On the other hand, if there is
too much subjectivity and private need, then the health-giving contact
and affirmative energies of the working man and woman would be inaccessible to the poet-prophet, and his poetry and spiritual life will sink
into solipsism or into the insularity that Whitman associated with the
feudal pattern of greatness from the past. The objective is to contain the
polar tension so that one's life and art express a synthesis.

V

That synthesis of self and world, with excesses of selfhood and of
material detail contained in a boundless new form, is what we find in
"Song of Myself." Typically, in "Song of Myself" the synthesis of self and
world results in an aroused, dematerialized sense of reality that is an
expression of the mystical, rhapsodic state of the poet. Neither national
life nor urban life is the subject of the poem; it is rather a higher dimension of reality that brings to the material world fresh spiritual eyesight.[22]
Yet despite this mystical apprehension of things, the fragmentary, shifting
form and the many-sided picture of existence in "Song of Myself" suggests an analogue with the expanding variousness of both city and national life. As Whitman would say later in his 1876 preface, the "form
has strictly grown from my purports and facts, and is the analogy of
them" (Prose, 2:473). Sprawling, multifaceted, eruptive, langorous, his
form imitates the shifting patterns and changes of pace of contemporary
life. And his form is not only "the arbiter of the diverse," it is "the key"
(LG, p. 712), the unifying element.[23]
    What is the logic and pathway of the poet's intuition of a higher
unity? The poet is not trying to trace the steps that led to his illumination
nor to systematically analyze it. Only by following the stream of associations and impulses that come to him in discrete bundles of cohesive "ensemble-individuality" (Prose, 2:396)[24] can he hope to suggest its wordless
power.
    Trying to articulate the scope and contours of a vision that slides
from the seen to the unseen, Whitman's speaker is sometimes also propelled into immodest and transcendental claims such as, "I am an acme
of things accomplish'd, and I am encloser of things to be" (LG, p. 80,

l. 1148). But his vision is not only transcendental; it interpenetrates the material world, at times, even finding complete embodiment and repose within it. As all kinds of people and objects become included in the poet's song of himself, they enable the speaker to dramatize the unbounded dimensions of his vision and the mythic identity he envisions for himself as "kosmos" (*LG*, p. 52, l. 497) and democratic exemplum.

So long as the poem remains at the same mystic, rhapsodic frequency, the unpredictable shifts of subject matter from dung heap to bright sun do not present an impediment to the impulse of the mythic poet to celebrate the world-as-himself. They abet it by enabling him to convey the multidirectional, multidimensional quality of his Muse. For the "afflatus surging and surging" (*LG*, p. 52, l. 505) through the speaker carries him into amorous, reverential, or curious contact with every living human and object in the universe:

> In me the caresser of life wherever moving, backward as well as
>   forward sluing,
> To niches aside and junior bending, not a person or object missing,
> Absorbing all to myself and for this song.
>
> (*LG*, p. 40, ll. 232–34)

Either he "absorbs" objects because they embody the new physical universe he is seeing and has only to say them to celebrate them; or he allows "the converging objects of the universe perpetually" (*LG*, p. 47, l. 404) to flow through him, because they correspond with, they help to express, the new dimension of his immaterial vision. It matters little what the object is. What matters is that the object reveal a special nuance of the poet's vision or that the poet's vision reveal a new wonderful surface or depth in the object.

We can best describe the particular lens or intensification of individuality that informs "Song of Myself" as a mystic/mythic Personalism. This unifying Personalism, finding correspondences wherever it looks, rises out of a spiritual height rather than emerging—as will be the case for the three other Personalisms we examine—out of an atomistic depth of selfhood and despair. The synthesis of a mystic/mythic Personalism with the world of things is the main current of "Song of Myself." For example, the photorealism of the great human catalog in Section 15 allows the poet to make himself one with a boundless human procession, and to do so in a manner that complements rather than contradicts the poem's mystic plane of apprehension. Only by corresponding with the fullest imaginable human plenitude can the love-filled mystery that the poet feels be conveyed. Furthermore, the poet believes that there will "never be any more perfection than there is now" (*LG*, p. 30, 1. 42), and that the most ardent way to dramatize this fact is to identify with the downtrodden and diseased.

Eventually, Whitman encounters his greatest difficulty when the impulse for the broadest possible participativeness in human existence leads him one step farther—into wanting to enter and to take up the tragedy, sickness, and death of others. Then the passionate desire for oneness with humankind threatens despair and disintegration. It threatens to pull him apart, to tear him into painful fragments for which there is no redeeming sense of wholeness or transcendental solace. It threatens atomistic despair.

The messianic impulse prompts the speaker in Sections 33–38 to leave his mystical pride and to enter a more vulnerable, exposed reality, where he sees himself "in prison shaped like another man" (*LG*, p. 71, 1. 948), or where he becomes the cholera patient taking his last gasp (*LG*, p. 72, ll. 954–55). He wants to make the suffering of others his. By Section 38, however, the growing deviation from a mystic Personalism leaves him feeling overwhelmed by his Christ-like impulse. The 1855 version of the poem had begun this section with the ejaculation, "O Christ! My fit is mastering me!"[25] The 1881 edition drops this cry. Yet, on the whole, by means of cuts and editing, it sharpens the sense of the poet being overwhelmed by the tug of his boundless sympathies. Section 38 in the final arrangement of the poem begins with the cry, "Enough! enough! enough!" and then announces (as did the first edition) that he finds himself "on the verge of a usual mistake" (*LG*, p. 72, 1. 962). What is this mistake? It is his propensity for identifying too fully with the suffering of those he loves. Yet he cannot fully reject the Christ model; his love of man runs too deep; and his illumination has already shown him that "a kelson of the creation is love" (*LG*, p. 33, 1. 95). He therefore laments: Would "that I could forget the trickling tears and the blows of the bludgeons and hammers!" Would "that I could look with a separate look on my own crucifixion and bloody crowning" (*LG*, p. 72, ll. 964–65). But he cannot.[26] The clue to his discovery of the right relation to the Christ model occurs in the next lines when he says, "I remember now," which is followed by his resumed enactment of the Christ myth on a new footing:

I resume the overstaid fraction,
The grave of rock multiplies what has been confided to it, or to any
    graves,
Corpses rise, gashes heal, fastenings roll from me.

I troop forth replenish'd with supreme power, one of the average
    unending procession

                                        (*LG*, p. 72, ll. 966–70)

What he remembers is his mystical vision in which suffering is only a *part*
of life. In Section 4 he had been able to see that sickness, battles, fitful
events, and the like "are not the Me Myself" (*LG*, p. 32, ll. 71–74). In
Sections 37–38 he loses sight of this fact. In the earlier section, the finite
self of the poet had been filled with the infinitude of his vision, so that
"the Me myself" was a balanced, detached, fulfilled being who knew
pain and death thoroughly but who could see through them, beyond
them. Thus, the poet is able to remember that his religion is a religion of
life, not afterlife. The specific insight is that one must have sympathy *for*
but not *with* the unhealthy in mind and body. The poet may merge with
them in imaginative sympathy—he can "resume the overstaid," the over-
solicitous selfhood—but he cannot do so to the extent of vacating his
own mystical vision of the world as full of perfection now. If Christ died
for humankind, the poet must live for it.[27]

In Section 28, describing a nightmare or a fantasied sexual assault
upon the speaker by a group, there is another instance of a highly responsive individual overwhelmed by the consequences of his sensitive
nature. Here the sensitivity is sensuous and sexual rather than emotive
and sympathetic. "To touch my person to some one else's is about as
much as I can stand" (*LG*, p. 57, l. 618), the speaker says about himself
immediately before Section 28 describes his responses to suddenly being
touched all over and by many seducers. And the result in Section 28 is a
tumultuous experience—passive, often frightened, and thrilled—in
which physical and psychological boundaries are violated and many partially described acts of oral and phallic sex are hinted at. In the end, however, the speaker accepts responsibility for having wished for or sought
out the experience: "I went myself first to the headland, my own hands
carried me there" (*LG*, p. 58, l. 638). Whether, then, this is a gang rape
or a desired rough seduction, and whether it is the record of a sleeping nightmare or a waking fantasy—or even, possibly, a biographical
event—the ultimate psychological consequence seems to be a renewed

condition, likened first to sprouts after rain "by the curb prolific and vital," and then embodied in the vatic utterance "Landscapes projected
masculine, full-sized and golden" (*LG*, p. 58, l. 647). Deep, dangerous
experience has been translated into new poetic powers.

In both of these crises of excessive sympathy and dangerous desire,
the emergence of a state threatening to the integrity of the self occurs.
This atomistic condition asserts itself more powerfully in subsequent editions of *Leaves of Grass* and is met with different kinds of Personalism that
enable Whitman to hold his vision together. But in "Song of Myself" the
intractable problems of the self begin to emerge; and helpful here in understanding this emergence is M. Jimmie Killingsworth's description of
the double nature of Whitman's sexuality and imagination. One drive
Killingsworth sees in Whitman is a social, revolutionary sympathy that
wishes to merge with others and liberate them—what I see as Whitman's
response to the segmentary fragmentation of his time. The other drive
Killingsworth sees is conservative and antisocial, wishing to protect the
integrity of the self from dilution or destruction—what I see as Whitman's affirmation of unique identity and his impulse to strengthen the
self, even if it means prideful difference.[28] In the above two sections of
"Song of Myself" describing the crises of excessive sympathy and anarchic sexual desire, the wish to merge is confronted with dangerous consequences. Whitman is forced to accept or reject these tendencies because
they threaten to destroy the integrity of the self. And, tellingly, he does
not reject them. Within the mystic/mythic Personalism of "Song of Myself," he feels that the powers of spiritual and poetic vision are adequate
to offset or synthesize these tendencies into a truer, more deeply human
vision. The lacerations of self from too much sympathy and the destruction of the ego from the release of powerful anarchic desires are
integrated in Whitman's poetry by a transcendental spirit that encompasses all.

VI

The strange turn that Whitman's poetry takes in the "Calamus"
poems in the third edition of *Leaves of Grass* (1860) is the backdrop to his
treatment of the theme of many and one in "Out of the Cradle Endlessly
Rocking." The "Calamus" poems are noteworthy for their departure
from the long form with successive imagery and slow cumulative build-

ing of sentiment. They are, for the most part, brief confessional lyrics about the joy and anguish, prideful assertion and smarting shame, of Whitman's homosexual experience. What the autobiographical details are about his sex life or about a possible love affair that left him desolate and tormented in 1858–59 we do not know. Yet his cathartic lyrics are quite direct:

(I loved a certain person ardently and my love was not return'd,
Yet out of that I have written these songs.)
("Sometimes with One I Love," *LG*, p. 134, ll. 3–4)

Here the frailest leaves of me and yet my strongest lasting,
Here I shade and hide my thoughts, I myself do not expose them,
And yet they expose me more than all my other poems.
("Here the Frailest Leaves of Me," *LG*, p. 131, ll. 1–3)

Candid from me falling, drip, bleeding drops,
From wounds made to free you whence you were prison'd,

From my face, from my forehead and lips,
From my breast, from within where I was conceal'd, press forth red
    drops, confession drops,
Stain every page, stain every song I sing, every word I say, bloody
    drops,
Let them know your scarlet heat, let them glisten,
Saturate them with yourself all ashamed and wet,
Glow upon all I have written or shall write, bleeding drops,
Let it all be seen in your light, blushing drops.
("Trickle Drops," *LG*, p. 125, ll. 3–11)

Whitman's willingness to allow his secret wounds to flow onto the page, despite their potential to humiliate, is striking. Clearly he is not the same poet, full of "afflatus" and long unscrolling sections, of the 1855 and 1856 editions. Quite possibly, it is the absence of universal acclaim that has devastated him and turned him toward his hungry psychic needs. (We also see devastation and tyrannous psychic needs in Melville's *Pierre or The Ambiguities* (1852), begun only months after *Moby-Dick* was completed.) Whatever may be the explanation, it is clear Whitman lapsed, for a while, from world visionary into a finite human being in the grip of a personal suffering that threatened him with a "sickness unto death." We do not know enough about what was occurring inside him to explain confidently his veering toward the theme of death—death as a corollary of love—that emerges in the 1860 edition of his poems.[29] Whitman's treatment of death here is quite different from the psychological realism of the 1855 poem "To Think of Time" and from the visual realism of his later Civil War poems. What we do know about this period is that Whitman was a habitué of Pfaff's German Restaurant along with other journalists, artists, and "Bohemians";[30] that he held his last job as a newspaper editor in 1858;[31] and that in mid-April 1861, when news of the attack on Fort Sumpter reached New York City, he foreswore his drinking and "late suppers" for "a pure, perfect, sweet, clear-blooded robust body."[32] As background to this period, it is also probably worth introducing here the undestroyed diary notation of a later period when Whitman was suffering over his attachment to the young Peter Doyle: "Depress the adhesive nature. . . . It is in excess—making life a torment. . . . All this diseased, feverish disproportionate *adhesiveness.*"[33] As the "Calamus" poems reveal, he was in a similar state for a period of time in the late 1850s.

Yet despite spottiness of biographical detail, what is crystal clear is that Whitman accepted this emotional conundrum as a viable poetic point of view, as an intensification of his individuality that his poetic theory required. If a man "slights . . . the precious idiocrasy and special nativity and intention that he is, the man's self, the main thing, is a failure" he said in *Democratic Vistas*. Counterbalancing the poet's desire to absorb must be a strong, coalescing individual vision—Personalism; in this case, homosexual Personalism—which gives his viewpoint profundity and depth and leads it to "communion with the mysteries, the eternal problems, whence? whither?" (*Prose*, 2:399). To his credit, Whitman was willing to embrace his "idiocrasy." As an artist, he was sufficiently yielding to his hidden inner selves to know that his homosexuality was a basic truth of his nature and that without this truth he would repress, he would divest himself of, one of the wellsprings of his poetic power.[34]

Yet Whitman's experiment in confessional directness has had the ironic result of creating dissatisfaction with his honesty because it was less than complete. And while it is unfair to judge Whitman's furtiveness without considering the cultural context in which his poems were written, one does come away from the "Calamus" group with a critical reservation. Whitman sometimes misunderstands at the same time as he probes, and he sometimes obscures as he exposes.[35] In certain "Calamus" poems, most notably in "Scented Herbage of My Breast" and "Out of the Cradle," we are confronted with the linking of love and death as being "purports essential" of life (*LG*, p. 115, l. 31). On the whole, critics have been respectful of this equation, perhaps remarking on its turgid metaphysical quality, yet in large part acceding to it. Yet why does loss of love lead to abject fatalism rather than to suffering for a time and then returning to the flow of life? Why does the hardiness and the resilience of the former Whitman not pertain here? The answer may be—and here we can only speculate—that as a predominantly homosexual man in nineteenth-century America, Whitman, lacking any group identity or support, is overwhelmed by his isolation and compensates by transforming his psychic despair into a universal, self-justifying truth. One of the aspects of Whitman's homosexuality that is most interesting is the curiously involuted combination of freedom and furtiveness he felt in expressing his sexual orientation. Candor and self-delusion were able to coexist in Whitman's attitude toward his sexuality. Strange as it may sound, his homosexuality did and did not exist. Because of the "cognitive vacuum"[36] that seems to have existed at the time in the public consciousness about homosexuality, Whitman was at once free to express and to deny he had homosexual sentiments. Sometimes this situation even appears to result in his forgetting that his sexual orientation was anomalous or idiosyncratic and in his attributing to it a universality that it does not quite possess.[37]

Recent scholarship is helpful here in providing additional background to situate Whitman's sexual outlook historically. While there were undoubtedly homosexual acts occurring between men, there were no individuals or groups identified as homosexuals in mid-nineteenth-century America. The term itself was first used in German legal and medical circles in 1869.[38] Until the latter part of nineteenth century, the range of emotions and expressions of affection that were appropriate in male friendship was far broader than it is today. Passionate same-sex friendships, some of which undoubtedly included sexual activity, were publicly indistinguishable from the broad, hazily defined range of homosocial relationships. The continuum of acceptable feeling narrowed only with the "medicalization of same-sex relationships"[39] by European psychologists like Krafft-Ebbing and with the resulting stigmatization of certain behavior as perverse and diseased. Historians do not believe that a subculture of American homosexuals even existed until this process of social categorization rendered homosexuals self-consciously aware of themselves around the turn of the century.[40] Whitman's dissimulation in his 1890 letter to John Addington Symonds regarding the meaning of the

"Calamus" poems may well reflect this growing atmosphere of shame and secretiveness in the 1890s. Havelock Ellis says about this letter in *Sexual Inversion* (1896) that "it would seem . . . that Whitman had never realized that there is any relationship whatever between the passionate emotion of physical contact from man to man, as he had experienced it and sung it, and the act which with other people he would regard as a crime against nature." Ellis goes on to say that Whitman "would most certainly have refused to admit that he was the subject of inverted sexuality. It remains true, however, that 'manly love' occupies in his work a predominance which it would scarcely hold in the feelings of the 'average man,' whom Whitman wishes to honor." Ellis concludes that while "It remains somewhat difficult to classify him from the sexual point of view, . . . we can scarcely fail to recognize the presence of a homosexual tendency."[41]

"Scented Herbage of My Breast" introduces the theme of death as an inescapable corollary of the theme of love. Lacking the extreme condensation of "Out of the Cradle," it offers a more explicit instance of the confusion and despair that lead to the love-death equation in "Out of the Cradle." "Scented Herbage," moreover, offers the basis to hypothesize that depression, arrested sexual development,[42] and the sense of life of a homosexual in nineteenth-century America as an emotional dead-end have a lot more to do with this turn toward death than any universal insight on Whitman's part.

The following passage in "Scented Herbage" insists on more growth and confidence for his homosexual emotions and for the poems these emotions will produce. The scented leaves—calamus is an odiferous prairie spear grass—are emblematic of his repression:

> Grow up taller sweet leaves that I may see! grow up out of my breast!
> Spring away from the conceal'd heart there!
> Do not fold yourself so in your pink-tinged roots timid leaves!
> Do not remain down there so ashamed, herbage of my breast!
> Come I am determin'd to unbare this broad breast of mine, I have long
>   enough stifled and choked.
>
> (*LG*, p. 114, ll. 17–21)

Suggestive of the desire to expose a fully erect phallus and to overcome the timid "pink-tinged roots" of sexual underdevelopment, this passage contains no actual connection with the theme of death that encloses it at the beginning and end. The poet's rejection of a poetry of symbolism for a program poetry when he says, "Emblematic and capricious blades I leave you . . . / I will say what I have to say by itself" (*LG*, p. 114, ll. 22–23) also suggests that he takes up the theme of death because he is unable or unwilling to probe any deeper into this troubled psychic terrain. Balked by "what I was calling life" (*LG*, p. 115, l. 30), he redefines life as disappointment and death.

In a poem about intimations of mortality at middle age the linkage with death would be fitting; but fused to a poem whose purpose is to permit "slender" leaves "to tell in your own way of the heart that is under you" (*LG*, p. 114, l. 7)—to talk openly about homosexual feelings and suffering—the ponderous linkage with death is less than coherent. Other "Calamus" poems contain descriptions of tender contact between lovers, moments of face-burning shame and heart-rasping anguish; they may not be great poetry—in some instances they are little more than notebook jottings; but the naked honesty and poignancy of the lyric mode is inescapable. Yet in "Scented Herbage" Whitman's attempt to give strong statement to his homosexual heart becomes quite clouded by a morbid fatalism. The real cause would seem to be not that death is always the obverse side of love, but rather that pessimism had prevailed about ever finding satisfaction for his longing for a partner. "[Y]ou are not happiness, / You are often more bitter than I can bear" (*LG*, p. 114, ll. 8–9), he confesses about these "calamus" feelings. And when their gratification in his life became no more than the repeated taste of ashes from a "diseased, feverish" torment, he transposes his hopeless longing for a partner into a longing for death as a substitute and release.[43]

"Out of the Cradle Endlessly Rocking" is an allegory about the formation of a certain kind of poet and, although further along, rises from the same crucible as the "Calamus" poems.[44] First published in the *New York Saturday Press* as "A Child's Reminiscence" in late December 1859, it returns to the long, more impersonal form and style of all of Whitman's major poems. Yet the kind of poet whose genesis is being depicted is different from the rhapsodic mystic of "Song of Myself." Where union presses close everywhere in that poem and celebration is its motive, in "Out of the Cradle" separation and suffering are the wellsprings. As Stephen Whicher has contended, "Out of the Cradle" involves the recovery of the poet's vocation on a new, tragic footing,[45] a footing, I would add, which asserts a new Personalism and a new view of the relation of the poet to the diversity of the world.

This new Personalism, an outgrowth of the homosexual experience of loneliness in the "Calamus" group, is a tragic Personalism. And the new relation of one to many rising out of this new Personalism is a dark insight that aligns all objects in its field around this dominant vision much as a magnet aligns iron filings. Such is the significance of the long catalog of "ensemble-individuality" at the opening of "Out of the Cradle":

> Out of the cradle endlessly rocking,
> Out of the mocking-bird's throat, the musical shuttle,
> Out of the Ninth-month midnight,
> Over the sterile sands and the fields beyond, where the child leaving his
>   bed wander'd alone, bareheaded, barefoot,
> Down from the shower'd halo,
> Up from the mystic play of shadows twining and twisting as if they
>   were alive,
> Out from the patches of briers and blackberries,
> From the memories of the bird that chanted to me.
>
> (*LG*, pp. 246–47, ll. 1–8)

Although we do not know yet what is the "key" of the poet's intensification of viewpoint, we do know from the prepositional parallelisms that an intensification of viewpoint with a strong ordering power over image and memory has taken place. Nearer the end of the poem, we learn that the correspondences with each object or memory in the opening section have been artistically united by the "key" realities of separation and death.[46] The end, in other words, reveals the vision that informs the poem from the outset: the poem is a retrospective view of the poet's genesis in childhood.

As the little boy slips down to the beach to listen to the desolate cries of the he-bird calling for his lost mate, he discovers a resonant tragic longing in himself; henceforth it will color his perception of life and become the master-theme of his view of existence and poetry:

> Demon or bird! (said the boy's soul,)
> Is it indeed toward your mate you sing? or is it really to me?
> For I, that was a child, my tongue's use sleeping, now I have heard
>   you,

Now in a moment I know what I am for, I awake,
And already a thousand singers, a thousand songs, clearer, louder and
   more sorrowful than yours,
A thousand warbling echoes have started to live within me, never to
   die.
(LG, p. 251, ll. 144–49)

The "thousand singers," the "thousand songs" within the poet's heart
and mind, will be united by the pained knowledge that has started to life
in the child. The bird's song "projects" the poet-as-child into life because
of the profound correspondence between the plight of the bird and the
emerging sympathies of the child. The bird's song contains a melancholy
essence of nature that the child's soul also participates in:

O you singer solitary, singing by yourself, projecting me,
O solitary me listening, never more shall I cease perpetuating you,
Never more shall I escape, never more the reverberations,
Never more the cries of unsatisfied love be absent from me,
Never again leave me to be the peaceful child I was before what there
   in the night.
(LG, p. 251, ll. 150–55)

At this point, the adult poet, finished with his reminiscence of his
poetic awakening, reveals he now needs something more. He has been
given vocation and vision, but he needs an answer to the aching incompleteness of his view of life. That answer, supplied by the sea, is the "low
and delicious word death" (LG, p. 251, l. 168). Deliverance for the poet
lies in the realization that as love is inevitably loss, so life inevitably leads
to death, to loss of life.[47] Hence the final apotheosis of life is its antithesis,
"death, death, death, death" (LG, p. 251, l. 169). Death is release; death
is escape from selfhood; death is easeful union with nature and spirit.

The embrace of death here, in contrast with "Scented Herbage," is
not involuted and evasive. It rises logically—if steeply—from the emotional details of the preceding narratives of bird and poet-as-he-bird.
Death is the final secret that nature holds for man. And if (as Whitman
seems to say in this poem, paraphrasing Emerson[48]) art is an experience
of nature "passed through the alembic of man,"[49] then this final secret is
indeed continuous with the derivation of a tragic poetry from a natural
creature.[50]

The ponderous final "clew" (LG, p. 252, l. 158) of death would again seem to be an "idiocrasy" of the poet's view of life. Gustav Bychowski, the Polish psycholanalyst, has linked this turning toward death as a return to the memory of the first union in the womb, to a "prenatal fixation."[51] Edwin Miller has noted that the mother-symbol, the sea, is the source of the "clew."[52] And D. H. Lawrence has observed that Whitman's desire to merge with everything leads inevitably to his desire to merge with death, the final negation of his separate individuality. Lawrence sees this merging with death as a necessary phase before the self can stand separately in the New World.[53]

We need to take the "clew" here from Lawrence and view Whitman's "idiocrasy" or limitation in this poem in positive terms. What Whitman cannot reach in "Out of the Cradle" and "Scented Herbage" is the ability to live with his finitude—his atomistic condition—in the world of experience and to find the sources of his poetry within his mortal condition. In his next important poem he makes that transition and reaches the apex of his poetic-philosophical development.

VII

"As I Ebb'd with the Ocean of Life" attains a height by conceding a depth of disintegration and despair. Published in *Atlantic Monthly* four months after "Out of the Cradle" and only a month before the third edition of *Leaves of Grass*, the poem embodies the crest of Whitman's reforming confidence and knowledge of self. Able to look backward and forward, it articulates both the worst doubts from his period of disintegration as well as his most profound insights into the reintegration of selfhood toward which he is moving. At the level of philosophic discourse, "As I Ebb'd" commits itself to defining fixed stages of subject-object relations; yet, at its end, it moves into a dialectical process that involves groping, intuitively, provisionally, toward a new synthesis. The conclusion of "As I Ebb" is that there is no unity in multiplicity. Man is finite, life is random, and poetic truth is fragmentary and discontinuous, without the support of broad mythic significance. Yet despite all this, Whitman is able to indicate a perspective in which the oceanic resources of poetry still exist for him. Man is debris, but he is also an ocean that can churn up debris, his poems.

The first section begins to establish the symbol clusters of sea-spirit-mother and land-matter-father. Although the poet's life is "ebbing" and the season is, fittingly, autumn, the "electric self out of the pride of which I utter poems" (*LG*, p. 253, l. 7) is still sufficiently vigorous to seize him. The meeting place of sea and land becomes symbolic as he walks the shoreline of the meeting of spirit and matter everywhere in the world but, most important, most specifically, in himself, the poet. Even the flotsam and jetsam of the globe, disconnected from any meaningful phenomena on land, do not thwart his poetic confidence because he has been filled by spirit. With his "old thought of likenesses" (*LG*, p. 254, l. 14) the long walk is rich in correspondence, including the significance of the debris as a "type" for his poems:

> These you presented to me you fish-shaped island,
> As I wended the shores I know,
> As I walk'd with the electric self seeking types.
> $\qquad$ (*LG*, p. 254, ll. 15–17)

Stanza 2 tells us there are also "shores I know not." If the first stanza returns to the mystic/mythic Personalism of "Song of Myself," the second stanza enters the tragic Personalism of "Out of the Cradle." As the "oceanic spirit" abandons him, the actual ocean looms and menaces with the dirge of wrecked lives. His view of himself is reduced to "a little wash'd-up drift" and his view of poetry to gathering "a few sands and dead leaves." As drift himself, he has become a particle among other particles, and his poetry has become no more than the result of a lateral "merge" with "sands and drift," matter brushing up against adjacent matter (*LG*, p. 254, ll. 18–24).

In Stanza 1, he was in possession of a bird's-eye view: identity between spirit and matter enabled him to swoop through the center of the universe and its grand polysemous meanings. In Section 2, he has the crab's view of the seaweed, the beetle's view of the grass. And without spiritual insight into matter, doubts descend upon him. He feels mocked and shamed at how confidently he had dared to open his mouth. He realizes that the "Me myself" he thought he had discovered in "Song of Myself" lacked true revelation. "[T]he real Me stands yet untouch'd, untold, altogether unreach'd." He feels "I have not really understood any thing, not a single object, and that no man ever can." Life is opaque. And the magnitude of his springtime confidence results now in an equally grandiloquent statement of self-mockery. He imagines his real self pointing "with peals of distant ironical laughter" at his poems (identified with the transparent liquid of the sea) and indicating that they are really a manifestation not of an aqueous spirit, but of opaque matter, of "the sand beneath" (*LG*, p. 254, ll. 25–34).

In his preceding poem at this point of doubt Whitman retreated for his answer to the maternal ocean. Here too he seeks an answer, but in Stanza 3, significantly, he turns to the land that he associates with the father. He identifies with the paternal body rather than the maternal spirit. He has been part of the "measureless float," the Oversoul, but now he is matter, body, identity; and as he has come to understand it, he is also now finite and powerless drift:

> You friable shore with trails of debris,
> You fish-shaped island, I take what is underfoot,
> What is yours is mine my father.
>
> I too Paumanok,
> I too have bubbled up, floated the measureless float, and been wash'd
>   on your shores,
> I too am but a trail of drift and debris,
> I too leave little wrecks upon you, you fish-shaped island.
>
> (*LG*, p. 255, ll. 38–44)

As a product of the "measureless float," he is born of spirit, but he finds it incomplete to think of himself as spirit when his life has seen the contingencies, the "wrecks," to which matter is subject. Consequently, he clings to the father for the "secret of the murmuring I envy," some clue to the reconciliation of the spiritual with the material dimensions of life (represented by the wavelets washing upon the sandy shore). The passionate embrace and acceptance of the father as the source of his need are striking and unmistakably progressive. Whitman's poems have always returned—regressed?—to the maternal and viewed fathers as rejecting and threatening.[54]

The integration of the two principles occurs in the final section of Stanza 4 and warrants closer analysis than it generally receives.[55] Conceding man's place in the universe as drift, the last section of the poem asks: What is man? And what are his poems? The poet tries to provide an answer through the process of a symbolist journey into the world of debris, and through succumbing to a new lens, a new Personalism, formed from a fragmented sense of self. Debris becomes a referent for man's tragic condition and for the materials of his imagination—something close to the "foul rag-and-bone shop of the heart" in Yeats' "The Circus Animals' Desertion."[56] One key to understanding this section is to realize that we are in the midst of a poem about the formation of poetry — poetry as it is churned up from the spiritual and material depths. And the other essential insight is to remember that the ocean here is both an actual ocean and the internal oceanic resource of the imagination Whitman is trying to reclaim, despite his acceptance of himself and his poems as little more than drift.

The new lens of fragmented Personalism in this stanza enables the poet to equate himself and his poems ("Me and mine") to the "loose windrows" he sees at his feet. But the loose windrows are surrounded by "froth, snowy white, and bubbles," and these make the poet think not only of purposelessness but of death, "little corpses." That his pain and finitude lead him to think of death we have seen before; now, however, a gripping movement occurs in which the poet envisions himself as a corpse washed up like debris:

> Me and mine, loose windrows, little corpses,
> Froth, snowy white, and bubbles,
> (See, from my dead lips the ooze exuding at last,
> See, the prismatic colors glistening and rolling.)
> (LG, p. 256, ll. 57–60)

The minute realism of this vision including the sun-tinted colors in the frothy bubbles suggests there is no escape from this grotesque reality, no evasion into the transcendental. Man dies. Yet some prismatic and glistening possibility seems dimly suggested as the poetic metamorphoses continue in this journey of the imagination. The sense that we are witnessing the reemergence of an internal oceanic source asserts itself as the poet says next that "me and mine" are

>   . . . fragments
> Buoy'd hither from many moods, one contradicting another,
> From the storm, the long calm, the darkness, the swell,
> Musing, pondering, a breath, a briny tear, a dab of liquid or soil,
> Up just as much out of fathomless workings fermented and thrown,
> A limp blossom or two, torn, just as much over waves floating, drifted
>   at random.
> (LG, p. 256, ll. 61–66)

We note the emphasis on the fragmentary nature of life, on the multiple and contradictory moods out of which poetry is created. We note the emphasis on the rising power and amplitude of an oceanic element (it is impossible to separate an internal from an actual ocean); we note the allusion to man and nature (tears and soil) as raw materials for poems; and we note the emergence of beauty, a "limp blossom or two, torn, . . . floating . . . at random" in this churning elemental process of poetic birth.[57]

There is nothing broad, stable, or uplifting about this vision of the genesis of poetry, up from the elements of imagination and matter. The ocean of life, inside as well as out, is cataclysmic, capricious, and fragmentary. Yet selfhood and poetry are marginally possible for the adult who can accept his finitude and mortality, and who can see he is a particle among particles. Spiritual nature returns within him then with its oceanic powers. From mortal lips "prismatic colors" of poems can emerge. As well as a man who is only debris, blind "whence" he goes, the poet is also an "ocean" who churns up poems.

The poet must renounce the "arrogant" goal of imposing philosophical and cultural unity on the diversity of life. He must also accept an art comprised of moving perceptions of moving objects. If he can accept relativism and renounce his illusion of omnipotence, then the power of poetry will return. And the poet's responsibility to future generations, to place poems at their feet across the ocean of time, can be completed.[58]

Did Whitman write other poems out of this fragmented Personalism? The Civil War poems certainly deal with death as a naturalistic reality; yet rather than dwell on the fragmentary chaos of war, they assuage the anguish through the controlling sentiment of the "wound-dresser." As for "When Lilacs Last in the Dooryard Bloom'd," it too is not a realization of this fragmented perspective, for that elegy is a perfect wreath of symbols and lacks the existential view of existence as drift and debris.

Acquiescence to relativism was too harsh and unstable an outlook for Whitman. He always needed some unifying sentiment, even if it was no more than the idea implied in his all-inclusive form. Like Emerson, Whitman takes us to the perimeter, to the verge of the modern, but he never takes us to the bare open spaces beyond.

VIII

A different relationship between the many and the one has been implicit in my analysis of each of the four poetic viewpoints or "Personalisms." In the mystic/mythic Personalism of "Song of Myself" the poet was the point of convergence of all aspects of reality, both material and immaterial. Reality came to completeness only when it passed through the poet and was reborn through the poet's utterance. The major problem faced by the poet was his need to discover a limit to his sympathetic embrace of life, so that he would not be torn apart by his sympathies and reduced to an aching atomism. Bringing unity to diversity, the Personalism of "Song of Myself" is also found with variations in other poems such as "Crossing Brooklyn Ferry" and "Song of the Open Road"; and it is perhaps epitomized in "By Blue Ontario's Shore," which was originally titled "Many in One," and which is a rewriting of the 1855 preface (see *LG*, pp. 711–12, ll. 61–115).

The homosexual Personalism of the "Calamus" poems moves in the very opposite direction, away from an inclusive motive. Its tendency is exclusive, isolating, atomistic—in ways escapist. In a surprising number of these poems a "Not . . . , but . . . " sentence structure is employed to list all the worldly gratifications that have been rejected in order that the wish to be alone with a lover can be pursued. In "City of Orgies" the poet asserts that not the exciting ensemble of modern urban life

> Not those, but as I pass O Manhattan, your frequent and swift flash of
>   eyes offering me love,
> Offering response to my own—these repay me,
> Lovers, continual lovers, only repay me.
>
> (LG, p. 126, ll. 7–9)

In "When I Heard at the Close of the Day," not his name being "receiv'd with plaudits in the capitol," nor carousing, nor accomplishing his plans makes him happy, "But the day when I rose at dawn . . ." and

> When I wander'd alone over the beach, and undressing bathed,
>   laughing with the cool waters, and saw the sun rise,
> And when I thought how my dear friend my lover was on his way
>   coming, O then I was happy
>
> (LG, p. 122, ll. 1–5)

The exclusive tendencies of the "Calamus" poems are abandoned soon enough and superseded by the inclusive tragic Personalism of "Out of the Cradle Endlessly Rocking." While stated in somewhat forced terms in "Scented Herbage of My Breast," the impossibility of "two together" finds an overpowering statement in "Out of the Cradle Endlessly Rocking." There pain of atomism provides the poetic energy, the dialectical antithesis, to go beyond the mystic/mythic Personalism prevalent in the first three editions of *Leaves of Grass*. To the "thousand singers" and "thousand songs" in the heart of the poet, pain imparts the tragic sense of life. It links the poet of springtime with the poet of the spirit's autumn. It reconciles the mystic and the tragic planes of existence, which were so difficult for the poet to reconcile in Sections 33–38 of "Song of Myself." There is unity in diversity again, but the unity is not based solely on correspondence; rather it is also based on the poet's recognition of division and disappointment and on the necessity to embrace the ultimate division, death. In "Out of the Cradle," death is man's only means of reconciling the self with the world; man's only basis for complete merger with nature and spirit; man's only freedom from the compulsion for love.

The fragmented Personalism of "As I Ebb'd with the Ocean of Life" provides a yet more satisfactory solution this side of death. It accepts the finitude and mortality of man and acknowledges that matter is sometimes hostile and opaque. Nevertheless it seeks to absorb this otherness, which is alien and destructive toward man's spiritual well-being, into a poetic viewpoint that preserves unity within diversity. The key element is the acceptance of painful human finitude. First sensed in Sections 28 and 33–38 in *Song of Myself*; more evident in the homosexual poems; and still more explicit in the theme of pain, loss, and death in "Out of the Cradle"; atomistic fragmentation is most fully integrated with the segmentary amplitude of life in "As I Ebb'd." Only in this poem is the poetic merger of multiplicity and isolated individuality fully achieved. The sense of multiplicity submits completely there to the gritty realities of loneliness, psychological difference, and mortality.

The atomistic sense of self on the streets of New York City only slowly works its way up to the surface of Whitman's poetry, but when it does in "As I Ebb'd," we have the fullest integration of his twin visions of life. The challenge has been for the poet to find the truest Personalism with which to embrace modern life; and in the fragmented Personalism of "As I Ebb'd," the collective view and the personal view come together.

Personalism gave Whitman the depth of vision to try to hold his poetic world together. Each time he lapsed into fragmentation, he was able to find a substratum of the self and a point of view that enabled him to make his poetry cohere. Critical to success was his adherence to the view of the poet as unifier and to the diversitarian, inclusive form. But these would not have been enough without the mystic love, the homosexual longing, the tragic sympathy, and the "oceanic" finitude that bring to his poems strong emotional power and sustained perspective. Like the modes of nature that undergird Melville's fragmentary vision, Personalism was Whitman's ultimate strength.

6

Disconnection and Reconnection
in the Poetry of Emily Dickinson

I

Emily Dickinson's poetry exemplifies an extreme instance of atomistic fragmentation. While Whitman fell out of the vibrant weave of self and world, moving from a celebration of multiplicity to the challenging effort of integrating atomistic vision, Dickinson begins and ends in isolated individuality, in particularity, in atomism. She can recover connection through poetry but there is no afflatus, no protective muse, no persistently energizing masculine power or maternal goddess[1] to lift her out of her finitude and assure her of poetic empowerment. Deracination was a large part of her poetic condition and the gambit to achieve reconnection was always a necessary part of her poetic process.

Between 1830 when Emily Dickinson was born and 1862 when she reached white heat as a poet, there were at least eleven years when religious revivals occurred at Amherst College and in the village church.[2] The First Church of Amherst, where the Dickinsons worshiped, was typical of Congregational churches in New England. From the late 1790s the revival spirit of the Second Great Awakening had been sweeping the Connecticut River Valley.[3] Not characterized by the hysteria, the physical distortions, the inflamed oratory or camp meetings that had discredited the first awakening, the pattern of conversion in the second involved pious prayer meetings and conferences in churches and homes.[4] A spiritual anxiety involving soul-searching and prayer would enter a community, followed by individual acts of repentance and eventual "awakening." Neighbor after neighbor found the light within him- or herself.[5] Spread by word of mouth, by newspapers and itinerant revival preachers, or by publications such as the *Connecticut Evangelical Magazine* (first published in 1800) and Bennet Tyler's *New England Revivals* (1846), the sense that God had come down among men traveled between towns and villages. According to Tyler, there was great uniformity in the "origin and progress" of these revivals; "in the means used to promote them; in the exercises of the subjects, both previous and subsequent to conversion; and in the permanency of the fruits."[6] Calmness, sobriety, "spiritual seriousness," and "reformation of morals" were the common results.[7]

Although all of Emily Dickinson's immediate family were church members by the time she was twenty-five,[8] she never underwent a conversion herself. She never became a "church member," able to participate in the communion service and partake of the eucharistic sacraments. According to the fairly rigid standards of the First Church of Amherst in the 1840s and 1850s, she was among those generally expected to leave the church after the sermon.[9] Emily continued to attend church periodically until the early 1860s, by which time she had begun to withdraw generally from community life.

Although she attended church, Dickinson's correspondence with her friends reveals that from her early teens to her twentieth year she felt under periodic pressure to justify to herself as well as others her inability to "become a Christian."[10] Early in 1846 she responds in a letter to her friend and classmate in Amherst Academy, Abiah Root, about Abiah's leaning toward religious conversion. Dickinson claims to have "had the same feelings myself. . . . I was almost persuaded to be a christian. I thought I never again could be thoughtless and worldly—and I can say that I never enjoyed such perfect peace and happiness as the short time in which I felt I had found my savior. But I soon forgot my morning prayer or else it was irksome to me. One by one my old habits returned and I cared less for religion than ever" (*L* 10, p. 27). She goes on to describe the religious climate in Amherst at that time, and then to reveal her extreme cautiousness lest she be swept away:

Last winter there was a revival here. The meetings were thronged by people old and young. It seemed as if those who sneered loudest at serious things were soonest brought to see their power, and to make Christ their portion. It was really wonderful to see how near heaven came to sinful mortals. Many who felt there was nothing in religion determined to go once & see if there was anything in it, and they were melted at once.

Perhaps you will not believe it Dear A. but I attended none of the meetings last winter. I felt that I was so easily excited that I might again be deceived and I dared not trust myself. (*L* 10, pp. 27–28)

Three months later, learning about Abiah's "decision in favor of Christ," Dickinson remembers again "the few short moments in which I loved my Saviour" and how it was her "greatest pleasure to commune alone with the great God & to feel that he would listen to my prayers." She then reveals in greater detail her perversely secular tendencies:

But the world allured me & in an unguarded moment I listened to her syren voice. From that moment I seemed to lose my interest in heavenly things by degrees. Prayer in which I had taken such delight became a task & the small circle who met for prayer missed me from their number. Friends reasoned with me & told me of the danger I was in of grieving away the Holy spirit of God. I felt my danger & was alarmed in view of it, but I had rambled too far to return & ever since my heart has been growing harder & more distant from the truth & now I have bitterly to lament my folly—& also my own indifferent state at the present time.

I feel that I am sailing upon the brink of an awful precipice, from which I cannot escape & over which I fear my tiny boat will soon glide if I do not receive help from above. (*L* 11, pp. 30–31)

Peer and community pressure to convert was probably greatest during the ten months Dickinson spent at the Mount Holyoke Female Seminary from the autumn of 1847 to the summer of 1848. The students were grouped in three catagories: Christians, "Hopers," and "No-hopers."[11] Of 230 students attending, ninety began the year "without hope" and at the end only thirty were still "left out of Christ."[12] The school's head, Mary Lyon, held special weekly meetings, at least one of which Dickinson is known to have attended after hearing a moving sermon by a visiting minister. It was a "very solemn meeting," the school's associate principal recorded, for "those who felt unusually anxious to choose the service of God that night."[13] Yet despite Dickinson's strong response to the revival minister, letters of her classmates indicate that while other girls were finding the still, small voice within them, Emily "still feels no more interest" and "still *appears* unconcerned."[14] By May 1848 a letter to Abiah reveals growing uneasiness about the loss of opportunity to profit from this communally ritualized admission into the Congregational Church:

> I tremble when I think how soon the weeks and days of this term will all have been spent, and my fate will be sealed, perhaps. I have neglected the *one thing needful* when all were obtaining it, and I may never, never again pass through such a season as was granted us last winter. Abiah, you may be surprised to hear me speak as I do, knowing that I express no interest in the all-important subject, but I am not happy, and I regret that last term, when the golden opportunity was mine. (*L* 23 [postscript], p. 67)

In letters written during a revival in 1850, once Dickinson was back in Amherst, it becomes apparent that a highly individualized sense of identity has begun to form within her, which made conformity to a religious group impossible. For this reason, it is important to describe the sense of imaginative connection that was taking place in her as well as to focus on the sense of religious disconnection emerging between her and her church. As is revealed in four letters written throughout 1850 to her Amherst Academy friends, Abiah Root (*L* 31, 36, 39) and Jane Humphrey (*L* 35), what might be called a "dark" conversion to the world of the imagination was occurring. A complicated mixture of feelings of discovery and disobedience emerges in these letters of Dickinson's nineteenth year. Dickinson repeatedly mentions daring to "do strange things—bold things," of heeding "beautiful tempters" (*L* 35, p. 95); she mentions "dreaming a *golden* dream, with eyes all the while open" (*L* 36, p. 99), and of discerning a "golden thread . . . which will fade away into Heaven while you hold it, and from there come back" (L 35, p. 95); and she mentions Satan and snakes. In one of two letters about snakes, she says to Abiah: "a snake bite is a serious matter, and there cant be too much said, or done about it. The big serpent bites the deepest, and we get so accustomed to it's [sic] bites that we dont mind about them" (*L* 31, p. 88). The meaning of this strange constellation of images about discovery and disobedience is contained in the passage immediately prior to the one just quoted about snake bites, and is the conclusion of a page and a half of sustained adventurous fantasy in which Dickinson personifies a head cold as a visitor from Switzerland, a hallucinated imp, who attaches himself to her shawl on a walk and then comes to inhabit her room and sit on the edge of the bed. It is a wild, schizoid-type fantasy; but she then pulls in the reins, to tell Abiah before the snake passage: "Now my dear friend, let me tell you that these last thoughts are fictions—vain imaginations to lead astray foolish young women. They are flowers of speech, they both *make*, and *tell* deliberate falsehoods, avoid them as the snake, and turn aside as from the *Bottle* snake. . . . Honestly, tho' a snake bite is a serious matter" (*L* 31, p. 88).

If we recognize that in this letter to Abiah Root she is minimizing and deriding the very "bold things" and "beautiful tempters" she confesses with exotic pleasure to Jane Humphrey, then we realize that while she feels that imaginative activity, which both *makes* and *tells*, may be vain fiction and dangerous to "foolish young women," she does not see herself in the endangered camp. Moreover, if we add to this oblique confession of her involvement with the world of the imagination, one other significant assertion from her letter to Jane Humphrey, then we have a more complete picture of her shift from seeking truth in public religious conversion to seeking it in the human mind, in the imagination, and, ultimately, in poetry. Dickinson, in this letter, asserts her faith in trusting human nature, her hope that human nature is not fallen and delusive as the doctrine of her church maintains, and that it is, for those willing to live by it, a more profound guide to spiritual truth and renewal than church membership. She says:

> I hope belief [in human nature] is not wicked, and assurance, and perfect trust. . . . I hope human nature has truth in it—Oh I pray it may not deceive—confide—cherish, have a great faith in—do you dream from all this what I mean? Nobody *thinks* of the joy, nobody *guesses* it, to all appearance old things are engrossing, and new ones are not revealed, but there *now* is nothing old, things are budding, and springing, and singing, and you rather think you are in a green grove. (*L* 35, p. 95)

In other words, the golden thread, the dreaming, the bold temptation, the snake bite are all images related to the discovery of the independence and autonomy of the human mind and of the wild and limitless possibilities of the imagination when harnessed by art.[15] It leads beyond a "dark" conversion to a possible spiritual springtime, where "There is a morn by men unseen— / Whose maids upon remoter green /Keep their Seraphic May—".[16]

To call her dedication to the imagination a "dark" conversion is to borrow the guilty coloration her psyche gave to the discovery of self and to the early stirring of her efforts to become a poet. Her direction was, of course, toward religious poetry and a subjective pursuit of knowledge of God and immortality. What she reacted to with distaste about the religious activity around her was the aspect of group behavior underlying the ostensible emphasis on personally experienced conviction. She could hardly have respected the security with which her neighbors thought they were saved, once the church had examined them and accepted them as members. Also, how did they know Christ had truly come to them? And how, she may have wondered, could they spend a lifetime holding onto a past experience? Despite her basic tolerance, one can detect her misgivings in a letter to Jane Humphrey: "I cant tell you *what* they have found, but *they* think it is something precious. I wonder if it *is?*" (*L* 35, p. 94).

The revivalism of the times—what one historian describes as "antiritualistic revivalism" because of its emphasis on unmediated religious feeling[17]—did have its effect on Dickinson. In fact, its effect was even *more* private and *more* individualized than it was on her neighbors. Manifesting itself as an antidoctrinal and antiformalist religious impulse in the writing of poetry, Dickinson's approach was able to bring personal vision to the traditional Calvinist acquiescence to the mysterious and obscure nature of God. As Jane Donahue Eberwein says, Dickinson "withdrew increasingly from communal religious rituals—not because she ceased questing for God and all he offered her . . . but because she was probably the only person she knew who felt impelled to continue the quest."[18]

Yet contradictions do emerge between Puritan and premodern qualities in Dickinson. Carroll Smith-Rosenberg has observed from her research on the letters and diaries of women in the nineteenth century that there is, generally speaking, very little "generational conflict and criticism" between mother and daughter "until economic and intellectual change offered bourgeois daughters . . . viable alternatives to their mothers' domestic roles."[19] The stability of Dickinson's social and economic situation notwithstanding, her equation in late adolescence of the discovery of the power of the self with rebellion and disobedience is suggestive of the degree to which she possessed not only late Puritan religious tendencies but also premodern psychological ones reflecting her intellectual and cultural distance from her parents.

Before turning to the themes of disconnection and reconnection in Dickinson's poetry, there are two other forms of disconnention in Dickinson's life that should be discussed. Only touched on briefly so far, these are Dickinson's psychological disconnection from her parents and her disconnection from literary tradition.

Emily Dickinson's failure to obtain adequate psychological nourishment from her family is part of the explanation for both the extreme isolation of her later social existence and for the internalization and privatization of her poetry. In the psychological void created by an insufficient mother and professionally preoccupied father, Dickinson found herself without substantial underpinnings and compelled to get from imagination and poetry what she did not get from her parents. John Cody's psychoanalytic study emphasizes the "primal" maternal "deprivation"[20] Dickinson endured at an early age, the subsequent inadequacy of Mrs. Dickinson as a role model, and then the floundering of the young woman who seems to have vacillated between self-abnegation, outdoing her mother, and excluding "the question of femininity altogether as unworthy of attention" to identify with her father.[21] What Cody may not sufficiently emphasize is the hunger for her father's attention, which became coupled with an expectation of rejection and came to permeate her view of the (male) world.

Emily Dickinson's reluctance to pursue publication more aggressively, her emotionally exorbitant demands on friends,[22] and her pattern of falling in love with powerful, married men, all suggest a pronounced psychic wound revolving around her failure to obtain the right quality of parental attention, in particular from her father. This wound—what Freudians would call an "unresolved" fixation—was carried within Dickinson, who guarded it carefully, rarely exposing it, or doing so only under selected circumstances such as in letters or in fantasized love affairs. In some of Dickinson's poems that adopt the persona of the child there is a literary reenactment of what was probably originally a situation involving a talkative, demanding little girl and an inner-directed, over-tired father "too busy with his Briefs" (L 261, p. 404). In several poems akin to the following one, there is a premium placed on silence, good behavior, and singing softly; and on the part of God (the Father) there is the power to banish or withhold nurture for disobedience:

> Why—do they shut Me out of Heaven?
> Did I sing—too loud?
> But—I can say a little "Minor"
> Timid as a Bird!

Wouldn't the Angels try me—
Just—once—more—
Just—see—if I troubled them—
But don't—shut the door!

Oh, if I—were the Gentleman
In the "White Robe"—
And they—were the little Hand—that knocked—
Could—I—forbid?   (P 248)[23]

As Barbara Antonina Clarke Mossberg says about this poem, "It is significant that the child immediately assumes that her being 'shut out' is a
consequence of her failure to 'shut up' or at least be 'still.' The first
thought that occurs to her is 'Did I sing—too loud?' "[24] This is, of course,
a tentative biographical inference based on a writer's text. However, it
can be asserted with somewhat more evidence that Edward Dickinson
favored his son over his two daughters, that he missed Austin noticeably
when his son was away from home (see L 45, p. 119), and was greatly
invested in Austin's becoming a lawyer and remaining in Amherst to
practice.[25] To Emily, who knew early that her abilities "are neither few
nor small" (L 5, p. 10), hurt and resentment would have been the only
possible reaction to being less valued than her brother. And that gender
was in large part the reason for her father's preference, not more brains
or brighter wit, could have only added to the painfulness of her situation.[26]

Whether or not Sewall is correct that Edward Dickinson's authoritarianism was only "mild," and that "the legend of the dismal home and
the tyrannical father comes from later years,"[27] not when Emily was a
teenager, it appears that Emily's lively mind was not sufficiently enjoyed,
nor her emotional needs adequately welcomed,[28] and that the psychic
wound from her father's insensitivity and gender bias was a crucial aspect
of her later emotional situation. Based on this theory, we can make certain useful interpretations about the resources Dickinson substituted for
the sense of psychological insufficiency she experienced at the onset of
adulthood.

While Dickinson's girlfriends were finding teaching positions and
then marrying,[29] Emily was at home, with time on her hands, and—we
can surmise—beginning to explore the vivifying but isolating experience
of writing and thinking about writing poetry. She was becoming, as R. P.
Blackmur says, a "nuptial poet," married to herself.[30] And while on one

level, she had become, as Cody puts it, "blocked or arrested in some way,"[31] adopting the strategy of self-denial or "helpless victory" (see *L* 36, p. 98),[32] on another level, the writing of poetry and the processes of self-discovery had begun to provide compelling substitute gratification. As in her ambiguous love poems about marriage to Christ (*P* 1072, for example), literary and fantasized love objects replaced threatening adult realities. And as she was increasingly unable (or unwilling) to respond to actual relationships with young men (see *L* 36, p. 98), she slipped into a pattern of absorbing[33] the intimidating or inaccessible aspects of her life into a semiautonomous imaginative value system. After observing the manner in which she fashioned "a separate world of each" of her friendships, Richard Sewall remarks on the general approach to life that grew out of her high degree of internalization of her human relations:

> There is a hint here . . . not merely of the way she regarded her friends, but of the nature of reality itself and the methods she fashioned to cope with it. . . . She endowed each of her friends—the important ones—with whatever qualities her own nature required and, regardless of reciprocity, lived, for longer or shorter periods, within an ambience largely of her own creation . . . she could fill out in her imagination the gaps and blanks and frustrations with which actual human contact seems usually to have left her, and luxuriate in a "world" partly of her own creation.[34]

In addition to her emotional isolation, and compounding the sense of disconnection contributing to her poetry, Emily Dickinson struggled with a third form of disconnection in the process of locating her poetic voice and style, and this is the lack of a sustaining tradition in English or American letters for a woman lyric poet.

Neither in the Wordsworthian afflatus of William Cullen Bryant, nor in the learned variety and amplitude of Henry Wadsworth Longfellow, nor in the taut, more personal lyricism of Ralph Waldo Emerson would Dickinson have found deeply helpful guides into her own voice and style. While she read and learned from these poets, and while their own struggle to realize their talent cannot be minimized, these were, to state the obvious, male poets with more established sources of learning, encouragement, and recognition. Nor would she have obtained any important help by reading the popular poetry published in newspapers such as the *Springfield Republican*.[35] Such newspaper poetry is notable for its absence of distinguishing voice and vision, for its total reliance on standard subject matter, and on a mellifluous sentimentalism that would "treat" the subject without entering it. As Joanne Dobson and Sandra M. Gilbert have shown, there were certain subsidiary female traditions and even a female "community of expression"[36] that Dickinson was able to utilize. But these were not direct springboards into the "self-assertion" demanded by lyric poetry[37] so much as strategies for indirect expression or for projecting her complicated psychology of lyric power and personal denial into various personae.

Yet, at base, Dickinson was profoundly alone in her effort to realize her immense talent, without predecessors and without audience. Other than the hymnal tradition, which provided her with a standard of meter and rhyme, she seems to have had only a sense of her voice, strikingly manifested in the first lines of most of her poems. Idiosyncratic, off-beat, unpredictable, her voice seems to launch into the void with an inherent sense of uniqueness of mind and potential to draw notice.[38] Yet once her poem is launched, and often as part of its opening gambit, a plight of littleness and insignificance is simultaneously suggested, this sense of atomism or difficulty conveying the disabled and disconnected side of her poetic plight. Where in her male counterparts a guiding philosophy of life or stable poetic purpose would have carried the poem confidently to conclusion, in her poems, signs emerge of private effort to cobble vision from within limited internal circumstance—dashes that suggest painful intensity and anxious hesitation, capitalizations that convey a heightened and personal scheme of significance, irregular syntax that fulfills some intrinsic aptness of rhythm, uninflected verbs with a timeless slant on temporality, pronouns without referents, description of sensory or psychological effects with the causes and the world in which the causes exist omitted.

Just as her short, untitled poems seem surrounded on the page by empty space, the ground of Dickinson's being lacks certain enabling connections. Without a doctrinally stable idea of God, the psychological wherewithal to mature, or a female lyric tradition, her disconnection is at times so acute that it can be compared to the black holes described by contemporary astronomy—filled with such dense withdrawn mass that light has trouble escaping or is bent in the process. Her strategy for dealing with her psychological disconnection, however, complements her efforts at dealing with her literary disconnection. Compensating for her blocked psychological life by creating a highly internalized poetic universe also gives Dickinson the opportunity to attach new metaphorical meanings to certain experiences and relationships and pushes her in the protomodernist direction of fashioning reality anew out of language. Similarly, Dickinson's expression of her religious and psychological disconnection are mutually enabling. Her psychological disconnection bolsters her need to search for God in the existential pain of the present, forcing her to honor hunger as well as insight and pathetic weakness as well as bolts of vision. Out of impossibilities, a new art emerges.

II

Before looking at specific areas of Dickinson's poetry to study the drama between disconnection and reconnection, it will be worthwhile to devote some time to examining certain pervasive aspects of her poetic approach that reflect her estrangement. I have in mind aspects of her sensibility and her relation to representation and language that typify her atomistic vision—specifically, the feelings of smallness at the core of her sensibility, her poetry's disrelation from observable reality, and her poetry's reliance on language for reconnection.

One consequence of Dickinson's religious, psychological, and literary disconnection is a sensibility characterized by feelings of smallness and insignificance. "I'm nobody!" says the speaker in Poem 288. "Who are you? / Are you—Nobody—Too?" Expressing a human minimalism, bare and simple in diction, these poems dramatize a submissiveness to circumstance and a willingness to oblige others at the sacrifice of self (see, for example, *P* 540, 738, 941). They are not entirely expressions of self-denial and nobodiness, however. Usually, there is some hint of compensatory enlargement or wish for power. Yet the lack of *sufficient* enabling power, of belonging to a deprived gender, is at the heart of these "nobody" poems. They occur regularly until 1864, with at least thirty written by that year. The disappearance of this theme suggests that the enactment of powerlessness was no longer as gripping to Dickinson after the mid-1860s. The most telling of the group is the following:

> I was the slightest in the House—
> I took the smallest Room—
> At night, my little Lamp, and Book—
> And one Geranium—

So stationed I could catch the Mint
That never ceased to fall—
And just my Basket—
Let me think—I'm sure
That this was all—

I never spoke—unless addressed—
And then, 'twas brief and low—
I could not bear to live—aloud—
The Racket shamed me so—

And if it had not been so far
And any one I knew
Were going—I had often thought
How noteless—I could die—

(P 486)

It has been suggested that this poem is not simply psychobiography but that it utilizes the plight of a "character" to accentuate the pathos of its subject. Eberwein suggests the lonely nineteenth-century governess; I would suggest, as another possibility, a housemaid.[39] If this were so, there is certainly a nice irony in that the compensatory "Mint"—a metaphor for the poet's secret inspiration from Above—is in actuality the dust motes in lamplight that the maid will have to remove from the furniture the next day. Yet all we can really say with assurance[40] is that the poem portrays a discouraged and ignored young woman living in a house where the results of self-denial, mixed with shame and loneliness, are a death wish: "How noteless—I could die—." The sensibility of the "nobody" poems, prototypical of an important aspect of many of Dickinson's poems, combines an expression of insufficient human power with an irreducible claim for dignity and recognition.

Another literary consequence of the disconnections in Dickinson's life—on a totally different plane—is her attitude about representation. While her poetry often uses settings as a departure point, it hardly ever stays with the natural picture. Instead, her poetry veers into the world of metaphor and often builds one analogy on top of another. The disconnection of her poetry from mimetic goals can best be conveyed if we consider a passage superficially similar to Dickinson's poems. This passage, from a letter of the painter Georgia O'Keeffe, coordinates a long series of visual images into a pictorially and emotionally unified effect:

Tonight I walked into the sunset—to mail some letters—the whole sky—and there is so much of it out here—was just blazing—and grey blue clouds were riding all through the holiness of it—and the ugly little buildings and windmills looked great against it. . . .

The Eastern sky was all grey blue—bunches of clouds—different kinds of clouds—sticking around everywhere and the whole thing—lit up—first in one place—then in another with flashes of lightning . . . and some times sheet lightning with a sharp bright zigzag flashing across it—. I walked out past the last house—past the last locust tree—and sat on the fence for a long time—looking—just looking at—the lightning— you see there was nothing but sky and flat prairie land.[41]

Intended to convey O'Keeffe's awe at the American West, the unified effect of this passage can be ascribed to O'Keeffe's consistency of focus on the same external phenomena of clouds and sky, to her internal consistency in conveying the same feeling of awe throughout, and to her consistency of commitment to the one literary plane of impressionism to achieve her effect. Other than the inadvertently Dickinsonian opening line—"Tonight I walked into the sunset—to mail some letters," O'Keeffe's passage proves to be profoundly different from nearly all Dickinson's poems on sunsets,[42] none of which are alike, but about which one can cite a range of representative qualities.[43] Preeminent in Dickinson's approach to the subject is the characteristic of veering away from the natural picture into a series of metaphors and ideas that establish an autonomous realm, divergent from the originating scene. In Poem 628 this process is clear:

They called me to the Window, for
" 'Twas sunset"—Some one said—
I only saw a Sapphire Farm—
And just a Single Herd—

Of Opal Cattle—feeding far
Upon so vain a Hill—
As even while I looked—dissolved—
Nor Cattle were—nor Soil—

But in their stead—a Sea—displayed—
And Ships—of such a size
As Crew of Mountains—could afford—
And Decks—to seat the skies—

This—too—the Showman rubbed away—
And when I looked again—
Nor Farm—nor Opal Herd—was there—
Nor Mediterranean—   (*P* 628)

In the O'Keeffe passage, her relation to the subject continues to include "ugly little buildings" of a prosaic world and to remain true to a descriptive motive; in Dickinson's sunset poem, the "Hill" of reality is "vain"; she moves the scene into a world of subjective becoming and metaphoricality, into a series of visions of "Opal Herd" and "Mediterranean."

Sometimes, however, Dickinson's poems are intended, by means of metaphor, to help us visualize. Yet at these times, she is trying to carry us to a higher, more clarified seeing, part visual, part metaphysical. Her goal is to help us see in our mind's eye what can best be described as a metaphysical image-system, in which an idea of higher reality is suggested from slant and selective perceptions and analogies about physical reality. In "Whole Gulfs—of Red, and Fleets—of Red" violent, expressionistic slashes of naval imagery in the first stanza are subsumed by the end of the second into a comparison with a scheduled dramatic performance:

Whole Gulfs—of Red, and Fleets—of Red—
And Crews—of solid Blood—
Did place about the West—Tonight—
As 'twere specific Ground—

And They—appointed Creatures—
In Authorized Arrays—
Due—promptly—as a Drama—
That bows—and disappears—   (*P* 658)

Again, the intention is not like O'Keeffe's descriptive impressionism; it is to take us to a higher level of seeing that includes an indirect suggestion of a power orchestrating awesome natural events for unknowable purposes; and therefore the poem pushes beyond its naval analogue in an effort to suggest deeper mysteries, hidden causes, for which there is no referent.[44] Poem 228 exemplifies this pattern of moving from the visual, to the metaphorical or symbolist, to the metaphysical:

Blazing in Gold and quenching in Purple
Leaping like Leopards to the Sky

Then at the feet of the old Horizon
Laying her spotted face to die
Stooping as low as the Otter's Window
Touching the Roof and tinting the Barn
Kissing her Bonnet to the Meadow
And the Juggler of Day is gone. (*P* 228)

The rays of the sunset, at first likened to leopards leaping from low in the sky, actually then assume the identity of a leopard, with this extended metaphor controlling the next several lines. In the fifth line, the symbolist's plastic imagination takes over, describing the setting sun "low as the Otter's Window," a way of suggesting penetration so deep into the recesses of nature that the sun's head touches the roof. In the final line, the sun is compared to a juggler, which achieves a twofold allusion to the regularity of natural law on the one hand, and to the whim and mischievousness of a carnival performer on the other. Like the "Showman" and the dramatist of the two earlier poems, the "Juggler of Day" suggests a hidden cause for which there is no clear referent, only a mystery beyond human ken.[45]

In each of these sunset poems, we can see that since metaphysical reality is what Dickinson wants to describe, she promptly disconnects from the physical image. She wants to create an alignment that offers a metaphysical purchase on her subject, one that includes intellect and not just sense impression. She is willing to reconnect, but only after she has included her mind's bold slant. Mimetic disconnection is the first phase of her strategy; realigning herself with the materials central to her uniqueness as a poet is the second. Is there avoidance of the "ugly little buildings" of the quotidian world? Is her veering away from physical life motivated by a reflex to avoid the deprivations in her psychology? In part perhaps it is. But her attraction to misalignment is, at least, as strongly an expression of the power of her mind to find its originality and its original relations to things. Without confident and stable connections to the world around her, she tries to capitalize on her estranged condition.

The various disconnections in Dickinson's life also contribute to her sense of possessing a painfully unrooted or "plucked" viewpoint that ultimately shapes her view of the artist and the role of language. "If it had no pencil" (*P* 921) is one of Dickinson's poems with an "omitted center."[46] However, if we assume God is the unspecified "it," then the poem can sustain an interpretation:

If it had no pencil
Would it try mine—
Worn—now—and *dull*—sweet,
Writing much to thee.
If it had no word,
Would it make the Daisy
Most as big as I was,
When it plucked me.

The poem has a circular quality, since it is itself proof that God has not only plucked her life from her roots but *is* using her pencil to create through her. Alluding to God's contradictory ways—making a flower and then plucking its being from its roots—the poem suggests the incomprehensibility of God's design: he uproots and then counts on his unrooted creatures to express his lyric impulse. "Worn—now—and *dull*—sweet, / Writing much to thee" are the pivotal lines of this circular poem, since they reveal that the poet has, despite all, achieved a modicum of acceptance and pleasure in her role as martyr-poet. "Yet do I marvel at this curious thing: / To make a poet black, and bid him sing!" wrote Countee Cullen about his plight as a black lyric poet in 1925.[47] Something of this same sense of inherent contradiction, combined with a willingness to submit, characterizes Dickinson's situation as a female lyric poet in the previous century.

Once plucked, one is without sustaining roots; one is spiritually homeless; one is disconnected from normal assumptions, contacts, and practices. Yet as a result, one has the ability to explore otherness, enter dark places, and adapt to asymmetry. Again using a pronoun without a referent for the central concern of her poem, Dickinson describes the effort of the artist-martyr to "fit" "them"—the alien thoughts and feelings that suffering produces:

I fit for them—
I seek the Dark
Till I am thorough fit.
The labor is a sober one
With this sufficient sweet
That abstinence of mine produce
A purer food for them, if I succeed,
If not I had
The transport of the Aim—

(*P* 1109)

Abstinence, the result of withdrawal from life, promises a "purer food" for her intellectual and emotional struggle—if she succeeds. If not, "the transport of the Aim," that is, the raising of her sights from the everyday to the private arena of spiritual quest, will have heightened her sights. As the sign of her alienation, the unconnected pronouns of these poems embody and point to the problem outside the poem: the proximity of the nonhuman, the unnconnected forces in the universe and, ultimately, in ourselves. As Vivian R. Pollak puts it, quoting Dickinson, they are "Ourself behind ourself, concealed—" (*P* 670),[48] and they include the fear of death:

> While we were fearing it, it came—
> But came with less of fear
> Because that fearing it so long
> Had almost made it fair—
>
> There is a Fitting—a Dismay—
> A Fitting—a Despair—
> 'Tis harder knowing it is Due
> Than knowing it is Here.   (*P* 1277)

The ability to accommodate alien feelings and a sense of misalignment and asymmetry also enable the poet to transvaluate her situation. As the poet drifts and relocates herself in "reportless places," she discovers a new, resurrecting Joy:

> In many and reportless places
> We feel a Joy—
> Reportless, also, but sincere as Nature
> Or Deity—
>
> It comes, without a consternation—
> Dissolves—the same—
> But leaves a sumptuous Destitution—
> Without a Name—
>
> Profane it by a search—we cannot
> It has no home—
> Nor we who having once inhaled it—
> Thereafter roam.   (*P* 1382)

This "Joy" is "sincere as Nature / Or Deity" but it is different from the joy that God or the experience of nature produces; it is a chartless and spontaneous "Joy," unfamiliar and undefinable; and it dissolves as mysteriously as it comes, betraying a causality beyond the human ken. Yet even when it is gone, this new emotion leaves the poet comforted in her landscape of estrangement, feeling a new kind of loss and a new sense of possibility of reconnection.

Although language is at a loss to describe "reportless" feelings, language, by acknowledging its own limitations, is able to hint at truths beyond itself. In the most extreme situations, words are the only foothold. The word may be little more than the last refuge from fear, no more than the naming of the unravelling situation, but it does represent the only possibility for constructing *something* and establishing, minimally and at an ironic distance, a point of view:

> Escape is such a thankful Word
> I often in the Night
> Consider it unto myself
> No spectacle in sight
>
> Escape—it is the Basket
> In which the Heart is caught
> When down some aweful Battlement
> The rest of Life is dropt—
>
> 'Tis not to sight the savior
> It is to be the saved—
> And that is why I lay my Head
> Upon this trusty word—   (P 1347)

The reliance on language as the individual's only way to make order and meaning from the chaos of the world is, of course, at the heart of twentieth-century literary modernism. And that Dickinson is among the precursors of literary modernism is implied, to some extent, by each of the aspects of her disconnected poetic just discussed—by her antiheroic "nobody" poems; by her attraction to a quasi-symbolist, antimimetic aesthetic approach; by her view of the artist, like Kafka's "hunger artist," as a martyr seeking "purer food"; and by her experimental view of language as a fundamental and constitutive resource.[49]

Yet Dickinson's continuities with later European and Anglo-American literary modernism are less central here than the details of her specific case of atomistic fragmentation. I have suggested a few of the aspects of her sensibility, aesthetic approach, and angle of vision in order to sketch in her disconnected poetic. Dickinson's poems both express and stylistically embody this disconnection, yet they also involve her effort, spiritually and artistically, to achieve reconnection. Through protomodernist and other, more traditional, religious strategies, she struggles in poem after poem to find ways to overcome her disconnection and to achieve artistic and spiritual connectedness.

Other critics have, of course, developed ideas about Dickinson's poetry that parallel my concepts of disconnection and reconnection. A revealing instance can be found by looking at the way Charles Feidelson, David Porter, and Sharon Cameron gravitate to the themes of the intellectual impenetrability of the world and of literature as an autonomous realm. Feidelson, who did not include Dickinson in his work on American symbolism (although he well might have), nevertheless establishes the key themes of symbolic voyage and a universe hostile to meaning when he says about Melville that the "art of *Moby-Dick* depends on the frank acceptance of a methodological paradox," "that the realm of 'significance' rises from and returns to the dual reality of subject and object, which it would deny"; and, elsewhere, that "the basic ambiguity of Melville's mind was a double attitude toward the intellectual quest," that it was both necessary and doomed to fail.[50] The fusing vision of the voyaging mind, in Feidelson's thesis, discovers disjunction and the annihilation of meaning in the "dead, blind wall"[51] of an antagonistic universe. David Porter's *Dickinson: The Modern Idiom* (1981) observes the theme of material and metaphysical ignorance and the gap between language and perceived reality in Dickinson's poetry. Porter emphasizes Dickinson's "incomprehension" of life beyond sensational beauty and the "effects of . . . [a] divorce of language from the phenomenally experienced world."[52] And just as Feidelson saw modernist properties in Melville, Whitman, and Poe, Porter sees them in Dickinson's fragmented use of words, which he says she "joined in a chain that curves in and out of the intelligible and loops, finally, out of the real world into the autonomous system of language."[53] "Dissenting, disjunctive," "covering hysteria," "ready to collapse into chaos" are some of Porter's descriptions of Dickinson's use of language.[54] Finally, in Sharon Cameron's *Lyric Time* (1979), we find Porter's theme developed from a more theoretical, poststructuralist standpoint. Caught in a linguistically difficult role between muting loss and desire for absent immortality, Dickinson's poetry, in Cameron's view, evidences both disconnection and connection to this world and the next. Dickinson is pulled toward abstraction and obliquity in her view of self and world. "Since the immortal world cannot be seen," Cameron says, "it must be specified in lieu of any concrete form, discerned in the shape of a formal absence"; and the additional problem Dickinson faces, she adds, "because we are at a loss to see the invisible half alluded to," is that "the particularities of the temporal world, when it is invoked, can seem equally inscrutable."[55] In the "oblique dialectic of time and immortality," only "language fills the space vacated by" absence or human pain; only "language can indicate or intuit presence" or "can translate it out of its otherness."[56]

My own view of Dickinson's approach to disconnection and reconnection I would characterize as more psychological and Emersonian. As will become evident in the following sections of this chapter on reconnection, I see Dickinson able to work through a core of isolation at the center of her being. By means of an ethic of self-reliance and an aesthetic approach founded on a radical belief in self-relation, she is able to fully engage the only basic resource remaining to her, her "polar privacy" (P 1689).

The gap between Dickinson's incomparable body of poems and her significant personal limitations poses a particularly challenging critical problem. Emphasizing to this point Dickinson's deficiencies has been part of my larger plan of encompassing the complex and remarkable nature of her poetic achievement. In the balance of this chapter many of the subjects and recurring efforts that comprise Dickinson's lifelong struggle for reconnection will be examined. Melville, in *Moby-Dick*, talks about the cyclical nature of human development, how various metaphysical viewpoints are repeatedly visited in one's life.[57] Emerson, somewhat similarly, sees "temperament . . . as the iron wire on which the beads" of human moods are strung,"[58] reasoning, in addition, that while people's moods limit what they perceive, through the rotation of many moods, people can discover large possibilities about themselves and about the world. Dickinson, similarly, has certain cluster subjects and nodal viewpoints that she visits repeatedly in her creative life. By selecting certain of these clusters and placing them in a significant order, I hope to provide a picture of Dickinson's struggle to go beyond disconnection.[59]

III

One of the key reasons for selecting the terms "disconnection" and "reconnection" to particularize Dickinson's poetic atomism is their allusion to electrical current and to the absence or presence of energy conducive to spiritual and poetic power.[60] Emily Dickinson's life seems to have involved not only fundamental deprivations and rare talent but, if we are to take her "Master" letters and her poems at all autobiographically, traumatic romantic experience and powerful revelatory moments. Letters 233 and 248 to "Master," written with a "Tomahawk in my side," reveal "a love so big it scares." Powerless to secure the affection of Master, full of self-accusation ("Oh, did I offend it . . . Daisy—Daisy—offend it—who bends her smaller life to his"), she is drowning, clearly: "Oh how the sailor strains, when his boat is filling" (L 248, pp. 391–92). But, as is suggested by her poems, there are also, either prior to or more likely simultaneous with this crisis, moments of revelation that drew her to accept her calling as a poet. On one level, her sense of loss led her to become resigned to, wedded to, a model of a Christ-like sacrifice as the human path to higher truth: "If my Bark sink / 'Tis to another sea—" she says in Poem 1234. Yet, on another plane of her experience, she appears to have become energized by revelatory feelings that her genius was divinely ratified: "Mine—by the Right of the White Election! / Mine—by the Royal Seal! / . . . Mine—here—in Vision—and in Veto! / . . . Mine long as Ages steal!" (P 528).

Wendy Barker's assertion in *Lunacy of Light* (1987) seems correct that the public, daylight pursuit of the visionary gleam was not the predominant manner in which Dickinson experienced the poet's inspiring light.[61] Night, in the privacy of her room, is the scene of Dickinson's inspiration; and, as Barker has argued, it led to the tendency of the female poet not only to avoid the censorious, male-dominated light of day but to create through the imagination "*another kind* of light" in the darkness.[62]

Dickinson's poems about lightning comprise a group of such poems about created, not described, light; about electric influx of power; and about the fragmentary or filament-like nature of her poems, whose flashes of language seem often like synaptic fragments from a higher source to a fragment life.[63] In P 630 the electrical danger, the spiritual attraction, and pictorial vividness of her lightning and thunder poems are typified:

> The Lightning playeth—all the while—
> But when He singeth—then
> Ourselves are conscious He exists
> And we approach Him—stern—

With Insulators—and a Glove—
Whose short—sepulchral Bass
Alarms us—tho' His Yellow feet
May pass—and counterpass—

Upon the Ropes—above our Head
Continual—with the News—
Nor We so much as check our speech—
Nor stop to cross Ourselves—   (P 630)

The "sepulchral Bass" voice of the thunder and the "Yellow Feet" of the lightning derive from "mansions never quite disclosed" (P 1173) and are symbolic manifestations of a concealed divine power traveling from the sky to the earth. Yet Poem 1581 says that lightning-like spiritual energy has the power to strike in human experience—and to strike apocalyptically:

The farthest Thunder that I heard
Was nearer than the Sky
And rumbles still, though torrid Noons
Have lain their missiles by—
The Lightning that preceded it
Struck no one but myself—
But I would not exchange the Bolt
For all the rest of Life—
Indebtedness to Oxygen
The Happy may repay
But not the obligation
To Electricity—

"If I feel physically as if the top of my head were taken off, I know *that* is poetry," Dickinson told Higginson in one of her letters (L 342a, p. 474). In the above poem (P 1581), she goes on to say that the "gleam concomitant" and subtle "reverberation" sensed in daily life are explicable only in terms of analogy with lightning and thunder. The poem ends with the thought that life is undergirded by a power comparable to electricity:

It founds the Homes and decks the Days
And every clamor bright
Is but the gleam concomitant
Of that waylaying Light—

> The Thought is quiet as a Flake—
> A Crash without a Sound,
> How Life's reverberation
> Its Explanation found— (P 1581)

Another poem on the underlying divine light of life speaks of "The Love a Life can show Below" as "but a filament," an electrical fraction "Of that divine thing / That faints upon the face of Noon— / And smites the Tinder in the Sun— / And hinders Gabriel's Wing—"(P 673). And elsewhere Dickinson describes poems themselves as "filaments." In moments of exaltation, of "electric gale," the body itself becomes a soul:

> With Pinions of Disdain
> The soul can farther fly
> Than any feather specified
> In Ornithology—
> It wafts this sordid Flesh
> Beyond its dull—control
> And during its electric gale—
> The body is a soul—
> instructing by the same
> How little work it be—
> To put off filaments like this
> for immortality   (P 1431)

In uplifted moments, the body is instructed by the same electric principle as the soul; and just as the body can become electrified, so poems—like this one—can shed their materiality to become "filaments like this / for immortality."

"Lightning—lets away / Power to perceive His Process / With Vitality" says Dickinson in Poem 925. If we substitute God for "Lightning," the positive pole of the religious poet's experience is succinctly described. The violent and electric nature of poetic and religious experience, however, necessitates that poetic truth be told with indirection. The indirect, "slant" approach allows the poet to "dazzle gradually" so that reader (and poet) are not vaporized:

> Tell all the Truth but tell it slant—
> Success in Circuit lies
> Too bright for our infirm Delight

The Truth's superb surprise
As Lightning to the Children eased
With explanation kind
The Truth must dazzle gradually
Or every man be blind— (*P* 1129)

A pursuit of life in its radical incandescence also requires a method of "Suddenness"; and lightning again provides Dickinson with the best illustration:

The Soul's distinct connection
With immortality
Is best disclosed by Danger
Or quick Calamity—

As Lightning on a Landscape
Exhibits Sheets of Place—
Not yet suspected—but for Flash—
And Click—and Suddenness.
(*P* 974)

Life's essential landscapes must be sensed with a luminous suddenness; they must be brilliantly original pictures of momentary events. Whether they are prelinguistic descriptions of a psychic state as in "It was not Death, for I stood up" (*P* 510) or linguistic simulacra of nature's exotic transience as in "A Route of Evanescence" (*P* 1463), the immediate sensation must be of "sheets of Place" that yield powerful insight. Lightning, consequently, is not only a natural image for the jolting effect of inspiration, but a key to the slant and sudden nature of Dickinson's method and style. Original poetry for Dickinson flares with energy and flashes with language; it is a "filament" of truth, an electrical fraction of a mysterious lightning-like source that, at times, "lets away / Power to perceive His Process / with Vitality," and at other times—when writing about debility—demands that the poet, like a battery, call on stored power to reveal the negative side of life.

In 1862–63, when Dickinson's psychological crisis seems, simultaneously, to have plunged her into her period of greatest productivity, being *"at the White Heat"* (*P* 365) seems to have inflamed her days with a sense of exhausted spiritual light. In Poem 362 a repeated sense of "reconnection" or influx results in a rare state of *too much* "lightning":

> It struck me—every Day—
> The Lightning was as new
> As if the Cloud that instant slit
> And let the Fire through—
>
> It burned Me—in the Night—
> It Blistered to My Dream—
> It sickened fresh upon my sight—
> With every Morn that came—
>
> I thought that Storm—was brief—
> The Maddest—quickest by—
> But Nature lost the Date of This—
> And left it in the Sky—   (*P* 362)

Too much timeless ecstasy, too much visitation, burns and sickens Dickinson's fresh sight. But this is the exception—perhaps the exception of a lifetime. Disconnection is her norm, reconnection the aspiration of her method, and divine influx usually little more than the flickering filament that is able—somehow—to sustain poetic activity. "Our faith comes in moments; our vice is habitual. Yet there is a depth in those brief moments, which constrains us to ascribe more reality to them than to all other experiences,"[64] Emerson said in "The Over-Soul." Emerson is describing here not only his own experience as a poet-philosopher but that of a religious lyric poet like Emily Dickinson. As Dickinson puts it:

> For each ecstatic instant
> We must an anguish pay
> In keen and quivering ratio
> To the extasy.
>
> For each beloved hour
> Sharp pittances of years—
> Bitter contested farthings—
> And Coffers heaped with Tears!
>   (*P* 125)

She says also in "Did our Best Moments last—" that they are given as

> stimulants—in
> Cases of Despair—
> Or Stupor—The Reserve—
> These Heavenly Moments are—

A Grant of the Divine—
That Certain as it Comes—
Withdraws—and leaves the dazzled Soul
In her unfurnished Rooms   (*P* 393)

What, then, was the nature of Dickinson's religious experiences? She is elusive on this point: "I found the words to every thought / I ever had—but One," she says in Poem 581, "And that—defies me— / As a Hand did try to chalk the Sun." Were Dickinson's revelatory experiences restricted to feeling divinely chosen at moments of composition, her genius laced at special times with an intimation of election? Or did her relevatory experiences actually extend to numinous events of the kind her lightning poems simulate? There is little doubt about the feeling of poetic election. Poems such as "Mine—by the Right of the White Election!" as well as several others (see *P* 306, 349, 431, 580) articulate the feeling of the poet's election. Yet we can only wonder whether she had more overt transcendental moments, based on "The farthest Thunder that I heard" (*P* 1581) and "It struck me—every Day—" (*P* 362). The key point, in the end, would seem to be that Dickinson did sometimes feel that she was a divine "filament," an electrical fraction, and that her talent was *possibly* linked to a higher source. Her only option, consequently, even at other times, when faced with extreme states of terror and isolation, was to accept the unceasing current of poetic ideas and language passing through her and to continue to illuminate consciousness and identity when "disconnected" as well as when charged by higher powers.

IV

Corresponding to the disconnection I have observed in Dickinson psychologically, religiously, and in terms of literary tradition, the poet also perceives profound aloneness at the core of her being. Out of this condition several important clusters of poems arise: those on "polar" isolation as a bracing or terrifying condition, those on emotional privation and compensatory spiritual gain, and those on incomplete growth. In each case an almost ontological loneliness and lack of important connection with life characterize the adversarial medium from which her poems derive, while reconstitution and reconnection are the experiences they struggle toward.

In the first group, the spiritual aloneness of the soul proves to be both the most extreme of human conditions and yet somehow the basis, the root, of its own resolution:

> There is a solitude of space
> A solitude of sea
> A solitude of death, but these
> Society shall be
> Compared with that profounder site
> That polar privacy
> A soul admitted to itself—
> Finite infinity.   (P 1695)

Only the soul is equal to itself and can answer its own problems. This Dickinsonian version of Emersonian self-reliance leads to innumerable lines about the soul's adequacy to itself: "How adequate unto itself / Its properties shall be" (P 822); "You cannot take itself / From any Human soul—" (P 1351); "with itself did cold engage" (P 1259); "Light is sufficient to itself—" (P 862); "Its Hour with itself / The Spirit never shows" (P 1225). The theme of pure self-relation—of no longer needing "props" because "adequate, erect, / The House supports itself" (P 1142)—has ramifications for Dickinson's view of the ideal relations of the self to a variety of aspects of life.[65] The soul must be its own object, select "her own Society— / then . . . [shut] the Door—" (P 303; see also P 746 and 803).

Confidence comes only after the poet has confronted herself in the deepest recesses of her psyche. Only then is self-reliance possible: "On a Columnar Self— / How ample to rely / In Tumult—or Extremity— / How good the Certainty" (P 789).[66] Only then can "Truth," like an electric current, sustain her:

> How excellent a Body, that
> Stands without a Bone—
>
> How vigorous a Force
> That holds without a Prop—
> Truth stays Herself—and every man
> That trusts Her—boldly up—
> > (P 780; see also 1142)

But the soul is not always equal to itself, or capable of reconnection. Its profound isolation can result in splintering, in a nightmarish dualism and lack of self-relation. "Ourself behind ourself" can produce a sense of terrified otherness, so that one feels like a haunted house (*P* 670), a grave (*P* 777), or a cavern (*P* 777, 891). Without contact with "Truth," without the coherence it brings, one faces a loneliness "whose worst alarm / Is lest itself should see— / And perish from before itself / For just a scrutiny—" (*P* 777). What is so terrifying? It is the awareness of abandonment by some profoundly needed presence, and it results in psychospiritual despair that feels infinite and without remedy (see also *P* 281, 293, 458). The transition from a spiritually confident relation with the world to one of concern about inadequacy is described in Poem 822:

This Consciousness that is aware
Of Neighbors and the Sun
Will be the one aware of Death
And that itself alone

Is traversing the interval
Experience between
And most profound experiment
Appointed unto Men—

How adequate unto itself
Its properties shall be
Itself unto itself and none
Shall make discovery.

Adventure most unto itself
The Soul condemned to be—
Attended by a single Hound
Its own identity.

Once consciousness is aware of death, it discovers that it is alone; that it must traverse life with only itself as a resource; and that it must face several questions: How adequate is it to itself and to the soul? How adequate to the myriad realities of life and death? How adequate to its immortal potential in art and afterlife? The poem narrows in Stanza 4 to the soul "condemned" to live with its cellmate, the I, the poet's individual identity, described tormentedly as "a single Hound." Suggesting a demanding, a hounding, conscience, this metaphor seems intended to convey the tremendous pressure of self-conscious effort within the poet trying to be the perfect equal of the soul. In Poem 894 Dickinson says, "Of Consciousness, her aweful Mate / The Soul cannot be rid—." Consciousness is the soul's mate. If aligned with soul, truth can pass through consciousness, rendering it an incandescent filament with a luminous potential. If unaligned, consciousness cannot fully see phenomenal reality (see *P* 733 and 1039), and splinters into nightmarishness. Consciousness loses its integrative ability; and feeling abandoned by God and its sense of election, consciousness sinks toward despair, madness, or suicide.

The recipient of attention by many Dickinson commentators—most notably, Richard Wilbur, John Cody, and Vivian R. Pollak—Dickinson's poems on alimentary deprivation are also an expression of certain aspects of her disconnection.[67] Cody has located the genesis of this symbol of insufficient psychic food in the early, deprived needs of the poet for maternal love;[68] but the symbol also takes on many wider implications emotionally, socially, sexually, spiritually, and creatively. Dickinson's life *lacked*. If it was not an ontological condition that she saw in everyone's life, it was certainly a truth of personality that permeated her viewpoint; and she was inclined to lay the blame on God for his economy (*P* 791) or on Nature for her meagerness (*P* 612, 726). Seeking, moreover, to make a virtue of necessity, Dickinson saw privation as a challenge to conceive a higher reward. This reward had two versions: the "finer want" for an afterlife (*P* 726) and the higher enrichment sought when normal desires are frustrated. If one can replace appetite with aspiration, then "an Ampler Coveting" is possible:

> God gave a Loaf to every Bird—
> But just a Crumb—to Me—
> I dare not eat it—tho' I starve—
> My poignant luxury—
>
> To own it—touch it—
> Prove the feat—that made the Pellet mine—
> Too happy—for my Sparrow's chance—
> For Ampler Coveting—   (*P* 791)

In a state of deprivation, control and reshaping of appetite can make the "Pellet" hers. It can enable her to transform starvation into a "Sparrow's chance" for higher aspiration. Lack becomes gain. Worldly disconnection becomes a gambit for poetic and spiritual reconnection.

Emphasizing the increased potential for spiritual fulfillment that comes with loss and distance, Richard Wilbur has argued that Dickinson is successful in embracing "the paradox that privation is more plentiful than plenty; that to renounce is to possess more."[69] Yet Wilbur's view succumbs too completely to Dickinson's view that the infinite soul can redeem the deprived life.[70] A useful corrective that will help draw a larger circle around this theme can be found in Pollak's belief that Dickinson was also aware of the consequences that resulted from exclusion of pleasure, including, at the extreme, the drying up of the social and psychological self.[71] Aware of this danger, Dickinson also possessed an opposite tendency concerned with articulating the hungers and thirsts of the psychological self, upon which the vitality and amplitude of the imagination feed.[72] To tease out Pollak's view, in other words, when Dickinson's "poetic vision was most comprehensive,"[73] tendencies of self-denial were counterbalanced by a willingness to consider desire more openly and to embrace linguistic amplitude—the imaginative equivalent of desire—with fuller satisfaction.[74]

Dickinson's poems on growth, power, and desire constitute the third group that arises from the center of disconnection corresponding to her sense of psychological and cultural deprivation. That rage existed beneath Dickinson's domestic privation is clear. Her volcano metaphor, being a "Vesuvius at Home" (P 1705), serves as her fiercest expression of her resentment. And concomitant with this violent rage was probably guilt and terror, deep-seated reactions that would have created a psychic abyss that rendered her growth abortive and her ability to achieve reconnection with power and desire muted and incomplete. Her poems on growth, power, and desire are far fewer than those on her smallness, her impoverishment, or her contemplation of immortality; yet these poems are important and warrant a place in an analysis of her struggle to achieve self-relation and reconnection.

The formulation of what complete growth would entail is not absent from the Dickinson canon. Consistent with her ideas on self-relation, it would involve each individual having to "achieve—Itself— / Through the solitary prowess of a Silent Life—":

Growth of Man—like Growth of Nature—
Gravitates within—

Atmosphere, and Sun endorse it—
But it stir—alone—

Each—its difficult Ideal
Must achieve—Itself—
Through the solitary prowess
Of a Silent Life—

Effort—is the sole condition—
Patience of Itself—
Patience of opposing forces—
And intact Belief—   (P 750)

More often, however, the "opposing forces" are not held intact by self-belief but exist in painful tension. In "The Zeroes—taught us—Phosphorus—" (P 689) "paralysis" is said to be "our primer—dumb / unto Vitality." And in Poem 1238, "in every company," is said to be "Power . . . like a bland Abyss." But still more revealing, because more particularized, is "I dreaded that first Robin, so," (P 348) where natural growth is inseparably linked with psychic pain. The onset of spring and its myriad sounds, sights, and swarming energies is linked with the difficult onset of female maturation:

I dreaded that first Robin, so,
But He is mastered, now,
I'm some accustomed to Him grown,
He hurts a little though—

I thought if I could only live
Till that first Shout got by—
Not all Pianos in the Wood
Had power to mangle me—

I dared not meet the Daffodils—
For fear their Yellow Gown
Would pierce me with a fashion
So foreign to my own—

I wished the Grass would hurry
So—when 'twas time to see—
He'd be too tall, the tallest one
Could stretch—to look at me—

I could not bear the Bees should come,
I wished they'd stay away

In those dim countries where they go,
What word had they, for me?

They're here, though; not a creature failed—
No Blossom stayed away

Related to her sexual awakening, clues to the speaker's psychic unease can be gleaned in the lusty shout of the first robin; in the hurtful competitive encounter with more fashionable daffodils; in the shrinking impulse from the peering eyes of tall grass; and in the dreaded swarming of hungry bees. Together they create the experience of a young woman overwhelmed by the underlying dimension of psychological and physical maturation.

Other poems supplement both aspects of this natural process—the intensification of sense and desire that comes with maturation and the exposure of a hidden psychic wound at the heart of a troubled womanhood. "Before I got my eyes put out" (P 327) describes how the "News" of the visual world "would strike me dead" if the poet had to look at nature with her newly acquired depth of vision; and Poem 1039 adopts the same idea of there being a potential in her for deeper, truer hearing: "I heard, as if I had no Ear / Until a Vital Word / Came all the way from Life to me / and then I knew I heard." Several poems also talk about wanting to avoid the painful knowledge of self provided by correspondence with nature. Poem 891 is quite explicit:

To my quick ear the Leaves—conferred—
The Bushes—they were Bells—
I could not find a Privacy
From Nature's sentinels—

In Cave if I presumed to hide
The Walls—begun to tell—
Creation seemed a mighty Crack—
To make me visible—

Another poem on wanting to avoid the pain of nature's revelations of self is "The Birds reported from the South" (P 743):

The Birds reported from the South—
A news express to Me—

A spicy Charge, My little Posts—
But I am deaf—Today—

The Flowers—appealed—a timid Throng—
I reinforced the Door—
Go blossom to the Bees—I said—
And trouble Me—no More—

The Summer Grace, for Notice strove—
Remote—Her best Array—
The Heart—to stimulate the Eye
Refused too utterly—

The two stated reasons for feeling overwhelmed by the onset of natural processes in nature and the self—the intensity of youthful sensation and the painful wounded core of the poet's psyche—combine to create an unbearable sense of exposure and failure of self-relation. In "I dreaded that first Robin, so" the second line reveals that she manages somewhat to master the tumult. But in the two preceding poems, she is unequal to her growth. "Growth of Man—like Growth of Nature—" is a "difficult ideal" that exceeds her capacity for inner strength.

Nevertheless, Dickinson's poems about desire certainly demonstrate the fact that a great lyric poet must have an adventurous imaginative relationship with desire, and that this relationship, even when offset by a powerful contrary impulse toward self-denial, must remain active. Dickinson says in Poem 904, "My need—was all I had—I said / The need did not reduce— / Because the food—exterminate— / The hunger—does not cease—." "Fondness" has a "ravenousness" to it, she observes in a letter to Maria Whitney in 1883, adding, "Is there not a sweet wolf within us that demands its food" (L 824, p. 777). About sexual desire, late in her life, she also wrote a poem about a phallic dream, atypical for its directness. She has found a worm in winter in her room, "Pink, lank, and warm," and secured him by a string. When she returns,

A snake with mottles rare
Surveyed my chamber floor
In feature as the worm before
But ringed with power—
The very string with which
I tied him—too
When he was mean and new
That string was there—

I shrank—"How fair you are"!
Propitiation's claw—
"Afraid," he hissed
"Of me"?
"No cordiality"—
He fathomed me—
Then to a Rhythm *Slim*
Secreted in his Form
As Patterns swim
Projected him.

That time I flew
Both eyes his way
Lest he pursue
Nor ever cease to run
Till in a distant Town
Towns on from mine
I set me down
This was a dream.   (*P* 1670)

"Cordiality," not fear, she claims is her attitude, her relation to this creature of naked potency. She would like to keep him at polite arm's length,
where she can be curious but cautious. However, as the snake's movements seem like projected patterns (from her mind? from the snake's
subtle nature?), she panics, ending her most naked literary encounter
with poetic power cast in phallic terms.

   The town in the above poem is somewhat reminiscent of the "Solid
Town" that turns back the rising sea of eros in "I started Early—Took my
Dog—" (*P* 520). If the snake in Poem 1670 is a Blakean snake, ultimately
symbolizing eternal vision ("ringed with power"), the town to which she
flees is a place where she can avoid connection with such powers. In
Poem 520, the "Solid Town" is the place of solid social reality in a bifur-
cated worldview that puts eros, fantasy, beauty, and risk on one side of
the mind and civilization, sacrifice, mimesis, and safety on the other. An
extremely courageous poem for an agoraphobic to write, it takes its
speaker out into a world where eyes fall on her body and she is envel-
oped in a tide of eros:

I started Early—Took my Dog
And visited the Sea—

The Mermaids in the Basement
Came out to look at me —

And Frigates — in the Upper Floor
Extended Hempen Hands —
Presuming Me to be a Mouse —
Aground — upon the Sands —

But no man moved Me — till the Tide
Went past my simple Shoe —
And past my Apron — and my Belt
And past my Bodice — too —

And made as He would eat me up —
As wholly as a Dew
Upon a Dandelion's Sleeve —
And then — I started — too —

As the tide assumes a more masculine and aggressive character, the female speaker imagines herself as fragile as a droplet of dew and in danger of being overtaken; but the "Solid Town," the world of social fact, discourages the sea from pursuing her farther:[75]

And He — He followed — close behind —
I felt His Silver Heel
Upon my Ankle — Then my Shoes
Would overflow with Pearl

Until We met the Solid Town —
No One He seemed to know —
And bowing — with a Mighty look —
At me — The Sea withdrew —

Not only is the dialectical relation between eros and social reality explicit in the above poem, but the latent anxiety about allowing eros into the open is amply expressed. On the other hand, in "My Life had stood — a Loaded Gun —" (P 754) the encounter with masculinity and sexuality is more opaque.[76] Full of ambiguous lyricism and displaced feeling, the poem lacks a dialectical counterterm that includes psychic unease or acknowledges social factors; and the result seems to be a poetic fantasy that veers toward symbolist decadence and confused meanings.[77]

Polarities of desire and denial/avoidance, accompanied by corresponding attitudes of amplitude or austerity regarding language and metaphor, pull the poet one way and then the other in her treatment of her subjects. Usually, the deep transactions between them arrive at a stand-off that Dickinson can formulate with sufficient rationality on the surface of her poem. Even though she is ostensibly starving from self-denial, she can claim that desire has actually won a "higher" victory. Or even though she almost drowns in erotic dreaming, she can claim it is safe to let eros loose because civilization is a barrier. Yet sometimes these submerged transactions between desire and denial result in opacity or self-delusion. One senses this self-beguilement in "My life had stood," where satisfaction is so ambiguously defined that one can read the poem as both celebration and critique of her frontier relationship and in neither reading account fully for the core of its dependent and sexless heterosexual love. One also senses this lack of awareness of her poem's affect in "As the Starved Maelstrom laps the Navies" (*P* 872), where the repellent images of animalistic appetite belie Dickinson's true feelings, despite her attempt to positively describe a Darwinian continuum between animal and human desire. Yet often, also, bold conceits, boldly asserted, yield brilliant results. Despite the contemporary reader's initial lack of sympathy with the parallelism of lover and divine bridegroom, sexual consummation and dying, wedding night anxiety and readying oneself for God, "A Wife—at Daybreak I shall be—" (*P* 461) successfully creates a complex poetic experience, fusing the spiritual with the secular as the virgin wife goes upstairs to give herself to her bridegroom. The key would seem to be how the proximate nature of the sexual subject is handled, and in "A Wife—at Daybreak I shall be—" it is handled with a great implicit candor:

A Wife—at Daybreak I shall be—
Sunrise—Has thou a Flag for me?
At Midnight, I am but a Maid,
How short it takes to make a Bride—
Then—Midnight, I have passed from thee
Unto the East, and Victory—

Midnight—Good Night! I hear them call,
The Angels bustle in the Hall—
Softly my Future climbs the Stair,
I fumble at my Childhood's prayer
So soon to be a Child no more—

Eternity, I'm coming—Sir,
Savior—I've seen the face—before!

V

As we move outside the self to consider Dickinson's relationship to landscape, there is a group of poems rising out of a phase of being in which a powerful connection exists with nature: "The Red upon the Hill," she says in Poem 155, "Taketh away my will— / . . . The Breaking of the Day / Addeth to my Degree—." Yet in correspondence a limitation exists, not in depth of sensation but in ability to penetrate "the Sign / Of Nature's Caravan" to grasp the hidden intent (P 1097). As in Dickinson's sunset poems, beguiling sensuous beauty is not to be confused with ultimate intention. In several of her best landscape poems,[78] a sense of painful disconnection occurs from a subtle change in light quality or in seasonal feeling, this subtle shift in optics or atmosphere producing a cessation of satisfied connection with nature. Where there was a feeling of correspondence, the realization of its illusory nature results in a "cleavage"[79] freighted with impenetrable meanings: "Heavenly Hurt, it gives us— / We can find no scar, / But internal difference, / Where the Meanings, are" (P 258).

In Poem 812, a March light of early spring "almost speaks to you" through the colors on a solitary field "That Science cannot overtake / But Human Nature feels." When it goes, it produces "A quality of loss / Affecting our Content / As trade had suddenly encroached / Upon a Sacrament." In Poem 1540, summer's lapsing is akin to the end of a human relationship, with an attenuation of feeling occurring as summer begins the process of withdrawal. The increasing distance and sense of ingathering of Nature to spend "with herself / Sequestered Afternoon" suggest the "Perfidy" of a relationship in which the other party has always intended to leave but has never said so. The end of summer is, in ways, a little death:

As imperceptibly as Grief
The Summer lapsed away—
Too imperceptible at last
To seem like Perfidy—
A Quietness distilled

As Twilight long begun,
Or Nature spending with herself
Sequestered Afternoon—
The Dusk drew earlier in—
The Morning foreign shone—
A courteous, yet harrowing Grace,
As Guest, that would be gone—

Absolute cleavage between self and nature is the jumping-off point for "Four Trees—upon a solitary Acre—" (P 742). This poem tries to empty itself as much as possible of a human observer. It is about the relation of four trees to an acre of land in a world without the human mind. It begins and ends in disconnection, its only reconnection being its successful definition of opaque relationships, of disrelation, of impenetrability. The randomly placed trees, in Dickinson's anticipation of modern field theory, merely "maintain" their difference from empty space:

Four Trees—upon a solitary Acre—
Without Design
Or Order, or Apparent Action—
Maintain—

The Sun—upon a Morning meets them—
The Wind—
No nearer Neighbor—have they
But God—

Only minimally definable relations exist:

The Acre gives them—Place—
They—Him—Attention of Passer by—
Of Shadow, or of Squirrel, haply—
Or Boy—

These relations involve the acre giving the four trees "Place" and the trees giving the acre the ability to capture attention by being a focal point in an otherwise empty landscape. But their deed or purpose in "General Nature" is unknown to them:

What Deed is Theirs unto the General Nature—
What Plan
They Severally—retard—or further—
Unknown—

If the plan of general nature is less than known to sentient creatures, obviously nature's plan is unknowable to trees. But as an exploration of local reality for its symbolic or "allegorical embodiment,"[80] this picture of four trees on a solitary acre envisions a chilling image of disrelation and disconnection.[81]

A final instance of Dickinson's effort to respond to disconnection with a poetry of reconnection involves moving yet farther out, beyond land-scape, to her relation to "circumference." Dickinson could not see im-mortality, but she could write poems that took her to the limit of mortal consciousness where she could, through intuition or fantasy, try to peer beyond.

One means was to begin in the very meagerness of her existence:

> I have no Life but this
> To Lead it here—
> Nor any Death—but lest
> Dispelled from there—
>
> Nor tie to Earths to come—
> Nor Action new—
> Except through this extent—
> The Realm of you—
>   (P 1398)

Through a series of negative definitions or exclusions, Dickinson man-ages to indicate something minimally expectant about what waits beyond and then a route—through a loved one or Christ. Poem 853 focuses on "parting with the rest" when one's life has already involved great privation:

> When One has given up One's life
> The parting with the rest
> Feels easy, as when the Day lets go,
> Entirely the West
>
> The Peaks, that lingered last
> Remain in Her regret
> As scarcely as the Iodine
> Upon the Cataract.   (P 853)

The key word of the first stanza is "entirely," which clarifies the subject as the final letting go in a life that has already been one of sacrifice; the key word of the second is "scarcely," which reveals the extent of the movement beyond living and into the circumference that the final image of "Iodine / Upon the Cataract" implies. Snows might have been a more apt image to convey the cold horizon of death-in-life; but an iodine cataract, a waterfall stained in blood, conveys a sense of waters connected with immortality (see also *P* 726) and of Christ's mediation of human suffering.

A poem such as "Because I could not stop for Death—" (*P* 712) dramatizes the journey between life and eternity, creating for us an experience of increasing physical distance and altered temporal perspectives. Conceiving death as a line, Poem 160 fantasizes the experience of consciousness moving across the line, only to be called back, and thenceforth able to view life with a double perspective:

> Just lost, when I was saved!
> Just felt the world go by!
> Just girt me for the onset with Eternity,
> When breath blew back,
> And on the other side
> I heard recede the disappointed tide!
>
> Therefore, as One returned, I feel
> Odd secrets of the line to tell!
> Some sailor, skirting foreign shores—
> Some pale Reporter, from the aweful doors
> Before the Seal!

Yet these poems do not reflect actual transformations as a result of contact with eternity; rather they are imaginative experiments, expressions of desire for reconnection, that substitute aspiration and fantasy for the real experience. Poem 271, on the other hand, rises from within a profoundly transformed and reconnected condition, much like the lightning poems cited earlier:

> A solemn thing—it was—I said—
> A woman—white—to be—

And wear—if God should count me fit—
Her blameless mystery—

A hallowed thing—to drop a life
Into the purple well—
Too plummetless—that it return—
Eternity—until—

I pondered how the bliss would look—
And would it feel as big—
When I could take it in my hand—
As hovering—seen—through fog—

And then—the size of this "small" life
The Sages—call it small—
Swelled—like Horizons—in my vest—
And I sneered—softly—"small"!

Although signified by the speaker's white dress, the transformation itself from smallness and renunciation to election and empowerment is hidden from us; however, the act of taking the bliss in her hand, of translating the plummetless sinking into the writing of poetry, is the crucial enabling act. As in Poem 1234 ("If my Bark sink / 'Tis to another sea— / Mortality's Ground Floor / Is immortality—"), reconnection comes when the poet lets her life drop away and allows some mysterious reality to buoy her up. Still, this is not enough, because eternity is ungraspable; the "bliss" feels too "big." Only when she grasps with poetry at the elusive thing that is described as a "hovering—seen—through fog—" does her small life swell "like Horizons." Only by remaining on this side of circumference and by pressing beyond with language can the poet acquire the enlargement of eternity in time.

Jane Eberwein has successfully studied many of Dickinson's poems in light of the poet's effort to move "circuit," the daily round, as close as possible to "circumference." "The design of her life," says Eberwein, "was a process of movement from her smallness . . . to circumference or the point of ultimate boundary between finite and infinite, the known and the mysterious, the human and the divine." Dickinson's method, moreover, involved distillation and contraction, until she exploded outward "toward the margins of the universe."[82] One of her many poems that begin in the tomb—that is, with the ultimate sense of disconnection from life—nicely illustrates the way confinement and smallness, not expansion, enable Dickinson to move into circumference:

A Coffin—is a small Domain,
Yet able to contain
A Citizen of Paradise
In its diminished Plane.

A Grave—is a restricted Breadth—
Yet ampler than the Sun
And all the Seas He populates
And Lands He looks upon

To Him who on its small Repose
Bestows a single Friend—
Circumference without Relief—
Or Estimate—or End—   (*P* 943)

VI

Walt Whitman's Personalism was his vehicle for mining the depths of the self and at the same time encompassing as much of the world's multiplicity as possible. Dickinson's approach can be described as *particularism*. Although she has abundant and multiple views of many subjects—sunsets, growth, landscapes—segmentary fragmentation is far less significant to Dickinson's poetic vision than the atomistic fragmentation that emanates from a sense of human finitude and incompleteness. Dickinson's approach is one of contraction not expansion. As Eberwein observes, expansion followed, but it followed usually as a result of compaction, as "Essential Oils—are wrung / The Attar from the Rose" (*P* 675). Dickinson felt alone with her many subjects because of her lack of literary predecessors; and her view of her subjects was consequently typified by qualities of uniqueness, idiosyncrasy, and a stark freshness tinged with a sense of absence, of something missing. As one looks at her many poems, Lucretian atoms drifting around in an ether of emptiness is what comes to mind, rather than pieces that cohere to give a composite picture of the universe. The individual poem is her goal, not a comprehensive worldview.

As suggested by Poem 1510, Dickinson wished, ideally, for each moment of poetry to represent a hard, simple confluence of forces:

How happy is the little Stone
That rambles in the Road alone,

> And doesn't care about Careers
> And Exigencies never fears—
> Whose Coat of elemental Brown
> A passing Universe put on,
> And independent as the Sun
> Associates or glows alone,
> Fulfilling absolute Decree
> In casual simplicity—   (P 1510)

A happy statement of her philosophy of spiritual self-reliance and self-relation, this poem's assertion of autonomy emerges in other phases of her poetry as well. From her austere poems about her insignificance ("I was a Phoebe—nothing more—," *P* 1009), to her densest poems about nature's mysteries ("Further in Summer than the Birds," *P* 1068), to her most exotic imagism about perception ("A Route of Evanescence," *P* 1463), her poems explore the spiritual and linguistic resources of self-sufficiency and self-referentiality. Poetry was her private realm against all that was missing for her in culture and development. Poetry was her higher purchase on fullness and fulfillment. Without poetry there would have been perpetual disconnection and leakage of vitality. Like "Jugs—a Universe's fracture / Could not jar or spill," Dickinson's poems are the result of a process similar to bees collecting pollen fuzz:

> Bees are Black, with Gilt Surcingles—
> Buccaneers of Buzz.
> Ride abroad in ostentation
> And subsist on Fuzz.
>
> Fuzz ordained—not Fuzz contingent—
> Marrows of the Hill.
> Jugs—a Universe's fracture
> Could not jar or spill.   (P 1405)

At the core of nature's creative dynamism, the flowers—"Marrows of the Hill"—are "ordained" not "contingent" food for bee or poet. And ambiguously positioned so that they refer to bees or flowers, the "Jugs" are ultimately neither but the result of both—the honey of poetry that "a Universe's fracture / Could not jar or spill." Bridging or representing dualism and subsisting on "ordained" food, Emily Dickinson's poems contain a fullness fashioned from the triumph of language over the abyss. A rare vitality rides abroad in Dickinson's poetry, filling the void with a new buzzing.

PART FOUR

Conclusions

7

Notes on Method; with Some Thoughts on the Diversitarian Spirit and Democracy

I

The works of literature examined in this study derive from a world of changing social and religious institutions and freshly evolving intellectual schemes. Gone are the state-supported orthodox churches with their fixed, pessimistic ideas about man; disappearing are the governing elites and the small, familiar cities and towns; gone is the comfortable relationship between reason and religion; gone is the idea of the spiritually unified self. In their place are competing religious denominations and sects, myriad foreign and native populations, transcendental philosophical intuitions, prebiblical discoveries in geology and paleontology, and an emerging reductivism and materialism in psychology.

Losing its traditional dogmas and figures of authority, this changing society produced a literature typified by relativism. The versions of relativism that emerged, moreover, were often strikingly different. Emerson's version was rooted in the psychological and spiritual, in shifting moods and opinions, and in plunging gulfs between periods of focus. Viewed at a distance so that his idealism can be seen as a defense against the onslaught of a materialist age, Emerson was, quite literally, seeking to assert mind over matter, man over society, subjective truth over social truth.[1] Somewhat different is Melville's version of relativism, rooted in the naturalistic and assuming metaphysical overtones as human consciousness grew overburdened by violence and tragedy. Despite Melville's presentation of oscillations in man and nature between "calms" and "storms," and despite the fragmentation in Melville's worldview, he also conceived of a powerful, vital connection between mind and matter; ultimately, he saw them as one mysterious dynamic force, which neither current epistemologies nor their working methods were able fully to comprehend. The mystery was too large, living, and inclusive of the observer. Whitman's relativism had two poles, the many and the one, the collective view and the individualist's view, the centrifugal approach and the centripetal approach. This bipolarity of vision was only integrated when Whitman saw a way for the painful and lonely atomism of the individual to be reconciled with his desire for merging and for poetic ensemble— when man, conceived as "debris," could still find a way to emit from his mouth the "prismatic colors" of the unifying spirit. Dickinson's relativism derived from her inexhaustible sense of imaginative difference. Whether it is that the mind will never have the same view of a subject twice, or that language will always be put to experience differently by such a determinedly original mind, the end result for Dickinson, despite a repetition of subjects and themes, was endless particularity—a variousness not simply of classifiable viewpoints but of highly realized metaphysical visions.

The thought-form of diversitarianism, formulated by European Romantics and enlarged by American democractic society, was an instrumental idea for American writers seeking to respond to contemporary life. Conceivably, Marxists might argue that the ultimate cause of the relativistic and fragmentary literature that emerges at midcentury is at base economic, since the idea of diversitarianism itself can be related to forces of early American industrial capitalism—to new labor pools flooding industrial cities, to loss of confidence in religious institutions as lives became more transient, to the expansion of foreign markets, and to introspective and mystical ideas about human aspiration once traditional relations with the land and social hierarchy deteriorated. But this economic analysis, while it may, to a significant extent, underscore contextual factors, fails to explain a critical dimension of the creation of the literary works in question. It does not explain—as a sophisticated Marxist would concede—how in imaginative terms writers dealt with the rapid growth, change, and fragmentation developing around them. In such a line of inquiry, the thought-form of diversity, amplified by American democracy culturally and politically, is also essential to understanding how writers were able to respond to the new heterogeneity of life and to the need to conceive of new integrative and assimilative forms that entertained multiple perspectives and communicated gaps of uncertainty in the face of multiple options. In other words, without a theory of artistic production that is both materialist and idealist, without a theory that can include both the material aspects of cultural multiplicity and the imaginative reordering of those "facts" in terms of variety, correspondence, dynamism, and abundance, the works of Emerson, Melville, Whitman, and Dickinson would not be sufficiently comprehensible. Marxism can offer a theory of realism, perhaps even an explanation (in terms of cooptation) of the artistic need for a thought-form to celebrate abundance and diversity, but not an explanation for the deeply original effort to respond to the overwhelming changes of contemporary life through fresh imaginative forms and visions.[2] Such a drive derives from deeper sources than ideologically controlled social motives and structures of meaning.

Leo Marx has suggested a method to uncover in literary analysis aspects of "covert" culture repressed because of their inconsistency with acknowledged, overt attitudes. "Literature may be studied," he says, "for what it betrays as well as what it depicts"; and may be approached "as a projection of covert" or "unstated ideas of a society."[3] In my description of Melville's, Whitman's, and to some extent Emerson's work as a representative analogy of the times, I have been concerned, somewhat similarly, with literary works that present an analogy of experience for Americans when faced with the increasing multiplicity and discord of American life. Prompted by the diversity of religious views, a variety of immigrant groups, the convergence of different classes and different political and philosophical views, writers were trying to find a form to recreate the "unstated" experience of being confronted, inundated by, competing perspectives.[4] Proof of the relation of literature to covert or implicit views of social reality is difficult to achieve. Leo Marx looks at repressed views of social reality revealed by imagery and metaphor. I have had to develop other lines of argument for each writer. Concerning Melville, I have pointed to parallel approaches to the abundant variety of life in Melville and in the urban journalist George G. Foster and called attention to the way Foster's diversitarian style and Melville's are quite similar, as though formed by and reacting to the same environment. Also regarding Melville, I have suggested a parallelism between the multiple religious options in the air during the Second Great Awakening and the vision of multiple metaphysical views of reality in *Moby-Dick* and would also point out the diversity of race, language, and point of view of Melville's characters aboard the *Pequod*, which he calls "an Anacharsis Clootz deputation from all the isles of the sea," and which Charles Olson elaborates on, describing them as " 'a people,' Clootz and Tom Paine's people, all races and colors functioning together, a forecastle reality of Americans."[5] But most important to my thesis is how Melville orchestrates the inter-action of matter and mind in the cetology section of *Moby-Dick*; how he creates a picture of natural reality as heterogeneous and vast and of the mind as possessing diverse ways to knowledge; how he then makes them intersect, like the grid of city streets; and how he specifies an allegorical interaction between mind and matter that is analogous to the experience of being confronted not only with a materialistic heterogeneous society, but with competing belief systems and interpretative schemes.

Whitman, obviously also, creates works that provide an explicit drama of merger between the soul and the material multiplicity of the times. While in "As I Ebb'd with the Ocean of Life," an allegory of the mind striving to penetrate opaque matter is explicit and focused, in "Song of Myself," although fluid and diffuse, the implied allegory is everywhere apparent as well. Emerson also was interested in painting the procession of society in terms of an allegory of mind and matter. In his introductory "Lecture on the Times," for example, he catalogs "the agitator, and the man of the old school, and the member of Congress, and the college-professor, the formidable editor, the priest, and reformer, the contempla-tive girl" but then tells us that each has to be measured by "spiritual law" and is, in the end, a shadowy form of a Platonic ideal that "flitted for a moment across a wall."[6] Merger for Emerson has a way in the end of reducing even the procession of society into pure spiritual consciousness.

"Allegory arises," says Stephen J. Greenblatt, "in periods of loss, pe-riods in which a once powerful theological, political, or familial authority is threatened with effacement."[7] Coming at this condition somewhat dif-ferently, one might ask why writers in an increasingly urban fragmentary society would not reflect a pluralistic, uncentered condition and prove incapable or uninclined to generate a coherent image of the world. Why should some writers seek to create a historical analogy and an epistemo-logical allegory from conditions of disintegration and disarray—"from the painful absence of that which it claims to recover"?[8] The answer would appear to be that their orientation was national rather than marginal and that they consequently sought to create an imaginative order for their fragmenting culture. Some current scholars may wish to contextualize these writers' motives in terms of a particular political issue such as slav-ery. Others may try to see these writers yielding to urban romantic allegories of the sort Peter Brooks finds in Balzac, or to a local, contingent allegory of loss and exile of the sort that Brooks (following Walter Benjamin) finds in the experience of Baudelaire's *flâneur*.[9] But it seems to me that the work of these writers often reflects thinking in national terms. Utilizing in new ways the traditional materials of their declining mainstream culture, such writers seek to prevent this decentering and fracturing by creating new imaginative forms and by devising new, more advanced aesthetic and spiritual responses to it. "The American writer," observes Lawrence Buell, "was charged with the mission of developing his or her talent from a position of social marginality that was supposed, nonetheless, to express itself, not as bohemianism but rather, as an articulation of national values"; he or she was supposed to both express individual vision and yet protect the communal need.[10] Against the threat of chaotic relativism and an extreme linear fragmentation, these writers are able to draw on deep resources in the Puritan past of symbol and allegory and in more recent European Romanticism of diversitarian thought-forms that celebrate, at one extreme, the social or natural multiplicity of existence and, at the other extreme, the unique and irreducible nature of the individual.

But we speak of the analogical representation of the experience of segmentary fragmentation. What of the instances when a writer felt isolated despite the vibrance of the cultural environment? At such times we have seen, especially in Whitman and Dickinson, the creation of literary forms steeped in a sense of psychic and artistic distinction in order to capture or offset the writer's isolation. In Whitman's homosexual poems, we find simple expression of the pain of isolation and the occasional joy of relief. In Dickinson this act of expression rises to become an expressive representation of the atomistic condition. Think of Dickinson's dashes and capitalizations and irregular syntax, her description of effects without causes or pronouns without referents. These, to some degree, comprise a self-conscious stylistic representation, albeit in gnomic form, of the individual struggle for expressive individuality despite anomie—a projection of a fragment life into a self-consciously fragmentary form. In Whitman's Personalism and in Dickinson's obsession with difference we see the effort to respond to the lonely isolation of the individual with internal depth and distinctiveness.

Hopefully, the four areas of background fragmentation I have delineated have, to some extent, coalesced in the reader's mind into a field of forces—forces that are relevant yet discontinuous, "out there," so to speak, from the vantage point of the reader's experience of the text. And, hopefully also, the cultural anchors spotlighted in each literary chapter have assumed a position more organically related to the "in hereness" of the texts themselves. In my scheme, the anchors provide a bridge between discontinuous general background and text, the midpoint in the continuum where context becomes constitutive.[11]

But background and anchor should have other value. In the case of Whitman, a notion of the New York City streets at midcentury provides a historical gauge against which to measure the nature and authenticity of Whitman's vision. Quite obviously, Whitman elides social divisions and political conflicts; yet his highly elaborated vision of a world of one flesh, held together by "adhesiveness" and "amativeness," becomes fully resonant only when one understands it as a quest for human solidarity that is meant to offset the disturbing divisions and estrangement brought on by immigration, industrial manufacturing, and national politics.[12] Indeed, much of Whitman's persona seems designed to bridge the gap between the harshness of historical actualities and his unique and ineluctably open human needs.

The breadth and depth of field afforded by my method also make it possible to see how the other writers in my study may have been influenced by a particular background context. One can certainly see the Second Great Awakening as a formative influence not only on Dickinson's antiformalist, antidoctrinal religious lyricism, but also on Emerson, Melville, and Whitman. Without the defining and provocative modalities of traditional religious ideas, and without the "individual spiritual immediatism"[13] that swept the United States, their imaginative visions are inconceivable. In a similar vein, the broad influence of urban life is evident as well. In conversation with the authors of *Literary New York*, Alfred Kazin is reported to have said, "I can't prove it but I'm sure New York is the single most important factor in American writing."[14] Probably, one has to allow for the enthusiasm of a native New Yorker. Yet to the degree that his intuition is true, my study has taken a first step in substantiating it with regard to the mid-nineteenth century.

Ramified differently in different contexts—"metropolitanized" by the city, "denominationalized" by religious freedom and popular revivals, "psychologized" by evolution, and "subjectivized" by philosophy—the ideal of diversity clearly played a major role in facilitating the reconstruction of the self and the view of social reality in mid-nineteenth-century America. Imaginative writers in particular were drawn to further amplify the cultural manifestations of diversified thinking already going on around them. And the consequence was innovation in the form, texture, and impact of literature in which a heightened value was placed upon multiplicity.

As to the still more overarching question of the representational relation between the fragmentation I have demonstrated in culture and the fragmentation I have demonstrated in literature, I have tried to show that certain literature was a representation and an expression, indeed an imaginative projection, of splintering within and without; that the fracturing was pervasive in this literature and helped extend the new views of social, intellectual, and psychological reality. However, if I were to try to define a unified theory of literary formation beyond the influence of the ideal of diversity, I would be violating my own diversitarianism as a scholar and critic. Differences in each writer's exposure and sensitivity to the facets of social and cultural reality, combined with the differences in the way each imaginatively constructs the world, render the question of representation largely an individual issue tied to the details of each writer's situation. No theory across the work of all four writers suggests itself to explain their minds and texts—an assertion that may be frustrating to certain cultural theorists, but which I see as an affirmation of empiricism that rejects overly detached formulations and overdetermined critical directions.

What I can offer, simultaneous with a summary of the protomodernist aspects of the writers I have treated, is a consolidation of my historical perspective. The emergence of the early forms of American modernism can then be seen from a social as well as artistic standpoint.

The romantic template of unity-in-diversity, as I have shown, enabled writers to assimilate increasingly complex and varied subject matter of both an intellectual and material nature. And when variety began to overwhelm the capacity of traditional modes of representation, organization, and discourse, the romantic pattern enabled writers to confidently seek new forms, some experimentally expansive, some experimentally fragmentary, some boldly heterogeneous, but each pursued with the assumption that new forms, organically realized from new material, could be created: the critical ingredients were innovativeness and vision. At some point, however, this elasticity of conception stretched to a philosophical and formal limit; and the resiliency of the romantic thought-forms of diversitarianism faced a more extreme crisis. As we saw, this crisis posed the problem of the endless succession of moods without prospect of redeeming transcendence on Emerson. It confronted Melville with the problem of coherence as he tried to represent discordant sides of experience as well as the clash of multiple approaches to it. It caused Whitman in "As I Ebb'd" to abandon correspondence in his approach to experience. It jolted Dickinson from disconnection to linguistic strategies for surviving spiritual amputation. And the results of this crisis are some of the early forms and philosophical adjustments of American modernism: Emerson's existentialist-like assertion of the total authority of individual subjective consciousness; Melville's technical improvisation of an encyclopedic, part-documentary form and a new self-contained method to encircle his problematical view of reality and art; Whitman's peek into the decentered realms of contingency, finitude, and estrangement; and Dickinson's language experiment.

What were the key historical factors surrounding this transition beyond the romantic paradigm? On the level of individual experience (represented by my chapter anchors), each writer was forced to confront accelerating social and environmental diversification as well as increased personal estrangement and division. And on the level of consciousness of society (represented by my context material), we have seen that each writer was confronted by a proliferation of controversies over revivalism, evolution, immigration, slavery, religious miracles, and Transcendentalism, and that the emerging print media exacerbated these controversies regionally and nationally. Philip Fisher's work on the concept of a demo-cractic social space, overwhelmed by immigrant diversity, and my own notion, influenced by his work, of democratic public space overwhelmed by a diversity of opinion,[15] both point to a growing sense of cultural debate and conflict. The concept of an intangible but very real space of public opinion, magnified by media, suggests that the controversies that filled the air and impinged on individual consciousness became the origin, the goad, for the new experimental forms that sought to mirror or simulate the sense of multiple and warring viewpoints agitating the cultural atmosphere. Hence we find the analogical level of the work of the writers studied not only alluding to the romantic problem of man's relation to nature (or the loss of nature) but to the fragmentation of religious life in America, to the imprint of urban diversity and the problem of urban discord, to the atomization of the individual, and to the increasing complexity and irreconcilability between intellectual schemes and new material realities.

Economic and intellectual change, institutional and individual frag-

mentation of identity, consciousness severed from stable social structures—these, then, are the elements out of which the first forms of American modernism emerged; these are the forces that drove our writers from
a faith in unity-in-diversity to adventurous experimentation in splintered
forms.

Several different levels of understanding have come into play in my
approach to the American Renaissance. A postmodern understanding of
the writers in question is different in some respects from a modernist
perspective, while in other respects only a historical approach, able to
grasp romantic and federalist views of American reality, is adequate to
interpreting what Emerson, Melville, Whitman, and Dickinson are saying. In our postmodern era of omnipresent mass media, with the space
of public consciousness an inescapable presence of daily life, we can only
now perhaps appreciate the incipient attempts to give form to the sense
of democratic public space that was becoming an increasing part of public
awareness and conscious experience. Another postmodern influence—
this one only different in degree from the conditions that contributed all
along to twentieth-century modernism—is the sense of intellectual, social, and material discord in the American metropolis. My personal experience is the best way to illustrate this point. Reading *Moby-Dick* 125
years after its publication, I found that inhabiting the postmodern environment of Manhattan was of invaluable help in responding to the protomodernist vision of life in Melville's masterpiece. While the world
around me made it possible for me to understand the shifting variety and
multivalenced perspectives in *Moby-Dick*, Melville's novel, I found, was
also a precipitant that enabled me to define for myself the structure of the
world around me—so full of stylistic, intellectual, and material diversity
and discord. In that convergence of horizons lies many of the seeds of
this book.

The democratic and romantic understandings of these works, on the
other hand, require an act of historical reconstruction, for they are inex-
tricably connected with eighteenth- and nineteenth-century elaborations
of American ideals. As I have shown, the correlation between the key
bases of vision in American literature and American political theory is
not insignificant. Paralleling the emphasis on individual rights and freedom is the emphasis in literature on self-reliance, self-relation, and the
realization of individual vision. And paralleling the importance given
to the flourishing of minority opinions as a protection of rights and
freedoms for all, there is in literature the celebration of diversity as the

necessary condition of pursuing truth in a relativistic situation. It is even tempting to seek clues in the literary definition of the problems of fragmentation resulting from too much self-sufficient individualism or too much diversity about how to face these dangers in our current social scene. While insights on these two planes of discourse are not ipso facto transferable, there are meaningful parallels. For example, it is noteworthy that while Emerson, Melville, and Whitman struggle against segmentary fragmentation, trying to give it some coherence, they do not try to solve the problem of fragmentation by stifling the fertility of multiplicity. And while Dickinson makes her isolated individual consciousness the foundation of artistic accomplishment, she is unable to ignore completely her lack of social fulfillment and lack of an audience for her poems: she never entirely denies her needs as a social being.

Yet despite the protomodernism of these writers, it is important not to lose sight of the largely romantic orientation each—except Dickinson—brings to their work. Preventing their materials from flying into chaotic confusion is, as we have seen, an important impulse in all four writers; and the thought-form used most commonly as a countervailing force to fragmentation is the romantic idea of correspondence. Correspondence between subject and object provides each with a basis to provide connections and achieve moments of coherence amidst representations of difference, discord, otherness, and violence. Emerson shows us that in allowing all our moods to play we will see into so many states of mind around us that we can approach universality. Melville shows us that the unending modalities of the mind and of nature are interrelated on a primitive level; and that when we can accept this evolutionary insight, the mind can encompass all of life in one structure and one vision—amputation, death, and shipwreck included. Whitman shows us how merger through love of the physical world closes the distance and softens its divisions. And Dickinson—at least in some of her poems—shows us the correspondences (and disjunctions) of spirit manifested in communion with seasonal landscapes and springtime eruptions. In most situations the splintering into local and anarchic disarray is avoided through the complementarity of mind and matter as an ordering principle, even though these moments of interrelation may clash with other, different moments and require a new heterogeneous aesthetic to bring them into larger "order."

Like correspondence, also important for these new ideas of

(dis)order to assimilate disjunction and disarray, is the romantic tendency to embrace open, organic approaches to form rather than adhere to pre-conceived, fixed ideas. The embrace of process as an important dynamic of form results at times, as Poirier has emphasized, in all ' .ruths" being reduced simply to change—to ideas of transition and metamorphosis that override a quest for substantive answers. One sees this awareness of in-escapable fluidity in Emerson's emphasis on "shooting the gulf" between moments of correspondent vision. One glimpses it in Melville's troubled cry in *Moby-Dick*: "There is no steady unretracing progress in this life; we do not advance through fixed gradations. . . . But once gone through, we trace the round again."[16] And one finds it in Dickinson, where the de-scription of the flux of the creative spirit is given preeminence over fixed forms and fixed referents:

> Pursuing you in your transitions,
> In other Motes—
> Of other Myths
> Your requisition be.
> The Prism never held the Hues,
> It only heard them play—[17]

We need to recognize with Dickinson that while "The Prism" is a necessary context, it is not identical with the multiple hues that play within it. To return to my analogy between literature and social thought: the multiple hues of creative vision or social diversity have a distinct life and character, although they disintegrate into fragmentary confusion without some "prism" within which they can discover their distinguish-ing traits. What this means about the importance of a representational framework in the artistic sphere or about a shared political and cultural tradition in the societal sphere, citizen-scholars are not always going to agree upon. Some see diversity itself as the American idea, while others insist there is, or there needs to be developed, a set of shared experiences, values, and traditions that can encompass our differences. My opinion, as a consequence of my reading of the literature, is that diversity alone will lead to conflict but that without the sanction of freedom of difference there cannot continue to be fresh vision or agreeable community. The tension or balance between individual freedom and society, and between minority and mainstream culture, will not stay the same. In the future different conditions and needs from without and within will redefine the desired equilibrium.

At the same time, we better continue to read our literature carefully, devotedly, and with a less zealous embrace of theory or politics. Having flirted with reading it under the exaggerated assumptions of deconstruction and ideological hegemony, we need to move closer to text and context, to a more open experience of reading and to the discovery of enlarged horizons through historical research rather than through a priori ideological assertions. Our literature, after all, is the deepest mirror of our identity—past, present, and future. In it the energies and forces of life take on form and meaning, and without encountering these forces again and again our powers of renewal will grow weaker and our resources as a nation will become less strong.

Notes

Chapter 1 Introduction: Diversity, Democracy, and the Nineteenth-Century Literary Imagination

1. See Arthur O. Lovejoy, *The Great Chain of Being: A Study of the History of an Idea* (Cambridge: Harvard University Press, 1936), chs. 9–10.

2. Ibid., p. 294.

3. Friedrich Schiller, "Letters upon the Aesthetical Education of Man," Letter 13, in *Essays Aesthetical and Philosophical*, n. trans. (London: George Bell, 1884), p. 63.

4. Friedrich Schleiermacher, *On Religion: Speeches to Its Cultured Despisers*, trans. John Oman (London: Kegan Paul, Trench, Trubner, 1893), Speech 5, p. 213.

5. Samuel Taylor Coleridge, *The Theory of Life*, in *Miscellanies, Aesthetic and Literary of Samuel Taylor Coleridge*, ed. T. Ashe (London: George Bell, 1885), pp. 384–85.

6. Theodore Parker, "A Discourse of the Transient and Permanent in Christianity," in *The Transcendentalists: An Anthology*, ed. Perry Miller (Cambridge: Harvard University Press, 1950), p. 264; the sermon was delivered on May 19, 1841, in the South Boston Church.

7. Theodore Parker, *Theodore Parker's Experience as a Minister*, in *Transcendentalists*, p. 492; written in 1859, this memoir-letter reflects Parker's view of Boston at an earlier, unspecified time.

8. *The Collected Works of Ralph Waldo Emerson*, ed. Alfred R. Ferguson et al. (Cambridge: Belknap–Harvard, 1983), 3:21.

9. Rather than invalidate their views, the fact that their journal was short-lived and their goals for it highly idealized only enhances the status of their ideas as representative of what was advanced and experimental at the time.

10. Lawrence Buell, *Literary Transcendentalism: Style and Vision in the American Renaissance* (Ithaca: Cornell University Press, 1973), p. 167.

11. See G. Harrison Orians, "The Rise of Romanticism, 1805–1855," in *Transitions in American Literary History*, ed. Harry Hayden Clark (New York: Octagon, 1967), pp. 187–91, 234–39.

12. For other ideas on the influence of democracy, see Larzer Ziff, *Literary Democracy: The Declaration of Cultural Independence in America* (New York: Viking, 1981).

13. *Collected Works of Ralph Waldo Emerson*, 3:22.

14. Alexis de Tocqueville, *Democracy in America*, ed. and abridged by Richard D. Heffner (New York: Mentor–New American Library, 1956), p. 163.

15. Orestes Augustus Brownson, *New Views of Christianity, Society, and the Church*, in *Transcendentalists*, p. 122; originally published as a booklet in 1836.

16. I have gotten this idea of a public space of consciousness created by media from Philip Fisher, "Appearing and Disappearing in Public: Social Space in Late-Nineteenth-Century Literature and Culture," in *Reconstructing American Literary History*, ed. Sacvan Bercovitch (Cambridge: Harvard University Press, 1986), pp. 155–88. While Fisher discusses the creation of a national space between the Civil War and World War I, I have found enough basis in my research to describe similar spaces of public consciousness in New York and Boston in the 1840s and 1850s. See, for instance, Gay Wilson Allen on New York journalism in the 1840s in *The Solitary Singer: A Critical Biography of Walt Whitman* (Chicago: University of Chicago Press, 1985), pp. 41–55. For Boston, consider the dimensions of the "miracles" controversy indicated by Perry Miller's huge selection of commentary in *Transcendentalists*, pp. 157–240. Fisher returns to this subject in "Democratic Social Space: Whitman, Melville, and the Promise of American Transparency," in *The New American Studies: Essays from ''Representations''*, ed. Philip Fisher (Berkeley: University of California Press, 1991), pp. 70–111.

17. Lovejoy, *Great Chain of Being*, pp. 308–10.

18. Thomas McFarland, *Romanticism and the Forms of Ruin: Wordsworth, Coleridge, and Modalities of Fragmentation* (Princeton: Princeton University Press, 1981), p. 7.

19. See Ann Douglas, *The Feminization of American Culture* (New York: Knopf, 1977), pp. 332–45; Anne C. Rose, *Transcendentalism as a Social Movement, 1830–1850* (New Haven: Yale University Press, 1981), pp. 229–33; Nathan O. Hatch, *The Democratization of American Christianity* (New Haven: Yale University Press, 1989), pp. 5, 7–8.

20. Ralph Waldo Emerson, *The Journals and Miscellaneous Notebooks of Ralph Waldo Emerson*, ed. William H. Gilman et al. (Cambridge: Belknap–Harvard, 1960–82), 5:337.

21. Fredric Jameson, *Marxism and Form: Twentieth-Century Dialectical Theories of Literature* (Princeton: Princeton University Press, 1971), pp. 4–5, 6–10.

22. I am thinking of two works: Michael Paul Rogin's *Subversive Genealogy: The Politics and Art of Herman Melville* (New York: Knopf, 1983); and Jonathan Arac's essay, "The Politics of *The Scarlet Letter*," in *Ideology and Classic American Literature*, ed. Sacvan Bercovitch and Myra Jehlen (Cambridge: Cambridge University Press, 1986), pp. 247–66.

23. Michael Davitt Bell in *The Development of American Romance* has called attention to the kinds of internal representation—spiritual and psychological mi-

mesis—practiced by Poe, Hawthorne, and Melville in the "self-conscious, experimental romance" each fashioned. Bell believes that "spiritual mimesis" growing out of interest in the expression of psychological states was the kind of "deviant" representation that drew them. Alienated emotionally or socially so that they were predisposed to a "sacrifice of relation" to social reality, these "romancers" experimented self-consciously with a form of romance that explored the effect of dissociating romantic ideas in aesthetics, epistemology, and metaphysics. See *The Development of American Romance: The Sacrifice of Relation* (Chicago: University of Chicago Press, 1980), pp. 33–39, 142, 148–49, 154–55. Working through the prism of genre, Bell, it seems to me, puts literary history on the bare bones of Charles Feidelson's epistemological dramas of "subject" and "object." See Charles Feidelson, Jr., *Symbolism and American Literature* (Chicago: University of Chicago Press, 1953). From Feidelson's seminal work, I want to go in a different direction.

24. Herman Melville, *Mardi: and A Voyage Thither*, ed. Harrison Hayford, Hershel Parker, and G. Thomas Tanselle (Evanston: Northwestern–Newberry Edition, 1970), p. 557.

25. Walt Whitman, "As I Ebb'd with the Ocean of Life," in *Leaves of Grass: Comprehensive Reader's Edition*, ed. Harold W. Blodgett and Sculley Bradley (New York: New York University Press, 1965), p. 256, ll. 61–62.

26. Paul Ricoeur, "Metaphor and the Central Problem of Hermeneutics," in *Hermeneutics and the Human Sciences: Essays on Language, Action and Interpretation*, ed. and trans. John B. Thompson (Cambridge: Cambridge University Press, 1981), p. 178.

27. Myra Jehlen, "Introduction: Beyond Transcendence," in *Ideology and Classical American Literature*, pp. 10, 13.

28. Daniel T. O'Hara, *Lionel Trilling: The Work of Liberation* (Madison: University of Wisconsin Press, 1988), pp. 8, 18, 27. O'Hara presents Trilling as a model of critical magnanimity toward texts and opponents.

29. I am thinking here, for example, of Donald Pease's chapter on *Moby-Dick* in *Visionary Compacts: American Renaissance Writings in Cultural Contexts* (Madison: University of Wisconsin Press, 1987), and Jonathan Arac's essay, "F. O. Matthiessen: Authorizing an American Renaissance," in *The American Renaissance Reconsidered: Selected Papers from the English Institute*, ed. Walter Benn Michaels and Donald E. Pease (Baltimore: Johns Hopkins University Press, 1985), pp. 113–56. Bizarre indeed is their scapegoating of Matthiessen, as if in overtly dramatizing their "anxiety of influence" they were revealing some profound truth about the critical struggle to reach one's own ideas. In Pease's chapter on *Moby-Dick*, if we subtract his contesting with Matthiessen, his own ideas on Melville's novel would fill no more than two pages. As for the linking of historical and literary motives without providing textual evidence, I am thinking of Arac's essay on Hawthorne in *Ideology and Classic American Literature*, pp. 247–66.

30. Here, for example, taken from the Sunday paper the week I write this paragraph, is a typical comment of a novelist: "I really am quite a political person outside my work. I'm a member of the National Organization for Women, and I'm much more of a feminist than my three daughters are. But in my work I try to forget about the urgency of politics and write about men and women." See

interview with Anne Bernays by Sarah Ferrell, "There's No Escaping Harvard," *New York Times Book Review, New York Times*, July 23, 1989, p. 25, cols. 1–3.

31. Jameson, *Marxism and Form*, p. 8; italics mine.

32. Two essays that seem to be zeroing in on the same critique can be found in *The New Historicism*, ed. H. Aram Veeser (New York and London: Routledge, 1989). See Frank Lentricchia's "Foucault's Legacy: A New Historicism?" especially p. 241; and Stanley Fish's "Commentary: The Young and the Restless," especially pp. 311–14.

A critique from within culture may not be as highly determined as some suppose. For the prison-house notion of language or culture overlooks the fact that many linguistic signs and cultural attitudes signify open rather than fixed states of being. Coming into being in culture or coming into being in a text is not an imprisoning process, although it may be a considerably determined one. Indeed, even if in the final analysis our sense of spontaneous discovery and enlargement in reading works of literature is an illusion of discovery and is really analogous to a computer responding to a program, it is nevertheless an illusion created by the coming into consciousness of a new sense of self and world. And that this is not pure being entering us from outside culture, but being predetermined by attitudes, values, and a sign system within culture, may not be as important as the qualitative experience itself, in which we feel a pleasurable influx of being. Again I would say that the practice of a critique from outside culture, in order to avoid a deterministic and conservative poetics and politics within culture, is a sterile illusion not worth pursuing.

33. Donald E. Pease, *Visionary Compacts* pp. 40–45.

34. Ibid., pp. 108–31.

35. James Madison, Federalist 51, *The Federalist Papers*, intro. Willmoore Kendall and George W. Carey (New Rochelle, N.Y.: Arlington House, 1966), p. 324. On this point, see also Sacvan Bercovitch, *The American Jeremiad* (Madison: University of Wisconsin Press, 1978), pp. 138–41.

36. Jehlen, "Introduction," p. 4.

37. *Brother Jonathan* 4 (1843): 469. Quoted in Edward K. Spann, *The New Metropolis: New York City, 1840–1857* (New York: Columbia University Press, 1981), pp. 43–44.

38. Fitz-Hugh Ludlow, "The American Metropolis," *Atlantic Monthly* 15 (1865): 87. Quoted in Spann, *New Metropolis*, p. 424.

Chapter 2   Fragmentation in American Social and Intellectual Life

1. Ira Rosenwaike, *Population History of New York City* (Syracuse: Syracuse University Press, 1972), pp. 36, 42.

2. Ibid., p. 42.

3. Ibid.

4. Edward K. Spann, *The New Metropolis: New York City, 1840–1857* (New York: Columbia University Press, 1981), p. 431.

5. Ibid., p. 105.

6. Douglas T. Miller, *Jacksonian Aristocracy: Class and Democracy in New York 1830–1860* (New York: Oxford University Press, 1967), p. 161.

7. Spann, *New Metropolis*, p. 426.

8. For an excellent essay on Foster's life, historical context, and literary influences, see Stuart M. Blumin, "Introduction," in *New York by Gas-Light and Other Urban Sketches*, ed. and with intro. by Stuart M. Blumin (Berkeley: University of California Press, 1990), pp. 1–61.

9. George G. Foster, *New York in Slices: By an Experienced Carver Being the Original Slices Published in the* New York Tribune (New York: William H. Graham, 1849), pp. 66–67.

10. Ibid., pp. 40–41.

11. Herman Melville, *Moby-Dick; or, The Whale*, ed. Harrison Hayford, Hershel Parker, and G. Thomas Tanselle (Evanston: Northwestern–Newberry Edition, 1988), ch. 72, p. 319.

12. Foster, *New York in Slices*, p. 56; italics mine.

13. In Jonathan Arac's discussion of the manner in which the city "overlays" Conrad's treatment of the sea, he remarks in passing that *"Moby-Dick . . .* began from Ishmael's urban discontents" and *"Pierre,* culminated in an infernal New York City." Arac's overall view, derived from Walter Benjamin, corresponds to my own intuition about Melville's and Whitman's treatment of the sea. Arac believes that "the historical experience that imprinted the urban crowd on all modern sensibilities" has done so "at least since the French Revolution." See Jonathan Arac, *Critical Genealogies: Historical Situations for Postmodern Literary Studies* (New York: Columbia University Press, 1987), pp. 177–89, especially pp. 183, 188–89 for above quotations.

14. Beginning on July 12, 1856, Whitman published a series of articles entitled "New York Dissected." The fourth article of the group, published on August 9 and titled "Broadway," describes the procession of different groups of people that pass down Broadway in a twenty-four-hour period, as though a camera were focused on the avenue and then the film shown in an accelerated fashion. The detailed variety Whitman indicates within each classified group, as well its emphasis on scale and vitality, typifies this style as urban diversitarian journalism. See *New York Dissected: A Sheaf of Recently Discovered Newspaper Articles by the Author of "Leaves of Grass,"* intro. and notes by Emory Holloway and Ralph Adimari (New York: Rufus Rockwell Wilson, 1936), pp. 119–24. See also the introduction, "Life Begins at Thirty-five," pp. 1–14. For a list of other journalism by Whitman on Broadway, see p. 222, n. 11.

15. See Carolyn L. Karcher, *Shadow over the Promised Land: Slavery, Race, and Violence in Melville's America* (Baton Rouge: Louisiana State University Press, 1980); Michael Paul Rogin, *Subversive Genealogy: The Politics and Art of Herman Melville* (New York: Knopf, 1983), pp. 102–51; Eric J. Sundquist, "Slavery, Revolution, and the American Renaissance," in *American Renaissance Reconsidered: Selected Papers from the English Institute*, ed. Walter Benn Michaels and Donald E.

Pease (Baltimore: Johns Hopkins University Press, 1985), pp. 1–33; Jonathan Arac, "The Politics of *The Scarlet Letter*," in *Ideology and Classic American Literature*, ed. Sacvan Bercovitch and Myra Jehlen (Cambridge: Cambridge University Press, 1986), pp. 247–66; Herbert J. Levine, "Union and Disunion in 'Song of Myself,' " *American Literature* 59 (1987): 570–89.

16. Foster, *New York in Slices*, p. 3.

17. Ibid., p. 7.

18. Joel Ross, *What I Saw in New York* (Auburn, N.Y., 1851), p. 179. Quoted in Spann, *New Metropolis*, p. 3.

19. Francis Trollope, *Domestic Manners of the Americans*, ed. Donald Smalley (New York: Knopf, 1949), p. 337; Charles Dickens, *American Notes and Pictures from Italy* (London: Oxford University Press, 1957), pp. 80–81.

20. *American Whig Review* 6 (1847): 240. Quoted in Spann, *New Metropolis*, p. 95.

21. Spann, *New Metropolis*, pp. 95–96.

22. *Evening Post*, July 17, 1852. Quoted in Spann, *New Metropolis*, p. 302.

23. Stephan Thernstrom, *Poverty and Progress: Social Mobility in a Nineteenth-Century City* (Cambridge: Harvard University Press, 1964), p. 33.

24. Ibid., pp. 15–16.

25. Phillip R. Yannella, "Socio-Economic Disarray and Literary Response: Concord and *Walden*," *Mosaic* 14 (1981): 1–24.

26. Spann, *New Metropolis*, p. 315.

27. Ibid., pp. 261–62.

28. See Foster, *New York in Slices*, p. 44; and David S. Reynolds, *Beneath the American Renaissance: The Subversive Imagination in the Age of Emerson and Melville* (New York: Knopf, 1988), pp. 463–66, 510.

29. See Sean Wilentz, *Chants Democratic: New York City & the Rise of the American Working Class, 1788–1850* (New York: Oxford University Press, 1984), pp. 255–65. For Wilentz on the "B'hoys," see pp. 300–301. For a picture of working-class women in Bowery life, see Christine Stansell, *City of Women: Sex and Class in New York, 1789–1860* (New York: Knopf, 1986), pp. 89–101.

30. Spann, *New Metropolis*, pp. 18–19.

31. Ibid., p. 158.

32. See Miller, *Jacksonian Aristocracy*, pp. 59–60.

33. Spann, *New Metropolis*, p. 148; see also Miller, *Jacksonian Aristocracy*, pp. 135–36.

34. Ibid., pp. 92–93.

35. Wilentz, *Chants Democratic*, pp. 323–24.

36. Spann, *New Metropolis*, pp. 365–66. A full-length scholarly study on Wood has recently been published: Jerome E. Mushkat, *Fernando Wood: A Political Biography* (Kent, Ohio: Kent State University Press, 1990). Spann is excellent as well; see *New Metropolis*, pp. 358–400.

37. See Charles Grandison Finney, *Memoirs of Rev. Charles G. Finney Written by Himself* (New York: A. S. Barnes, 1876), pp. 275–77, 280–83; *Lectures on Revival Religion*, ed. and with intro. by William G. McLoughlin (Cambridge: Belknap–Harvard, 1960). See also Carroll Smith-Rosenberg, *Religion and the Rise of the*

American City: The New York City Mission Movement, 1812–1870 (Ithaca: Cornell University Press, 1971), pp. 60–69, 86–92.

38. In discussing the religious context, it is necessary to go back to the beginning of the nineteenth century as a starting point for the Second Great Awakening.

39. Nathan O. Hatch, *The Democratization of American Christianity* (New Haven: Yale University Press, 1989), p. 9.

40. Sydney E. Ahlstrom, *A Religious History of the American People* (New Haven: Yale University Press, 1972), p. 361.

41. Hatch, *Democratization*, p. 15.

42. Charles Roy Keller, *The Second Great Awakening in Connecticut* (1942; rpt. n.p.: Archon, 1968), p. 37.

43. See "A Short History of the Life of Barton W. Stone Written by Himself," in *Voices from Cane Ridge*, ed. Rhodes Thompson, facsimile ed. (St. Louis: Bethany, 1954), pp. 69–72. Quoted in Ahlstrom, *Religious History*, pp. 434–35.

44. Peter Cartwright, *Autobiography of Peter Cartwright*, intro. by Charles L. Wallis (New York: Abingdon, 1956), p. 34.

45. Ibid.

46. Ahlstrom, *Religious History*, pp. 436–37.

47. Edwin Scott Gaustad, *Historical Atlas of Religion in America* (New York: Harper and Row, 1962), pp. 56–57.

48. Ahlstrom, *Religious History*, p. 381.

49. William Ellery Channing, *The Collected Poems of William Ellery Channing The Younger, 1817–1901*, ed. Walter Harding (Gainesville, Fla.: Scholars' Facsimiles & Reprints, 1967), p. 242. The poet is the namesake and nephew of the Boston Unitarian divine.

50. Philip Schaff, *The Principles of Protestantism*, Lancaster Series on the Mercerburg Theology, ed. Bard Thompson and George H. Bricker (Philadelphia and Boston: United Church Press, 1964), 1:140–41.

51. Ibid., p. 149.

52. The Second Great Awakening did have some vitalizing effects on traditional New England churches. Between 1830 and 1850, for example, Congregational and Episcopalian church membership roughly doubled and Presbyterian membership tripled. If we look exclusively at Presbyterian numbers there were roughly 13,500 members in 1800, 72,000 in 1820, and 500,000 in 1850 (Gaustad, *Historical Atlas*, pp. 87–92). The Congregational Church, whose strength was in New England, grew from about 100,000 in 1800, to 125,000 in 1830, to 240,000 in 1850 (ibid., p. 62). Nevertheless, there were already by 1830 approximately 300,000 Baptists and 511,000 Methodists (ibid., p. 67); and by 1850 there were 800,000 Baptists and 1.25 million Methodists. In terms of number of churches, the Seventh U.S. Census reveals that while there were 1,706 Congregational churches, 1,459 Episcopal churches, and 4,824 Presbyterian churches, there were 9,375 Baptist churches and 13,280 Methodist churches (ibid., p. 168).

53. Ibid., p. 89.

54. Ahlstrom, *Religious History*, pp. 456–58.

55. George M. Marsden, *The Evangelical Mind and the New School Presbyterian Experience: A Case Study of Thought and Theology in Nineteenth-Century America* (New Haven: Yale University Press, 1970), pp. 11, 117–20; Gaustad, *Historical Atlas*, p. 88.

56. Jerry Wayne Brown, *The Rise of Biblical Criticism in America, 1800–1870* (Middletown, Conn.: Wesleyan, 1969), p. 61.

57. Ibid., p. 65.

58. Ibid., p. 71.

59. Ahlstrom, *Religious History*, pp. 396–97.

60. For a selection of writings on the controversy about biblical miracles that raged from 1836 to 1841, see *The Transcendentalists: An Anthology*, ed. Perry Miller (Cambridge: Harvard University Press, 1950), pp. 157–246.

61. Connecticut did not abolish establishment until 1818 and Massachusetts until 1833.

62. Ann Douglas, *The Feminization of American Culture* (New York: Knopf, 1977), pp. 17–43; see especially pp. 41–42.

63. See Winthrup S. Hudson, *Religion in America* (New York: Charles Scribner's Sons, 1965), pp. 141–44.

64. When disestablishment came to Connecticut in 1818, Beecher felt, only briefly, he had come upon his darkest day: "For several days I suffered what no tongue can tell *for the best thing that ever happened to the State of Connecticut*. It cut the churches loose from dependence on state support. It threw them wholly on their own resources and on God.

They say ministers have lost their influence; the fact is, they have gained. By the voluntary efforts, societies, missions, and revivals, they exert a deeper influence than ever they could by queues, and shoe-buckles, and cocked hats, and gold-headed canes" (*The Autobiography of Lyman Beecher*, ed. Barbara M. Cross [Cambridge: Belknap–Harvard, 1961], 1:252–53).

65. Alexis de Tocqueville, *Democracy in America*, ed. and abridged by Richard D. Heffner (New York: Mentor–New American Library, 1956), p. 163; see also Whitney R. Cross, *The Burned-Over District: The Social and Intellectual History of Enthusiastic Religion in Western New York, 1800–1850* (Ithaca: Cornell University Press, 1950), pp. 81–82.

66. *From Boundlessness to Consolidation: The Transformation of American Culture 1848–1860* (Ann Arbor: William L. Clements Library, 1969), p. 6.

67. William Ellery Channing, "The Present Age," in *The Works of William Ellery Channing* (Boston: American Unitarian Association, 1903), 6:150–54.

68. Ahlstrom, *Religious History*, pp. 479–80. See also Ruth Alden Doan, *The Miller Heresy, Millennialism, and American Culture* (Philadelphia: Temple University Press, 1987).

69. Fawn M. Brodie, *No Man Knows My History: The Life of Joseph Smith, The Mormon Prophet*, 2d rev. ed. (New York: Knopf, 1971), p. 39.

70. Cross, *Burned-Over District*, pp. 33–36.

71. Ahlstrom, *Religious History*, pp. 491–500.

72. Ralph Waldo Emerson, "The Chardon Street Convention," in *The Com-*

plete Works of Ralph Waldo Emerson (Boston: Riverside–Houghton Mifflin, 1904), 10:374–75. Publicized widely, the subject of the first meeting was the Sabbath; meetings in the next two years were held to discuss the Church, the Ministry, and the Bible. See p. 584 for a note on the fourth convention meeting on issues pertaining to the miracles controversy. This report first appeared in "Chardon Street and the Bible," *The Dial* 3 (July 1842): 100–103.

73. *The Boston Evening Transcript,* November 18, 1840.

74. Cross, *Burned-Over District,* p. 41.

75. See ibid., pp. 93–100.

76. Ibid., pp. 104–9.

77. See Barbara Welter, "Defenders of the Faith: Women Novelists of Religious Controversy in the Nineteenth Century," in *Dimity Convictions: The American Woman in the Nineteenth Century* (Athens: Ohio University Press, 1976), pp. 103–29.

78. Cross, *Burned-Over District,* p. 37.

79. Douglas, *Feminization,* pp. 332–39; see also p. 94.

80. Ahlstrom, *Religious History,* pp. 548–49.

81. Lucy Smith, *Biographical Sketches of Joseph Smith the Prophet and His Progenitors for Many Generations* (Liverpool: n. pub., 1853), p. 37. Quoted in Brodie, *No Man Knows,* pp. 4–5.

82. Quoted in ibid., p. 26.

83. Ibid., pp. 12–14.

84. Joseph Smith and Heman C. Smith, *History of the Church of Jesus Christ of Latter Day Saints* (Lamoni, Iowa: n.pub., 1897–1908), pp. 5–7. Quoted in Brodie, *No Man Knows,* p. 22.

85. Mary Kupiec Cayton, *Emerson's Emergence: Self and Society in the Transformation of New England, 1800–1845* (Chapel Hill: University of North Carolina Press, 1989), pp. 83–111, especially pp. 108–11.

86. *The Journals and Miscellaneous Notebooks of Ralph Waldo Emerson,* ed. William Gilman et al. (Cambridge: Belknap–Harvard, 1960–82); entries are from 8:8, 86; 6:6.

87. Walt Whitman, *Walt Whitman, Prose Works 1892,* ed. Floyd Stovall (New York: New York University Press, 1963–64), 2:473.

88. George B. Hutchinson, *The Ecstatic Whitman: Literary Shamanism & the Crisis of the Union* (Columbus: Ohio State University Press, 1986), p. 24. For Hutchinson's attempt to link the socioeconomic disarray of Whitman's times with not only the revival movements, but with Whitman's own spiritual solution, see pp. 16–25 *et passim.*

89. For a representative statement about religion, see preface, 1872, to "As a Strong Bird on Pinions Free": "The time has certainly come to begin to discharge the idea of religion, in the United States, from mere ecclesiasticism, and from Sundays and churches and church-going, and assign it to that general position, chiefest, most indispensable, most exhilarating, to which the others are to be adjusted, inside of all human character, and education, and affairs. The people, especially the young men and women of America, must begin to learn that Religion, (like poetry,) is something far, far different from what they supposed. It is,

indeed, too important to the power and perpetuity of the New World to be consign'd any longer to the churches, old or new, Catholic or Protestant." See *Walt Whitman, Prose Works 1892*, 2:462–63.

90. James E. Cabot, *A Memoir of Ralph Waldo Emerson* (Boston: Houghton Mifflin, 1887), 1:244–45.

91. Peter Carafiol, *Transcendent Reason: James Marsh and the Forms of Romantic Thought* (Tallahassee: Florida State University Press–University Presses of Florida, 1982), pp. 13–14.

92. Daniel Walker Howe, *The Unitarian Conscience: Harvard Moral Philosophy, 1805–1861* (Cambridge: Harvard University Press, 1970), p. 31.

93. Herbert Hovenkamp, *Science and Religion in America, 1800–1860* (Philadelphia: University of Pennsylvania Press, 1978), p. 23.

94. Ibid., p. 27.

95. Alexander Kern, "The Rise of Transcendentalism, 1815–1860," in *Transitions in American Literary History*, ed. Harry Hayden Clark (New York: Octagon, 1967), pp. 274–75.

96. Charles Feidelson, Jr., *Symbolism and American Literature* (Chicago: University of Chicago Press, 1953), pp. 77–118.

97. Sherman Paul, *Emerson's Angle of Vision: Man and Nature in American Experience* (Cambridge: Harvard University Press, 1952), pp. 32–33.

98. Ralph Waldo Emerson, *Nature*, in *The Collected Works of Ralph Waldo Emerson*, ed. Robert E. Spiller and Alfred R. Ferguson (Cambridge: Belknap–Harvard, 1971), 1:17.

99. Margaret Fuller, "Selections from her *Memoirs*," in *Transcendentalists*, p. 337.

100. John Sullivan Dwight, "Music," in *Transcendentalists*, p. 412. See pp. 410–11 on Dwight's role as an enthusiast, critic, and theoretician of music in Transcendentalist culture.

101. See Lawrence Buell, *Literary Transcendentalism: Style and Vision in the American Renaissance* (Ithaca: Cornell University Press, 1973), p. 269; also p. 270.

102. Emerson, *Nature*, p. 10.

103. Ibid., p. 18.

104. Melville, *Moby-Dick; or, The Whale*, ch. 41, p. 184.

105. Quoted in M. H. Abrams, *The Mirror and the Lamp: Romantic Theory and the Critical Tradition* (London: Oxford University Press, 1953), p. 211.

106. See Robert Langbaum, "Freud and Sociobiology: Reflections on the Nature of Genius," in *The Word from Below: Essays on Modern Literature and Culture* (Madison: University of Wisconsin Press, 1987), p. 8; Abrams, *Mirror and the Lamp*, p. 222.

107. Jeffrey Steele, *The Representation of the Self in the American Renaissance* (Chapel Hill: University of North Carolina Press, 1987), p. 39.

108. Ibid., p. 14. Emerson's view of the unconscious, Steele argues, "is collective, not personal" (p. 17). Unlike Freud, but "like Jung, Emerson nourishes the vision of divinity buried in the heart of the psyche. He engages in psychological mythmaking, founded upon the development of depth psychology as a substi-

tute religion" (pp. 17–18). "Responding in similar ways to their respective senses of cultural crises, of decaying religious sensibility, both Emerson and Jung develop psychologies aimed at restoring faith. The goal of each is to inspire, to transform his audience by moving them from complacency to crisis and finally to a new awareness of individual spiritual potential" (p. 16). Especially in his claim that each work of Emerson's "defines a renewed being predicated upon the recovery and expression of divine powers found within the self" (p. 12), Steele's chapter is quite interesting—my only misgiving being that he seems to limit divinity to the psyche and forget about "spirit" circulating throughout nature as well.

109. Hovenkamp, *Science and Religion*, pp. 46–48.

110. John C. Burnham, "The Fragmenting of the Soul: Intellectual Prerequisites for Ideas of Dissociation in the United States," in *Paths into American Culture: Psychology, Medicine, and Morals* (Philadelphia: Temple University Press, 1988), p. 12.

111. Ibid., pp. 16–17, 22.

112. Alfred Lord Tennyson, "In Memoriam," in *Poems of Tennyson* (Boston: Houghton Mifflin–Riverside, 1958), Stanzas 120 and 118.

113. Charles Darwin, *The Descent of Man*, in *Darwin*, 2d ed., ed. Philip Appleman (New York: Norton, 1970), p. 208.

114. Beyond Freud, Darwin's influence led in the twentieth century to sociobiology, the systematic study of biology as a basis of social behavior. See Robert Langbaum's "Freud and Sociobiology," in *Word from Below*, pp. 3–19. Langbaum says: "Jung suggests that the sexual theory derived from some peculiar emotional need of Freud's. . . . For Freud the sexual theory was a guarantee that the 'unconscious' would not turn into another word for soul, that it would not be divorced from body. . . . The Jungian system did in fact turn the unconscious into soul. . . . Freud was reaffirming a monism that is scientific, romantic and to some extent Jewish and anti-ascetic . . . a monism that makes Freud, with his new way of connecting body to mind through the unconscious, the link between the romanticism and Darwinian biology that precede him and the sociobiology that follows him" (p. 19). More recently yet, it has led to comparative studies in genetics that have demonstrated a surprisingly high degree of commonality in the genetic codes between man and higher vertebrates, especially mammals, with the degree of similarity rising to over 99 percent in comparison of the genetic code of humans with our closest relative, the chimpanzee.

115. Langbaum, in another essay in *Word from Below*, shares my view. Defending the "romantic self" against deconstructionist attacks, he claims that "the romantic self remains valid because it came into being as a reaction against attacks on the self almost as devastating as today's attacks, and thus contains a protection against such attacks." He then goes on to assert that "twentieth-century writers . . . have made the romantic self more ruggedly substantial by working into it ideas of unconsciousness and primitive instincts derived from Darwin and Freud" ("Can We Still Talk about the Romantic Self?" p. 31).

116. Melville, *Moby-Dick; or, The Whale*, ch. 132, p. 542.

117. Leon Chai, *The Romantic Foundations of the American Renaissance* (Ithaca: Cornell University Press, 1987), p. 62.

118. Burnham, "Fragmenting of the Soul," pp. 14–15.

119. His interest in evolution is confined to the parallel unity of material and spiritual worlds revealed by scientific "classification." Emerson says in *Nature*, for example: "I cannot greatly honor minuteness in details, so long as there is no hint to explain the relation between things and thoughts; no ray upon the *metaphysics* of conchology, of botany, of the arts, to show the relation of the forms of flowers, shells, animals, architecture, to the mind, and build science upon ideas. In a cabinet of natural history, we become sensible of a certain occult recognition and sympathy in regard to the most unwieldly and eccentric forms of beasts, fish, and insects" (p. 40).

Chapter 3 Shooting the Gulf: Emerson's Sense of Experience

1. See Gary L. Collison, "Theodore Parker," in *The Transcendentalists: A Review of Research and Criticism*, ed. Joel Myerson (New York: MLA, 1984), pp. 228–30.

2. *The Collected Works of Ralph Waldo Emerson*, ed. Alfred R. Ferguson et al. (Cambridge: Belknap–Harvard, 1971–), p. 38; hereafter cited as *CW* with volume and page numbers. Other abbreviated references, cited by volume and page numbers, are as follows: *JMN*—*The Journals and Miscellaneous Notebooks of Ralph Waldo Emerson*, ed. William H. Gilman et al. (Cambridge: Belknap–Harvard, 1960–82); *W*—*The Complete Works of Ralph Waldo Emerson*, Centenary Ed., ed. Edward Waldo Emerson (Boston: Houghton Mifflin–Riverside, 1903–4); *EL*—*The Early Lectures of Ralph Waldo Emerson*, ed. Stephen E. Whicher, Robert E. Spiller, and Wallace E. Williams (Cambridge: Harvard University Press, 1959–71); *L*—*The Letters of Ralph Waldo Emerson*, ed. Ralph L. Rusk (New York: Columbia University Press, 1939).

3. See Robert Milder, "Emerson's Two Conversions," *ESQ* 33 (1st Quarter, 1987): 20–25.

4. Emerson's father died when he was eight; his aunt Mary Moody Emerson was the strongest model in his early life. His memory of his father, according to a letter to his brother, was fairly dim. See *L*, 4:178–79.

5. Gay Wilson Allen, *Waldo Emerson: A Biography* (New York: Viking, 1981), p. 147.

6. Milder, "Emerson's Two Conversions," pp. 20, 25–28.

7. Milder sees this as a continuing line of reformation begun by Jonathan Edwards in which not only intellect but "holy affections" were instrumental in finding grace; ibid., p. 26. See also Leon Chai, *The Romantic Foundations of the American Renaissance* (Ithaca: Cornell University Press, 1987), p. 65.

8. See ibid., pp. 280, 287.

9. See Arthur M. Schlesinger, Jr., *Orestes A. Brownson: A Pilgrim's Progress* (Boston: Little, Brown, 1939).

10. David Robinson, "Emerson's Natural Theology and the Paris Naturalists: Toward a Theory of Animated Nature," in *Critical Essays on Ralph Waldo Emerson*, ed. Robert E. Burkholder and Joel Myerson (Boston: G. K. Hall, 1983), pp. 501–2; see also p. 507.

11. Ibid., p. 507.

12. Ibid., pp. 510–11.

13. See Chai on romantic science, *Romantic Foundations*, pp. 140–55.

14. David Hume, *The Treatise of Human Nature*, in *Hume Selections*, ed. Charles W. Hendel, Jr. (New York: Charles Scribner's Sons, 1927), p. 85; Book 4, Section 5, "Personal Identity." On Emerson's ambivalent attitude toward Hume after his senior paper at Harvard, see Alexander Kern, "The Rise of Transcendentalism, 1815–1860," in *Transitions in American Literary History*, ed. Harry Hayden Clark (New York: Octagon, 1967), pp. 265–66. See also B. L. Packer, *Emerson's Fall: A New Interpretation of the Major Essays* (New York: Continuum, 1982), pp. 156–63.

15. John Michael, *Emerson and Skepticism: The Cipher of the World* (Baltimore: Johns Hopkins University Press, 1988), p. 44; see pp. 33–68, especially pp. 39–45.

16. Charles Lowell Young, *Emerson's Montaigne* (New York: Macmillan, 1941), pp. 18–19.

17. See Packer on the development and implications of the "axis of vision" formula, *Emerson's Fall*, pp. 72–84.

18. The most impressive alternative view is Carolyn Porter's thesis (*Seeing and Being: The Plight of the Participant Observer in Emerson, James, Adams, and Faulkner* [Middletown, Conn.: Wesleyan, 1981], pp. xi–xxii, 3–118, especially pp. xiv–xv, 24–25, 92–93, 106) that the cause of the alienation between the Me and the Not-Me was the emergence of industrial capitalism in New England. Porter attributes fragmentation to the reifying powers of capitalism that have divorced men from the external world and rendered them passive before its power. It is these same reifying powers within Emerson, she argues, that he resists through his idealist notion that man can remake his world. Yet Porter's definition of Emerson's problem subverts his own definition of it. She is unable to muster proof that Emerson attempts to "thwart a reifying process" whose effect he "felt keenly" or that he is trying to "call attention to these social forces" (p. xiv). For Emerson the social fragmentation he describes (particularly in the opening pages of "The American Scholar" address) is a symptom of a spiritual dilemma. Emerson's view of man's disunion is that it derives from a lack of contact with the spirit within and from an overdependence on external dogma and tradition. His diagnosis is intrapsychic and his recommendation is a new self-reliance that has "broken our god of tradition, and ceased from our god of rhetoric" (*CW*, 2:173). Emerson was interested in making "life at the heart" a source for "justly" organizing the fragmentation he saw "at the surface" (*JMN*, 7:6). As his refusal to join Brook Farm exemplifies, he did not believe in the reverse (a reorganization of social and economic forms as a means of reforming the heart). To approach Emerson in terms of economic causation and economic reform is to reverse his premises and impose one's own.

19. See Frederic Ives Carpenter, *Emerson Handbook* (New York: Hendricks House, 1953), pp. 108–203.

20. For instances of Emerson's idealism invading his social thought, see his response to utopian communities (*JMN*, 8:218, 250–51) and to abolitionists (*JMN*, 8:119). For instances of his realism turning inward on his private life, see

his comments on marriage and free love (*JMN*, 8:95) and on his close friends Bronson Alcott (*JMN*, 8:210–15) and Frederic Henry Hedge (*JMN*, 8:31).

21. To some degree, the death of Emerson's five-year-old son in the first weeks of 1842 must have affected the balance of his polar vision; however, the tension between the two forces was, as I have indicated, already well established. One needs to be especially cautious with assertions about the development of Emerson's thought based strictly on his published essays, for the source of these essays is often journal entries from an earlier biographical period. On the other hand, one must also consider why certain ideas have been featured in his essays and others neglected; the preeminence of certain ideas is certainly reason to attribute special significance to them in Emerson's development at the time the essay is published.

22. Packer, *Emerson's Fall*, p. 83.

23. See n. 64 for a discussion of Emerson's idealism.

24. It may diminish the impression that Emerson sometimes violates standards of rational discourse to realize that his professions of belief derive from experience as well as from a priori ideas. If "faith" means trust in something one has no direct knowledge of, then Emerson often uses the word loosely. He often means memory of revelation. (In the opening passage of "The Over-Soul," for example, Emerson's argument makes more sense if we read "faith" as "revelation." See *CW*, 1:213, for another example.) Moreover, it is important to realize that poetical as well as moral revelation was a source of affirmation for Emerson. As F. O. Matthiessen nicely documents in his discussion of the biographical context of Emerson's poem "Days," poetical inspiration characterized Emerson's notion of spiritual fullness and seemingly represented, more than direct revelation of God, the longed-for manna in his life (*American Renaissance* [London: Oxford University Press, 1941], pp. 55–64).

25. Originally published without a title in *The Centenary of the Birth of Ralph Waldo Emerson* (1903); rpt. "Emerson—The Brahmin View," in *Ralph Waldo Emerson: A Profile*, ed. Carl Bode (New York: Hill and Wang, 1968), p. 143.

26. I am essentially quoting Gay Wilson Allen here, who says, "Increasingly, to Emerson, life was consciousness" (*Waldo Emerson*, p. 161). Emerson says: "Life consists in what a man is thinking of all day" (*JMN*, 10:146).

27. Richard Poirier, *The Renewal of Literature: Emersonian Reflections* (New York: Random House, 1987), p. 11; see pp. 11–19.

28. Ibid., p. 50; quote is from *CW*, 1:59.

29. Ibid., p. 49.

30. Ibid., p. 17.

31. Ibid., p. 92. By troping Poirier means the "turning" of words away from predetermined directions and toward the creative detours that enable expression of individual power; see p. 131. He says also: "By the turning, the troping of it, language can be made into a sign not of human subservience but of human power" (p. 132).

32. Ibid., p. 87.

33. Ibid., p. 15. Poirier is drawing these terms from James' *Principles of Psychology*.

34. This is true at least in the first half of his book; in the second half, Poirier seems to concede the necessity of formulated thought and the dialectic between fluidity and form.

35. Stephen E. Whicher, *Freedom and Fate* (Philadelphia: University of Pennsylvania Press, 1953), p. 39. See also Henry F. Pommer, "The Contents and Basis of Emerson's Belief in Compensation," *PMLA* 77 (1962): 248–53.

36. Harry Hayden Clark, "Conservative and Mediatory Emphases in Emerson's Thought," in *Transcendentalism and Its Legacy*, ed. Myron Smith and T. H. Parsons (Ann Arbor: University of Michigan Press, 1966), p. 29.

37. Emerson read Victor Cousin in 1832 with the translation into English of *Introduction to the History of Philosophy* (*JMN*, 3:327). He also read some Cousin in French as early as 1828. He read Coleridge's *The Friend* and *Aids to Reflection* with the publication of the James Marsh edition in 1829. He read Carlyle in the late 1820s in anonymous articles, continued to read him once he knew his name, and then met him in August 1833. For documentation on this reading, see René Wellek, "Emerson and German Philosophy," *New England Quarterly* 16 (1943): 42, n. 5. See also Henry David Gray's description of the significant role of Frederic Henry Hedge in popularizing German philosophy among the Transcendentalists in *Emerson* (New York: Frederick Ungar, 1917), pp. 23–24.

38. Thomas McFarland, *Romanticism and the Forms of Ruin* (Princeton: Princeton University Press, 1981), p. 297.

39. Ibid., p. 302.

40. As Packer has shown, Newton's optics, as described by David Brewster in *A Life*, were also highly influential on Emerson's conception and language in formulating his notion of the "periodicity of vision"; see Packer, *Emerson's Fall*, pp. 72–78.

41. O. W. Firkins, *Ralph Waldo Emerson* (1915; rpt. New York: Russell and Russell, 1965), p. 177.

42. Friedrich Wilhelm Joseph Schelling, *On The World Soul* (1798), in *Sämmtliche Werks* (Stuttgart: J. G. Cotta'scher Verlag, 1856–61), 2:350, 347–48; trans. Alan White, *Schelling* (New Haven: Yale University Press, 1983), pp. 51, 52.

43. Francis Bacon, *The Works of Francis Bacon*, new ed., ed. James Spedding, R. L. Ellis, and D. D. Heath (London: Longmans, 1870), 1:165. Quoted by McFarland in his discussion of polarity, *Romanticism*, p. 339.

44. I want to indicate my debt here to McFarland, whose pages praising Coleridge for his temperate handling of the idea of polarity have enabled me to draw a larger circle around Emerson's thinking on polarity. Readers interested in later criticism of the polar thought of the German romantic philosophers should also see McFarland's discussion of the critique offered by Nietzsche (p. 340).

45. Gray, *Emerson*, p. 27.

46. Stanley Cavell, "Thinking of Emerson," in *The Senses of Walden: An Expanded Edition* (San Francisco: North Point Press, 1981), p. 125.

47. Firkins, *Emerson*, p. 329.

48. Packer, *Emerson's Fall*, pp. 203–5.

49. While he claims in "Montaigne" that "this parallelism of great and little . . . never react on each other, nor discover the smallest tendency to converge"

(*W*, 4:179), "tendency"—that certain slant of light in everyday affairs—does figure importantly in Emerson's argument elsewhere. "Most of life seems to be mere advertisement of faculty," he says in "Experience," suggesting that presence of spirit can be intuited amidst our daily movements; "information is given us not to sell ourselves cheap; that we are very great. *So, in particulars, our greatness is always in a tendency or direction, not in an action*" (*CW*, 3:42; italics mine). Spiritual influence finds its way into mundane affairs sometimes without any significant awareness of its workings: "We do not know today whether we are busy or idle. In times when we thought ourselves indolent, we have afterwards discovered, that much was accomplished, and much was begun in us. All our days are so unprofitable while they pass, that 'tis wonderful where or when we ever got anything of this which we call wisdom, poetry, virtue. We never got it on any dated calendar day" (*CW*, 3:27–28).

50. As I hope this essay demonstrates, Emerson's mind possessed the braided tendencies of the psychological and the philosophical thinker. The psychological side rendered him too tied to experience and too unsystematic to be considered a philosopher, yet the philosophical side rendered him too detached and interested in "higher" truth to be considered a psychologist. This description of Emerson as a psychophilosophical thinker should not be construed as an attack on John Dewey's description of Emerson as a poet-philosopher, in *Characters and Events*, ed. Joseph Ratner (New York: Holt, 1929), 1:69–77. I am offering it simply as another useful formulation from another angle of inquiry into Emerson's mental powers.

51. *Symbolism and American Literature* (Chicago: University of Chicago Press, 1953), p. 128.

52. For use of this provocative journal entry in the resolution of a critical problem in Emerson's thought, see Norman Miller, "Emerson's 'Each and All' Concept: A Reexamination," *New England Quarterly* 41 (1968): 381–92: rpt. in *Critical Essays*, pp. 346–54.

53. Frank Lentricchia, *After the New Criticism* (Chicago: University of Chicago Press, 1980), p. 298.

54. Geoffrey Hartman, preface, in *Deconstruction and Criticism* (New York: Continuum–Seabury, 1979), pp. vii–viii.

55. It is not easy to respond adequately to the authorial depression that the essay's opening section confesses to but does not follow up on. It would require tools of biographical criticism, it seems to me, not only the deconstructive assertion that in literature excesses of meaning rise from the text. For an example of more adequate responses, see Joel Porte, *Representative Man* (New York: Oxford University Press, 1979), pp. 179–86; Sharon Cameron, "Representing Grief: Emerson's 'Experience,'" in *The New American Studies: Essays from "Representations,"* ed. Philip Fisher (Berkeley: University of California Press, 1991), pp. 201–27; and Packer, *Emerson's Fall*, pp. 148–56.

56. Feidelson, *Symbolism*, pp. 146–50. Feidelson describes the theoretical implications of Emerson's poetics in the following manner: "Emerson had a theory of poetry which eliminated the particular poem, since it provided no means of halting the proliferation of metaphor or synecdoche. The poem he described,

constructed wholly on the principles of multiple meaning, was chimerical" (p. 149). See also Packer, *Emerson's Fall*, pp. 190, 193–95.

57. Poirier, *Renewal of Language*, pp. 16–17.

58. Ibid., p. 132.

59. Walter Kaufmann, *Existentialism: From Dostoevsky to Sartre* (New York: Meridian, 1956), p. 12.

60. Harold Fromm, "Emerson and Kierkegaard: The Problem of Historical Christianity," *Massachusetts Review* 9 (1968): 741–52. I have been particularly influenced by the following paragraph in Fromm: "The soul becomes! That is the basis for Emerson's thought, for his dialectic, and for Kierkegaard's hatred of the 'objective.' For, if nothing *is* but all is *becoming*, 'objective' thought tells us about a reality that does not exist. It tells us about a *thought* reality rather than an actual reality, for the thoughts perhaps stay the same, but things never do. So thoughts never refer to real things. For reality is experience, and experience, while it may be symbolized, cannot be communicated. From this springs Kierkegaard's doctrine that truth is subjectivity. And this serves well as a key to Emerson also: the soul *becomes*. Emerson, like Kierkegaard, is a psychological, not a philosophical writer. Both tell us about the mind, not about things (there are no things, only experience), and both use the method of psychological unfolding: the dialectical" (p. 747).

61. See Hermann Hummell, "Emerson and Nietzsche," *New England Quarterly* 19 (1946): 63–84. For a summary of the scholarship on this subject, see Carpenter, *Emerson Handbook*, pp. 246–49.

62. Kaufmann, *Existentialism*, pp. 21–22.

63. Alasdair MacIntyre, "Existentialism," in *Encyclopedia of Philosophy* (New York: Macmillan and Free Press, 1967), 3:147. See also James Collins, *The Existentialists* (Chicago: Regnery, 1952), pp. 1–37; John Wild, *The Challenge of Existentialism* (Bloomington: Indiana University Press, 1955), pp. 25–57.

64. That Emerson was a philosophical idealist "from beginning to end" can be supported within the limited scope of a note by looking briefly at his 1836 *Nature* and at his Harvard lectures of 1870–71, "The Natural History of Intellect," which are drawn from lectures in the 1850s in London and Boston.

I call Emerson a philosophical idealist despite his explanation of the limitations of idealism in Chapter 6 of *Nature* and his statement of a metaphysical view more satisfactory to him in Chapter 7, "Spirit." For a clarifying discussion of this "spiritualist" position, see Merton M. Sealts, Jr., "Mulberry Leaves and Satin: Emerson's Theory of the Creative Process," in *Studies in the American Renaissance, 1985*, ed. Joel Myerson (Charlottesville: University Press of Virginia, 1985), pp. 79–94, especially p. 81. Emerson's characterization of idealism in Chapter 6 does not see matter as composite and limits itself to Berkeleian "immaterialism," the extreme pole of subjective idealism, which holds that only sensations and ideas have immediate reality and that physical things do not exist distinct from the mind. In his chapter on idealism, Emerson omits epistemological gradations that include the object as well as the subject in a description of perception. As I see it, his purpose in this chapter is to suggest the strong tendency of idealism to precipitate "a noble doubt . . . whether nature outwardly exists" (*CW*, 1:29). He is able, thereby, to ascribe to idealism all the dangers of a subjective epistemology—egoism, separation from nature, alienation from God, and spiritual passivity (*CW*, 1:37–39)—and to ascribe positive, dynamic traits to his own position. "Spiritualism," he says, is "progressive," promotes "consanguinity" between man and nature, and finds spirit indwelling in the natural world (*CW*, 1:36–39). Yet the belief expressed in Chapter 7 that "spirit creates; that behind nature, throughout nature, spirit is present, . . . that spirit does not act upon us from without . . . but spiritually, or through ourselves" (*CW*, 1:38) is fully compatible with the philosophy of idealism that is derived from Plato. Like pantheism, "spiritualism" is a subdivision of idealism and falls within the generally accepted definition of idealism as "the view that mind and spiritual values are fundamental in the world as a whole" (H. B. Acton, "Idealism," in *Encyclopedia of Philosophy*, 4:110). Spirit is able to guide man and nature with its own higher direction because it contains "ideas" or another equally creative force derived from God. If it did not possess this higher power, it certainly could not offer man, as Emerson says in *Nature* spirit does, "access to the entire mind of the Creator" or opportunity to be "himself the creator in the finite" (*CW*, 1:38).

In "The Natural History of Intellect," Emerson's key term is not "spirit" but "Intellect," although he means the same thing. He uses "Intellect" there whenever he wants to refer to the common ground of man and nature and to the active agency that presses man and nature toward greater realization and knowledge of their "parallel unity" (*W*, 12:20). "Intellect builds the universe and is the key to all it contains" (*W*, 12:5), Emerson says. Several pages later, he asserts, "We figure to ourselves Intellect as an ethereal sea . . . carrying its whole virtue into every creek and inlet which it bathes. To this sea every human house has a water front" (*W*, 12:15). And as in his 1836 book, again we see that Emerson's characterization of this force includes the fact that divine "ideas" or "forms"—the heart of idealism—are contained in Intellect. "Who are we, and what is Nature," Emerson says, "have one answer in life that rushes into us" (*W*, 12:16). Emerson's goal is not achieved in "The History of Natural Intellect" of describing the "laws of the world" common to mind and nature (*W*, 12:3–4). Yet the philosophical idealism at the heart of his viewpoint is clear: man is part of natural history and his mind is an especially central part of it, because mind enables man to see "the laws and powers of Intellect" (*W*, 12:10) that form the world.

65. Fromm appears to agree: "What Kierkegaard and Emerson are doing is to make the mind the focus of reality. Despite Kierkegaard's rebellion against Hegel, his existentialism is as 'ideal' as Hegel's Logic. But what he has done is to deal with reality from the point of view of the mind rather than objectified categories of thought. As Kierkegaard read him, Hegel appeared to view reality as the mind made objective and manifesting itself as history and the history of thought. Kierkegaard has merely brought us back from the world to the whole psyche and told us that *no symbols, no categories* are adequate representations of the mind and that we must forget about embodiments altogether. Emerson has gone almost as far, but, being more of the German Idealist, he allows the embodiments more weight, while warning us to speed along to *new* embodiments" (pp. 750–51).

66. Aron Gurwitsch, "Husserl's Theory of the Intentionality of Conscious-

ness," in *Husserl: Intentionality and Cognitive Science*, ed. Hubert L. Dreyfus (Cambridge: MIT, 1982), pp. 59–72. If it were not for Emerson's need to include a spiritual and creative force in the cosmos, it would be valid to claim that Emerson would have discovered a more precise resolution of the status of objective reality in Husserl's theory of intentionality than he was able to specify in his own subjective idealism. Emerson's irresolution can be seen by contrasting the passage "Perhaps these subject-lenses have a creative power" (*CW*, 3:43–44) with the journal entry that begins "It is a small & mean thing to attempt too hardly to disprove the being of Matter" (*JMN*, 5:146).

Chapter 4 Multiplicity and Uncertainty in Melville's *Moby-Dick*

1. Herman Melville, *Moby-Dick; or, The Whale*, ed. Harrison Hayford, Hershel Parker, and G. Thomas Tanselle (Evanston: Northwestern–Newberry Edition, 1988), ch. 1, p. 7; henceforth references to *Moby-Dick* will appear in parentheses in the text.

2. Robert L. Caserio, *Plot, Story and the Novel: From Dickins and Poe to the Modern Period* (Princeton: Princeton University Press, 1979), p. 134. See ch. 5, "The Divine Inert: Melville." Caserio avoids describing Ishmael's sensibility and vision in terms of Romanticism, favoring, instead, an original terminology that enables him to link Melville's premodern qualities with later writers (see p. 166). I do not see, however, that his description is at odds with the romantic terminology I prefer to use.

3. My view of Ishmael as possessing a sensibility that is free yet content in passivity would seem to link me with what Donald E. Pease stereotypes as the "Cold War critics," who equate Ahab with totalitarian will and Ishmael with a freely developed sensibility, able to live in uncertainty and devoid of the need for decisive special action. However, once my (by now, fairly common) distinction is accepted between Ishmael the neophyte seaman in the plot and Ishmael the retrospective narrator-artist, Pease's criticism does not apply. For I quite agree with him that Ishmael the retrospective narrator has integrated Ahab's compulsion for final truth and deed and that Ahab's final deed is what frees Ishmael to roam in fluid sensibilities. What Pease does not quite say is that Ahab frees Ishmael to decisive action *as an artist*; and the reason he cannot say this is that for Pease artistic activity—if it is not talking about the social compact!—is not meaningful action; it is guilty of the solipsistic protomodernist sensibility that he is attacking. See Donald E. Pease, *Visionary Compacts: American Renaissance Writings in Cultural Context* (Madison: University of Wisconsin Press, 1987), pp. 40–44, 270–74.

For another still more recent analysis of Ishmael and Ahab that is largely psychological (although it does connect with the critic's social thesis about changes in American manhood), see David Leverenz, *Manhood and the American Renaissance* (Ithaca: Cornell University Press, 1989), pp. 279–306. Leverenz argues that Ishmael and Ahab "are doubles of a self that loathes itself," that is "obsessed with avenging . . . shattered manhood," and that expresses self-loathing "primarily as a craving to be dominated by unloving power." "Twinned in their desire to be beaten," says Leverenz, "Ishmael passively turns humiliation into fantasies of fraternity, while Ahab flaunts the bad aggressive self who deserves a whipping." Somewhere behind these psychological fears and cravings, moreover, lurks "the marketplace that drove" Melville's "patrician father to bankruptcy, insanity, and perhaps unconscious suicide" (pp. 280–81).

4. J. A. Ward, "The Function of the Cetological Chapters in *Moby-Dick*," *American Literature* 28 (1956): 167–68.

5. Herman Melville, *Mardi: and a Voyage Thither*, ed. Harrison Hayford, Hershel Parker, and G. Thomas Tanselle (Evanston: Northwestern–Newberry Edition, 1970), p. 557.

6. In discussing Ishmael's story and narration, it has been appropriate to refer to the narrative voice as "Ishmael" and to try to distinguish the narrative past from the narrative present. The motives and demeanor of the narrative persona in the cetology chapters can only be fully grasped, however, in terms of *Melville's* aesthetic and philosophic goals. Ishmael functions in cetology as a mask, a mouthpiece, a movable disguise for Melville's exposition. Consequently, I will be shifting in this section between the designation "Ishmael" and the designation "Melville," generally using "Melville" when speaking about underlying artistic goals, and "Ishmael" when speaking about specific acts of exposition on the part of the "I" voice. Common sense makes this somewhat inexact approach preferable to the artificiality of "Ishmael-Melville" or the absolute adherence to "Ishmael" no matter how strongly the force of the author's presence is sensed.

7. Edgar A. Dryden, *Melville's Thematics of Form: The Great Art of Telling the Truth* (Baltimore: Johns Hopkins University Press, 1968), p. 100.

8. Ibid., pp. 93–94.

9. For a discussion of Melville's literary models for cetology and for his handling of Ishmael's being "carried away" in the cause of knowing the whale, see Jane Mushabac, *Melville's Humor* (Hamden, Conn.: Archon, 1981).

10. Howard P. Vincent, *The Trying-Out of ''Moby-Dick''* (Carbondale: Southern Illinois University Press, 1949), p. 365.

11. Charles Feidelson, Jr., *Symbolism and American Literature* (Chicago: University of Chicago Press, 1953), p. 35.

12. Northrop Frye, *Anatomy of Criticism: Four Essays* (Princeton: Princeton University Press, 1957) p. 310. Frye classifies *Moby-Dick* as "romance-anatomy" (p. 313).

13. See M. H. Abrams, *The Mirror and the Lamp: Romantic Theory and the Critical Tradition* (London: Oxford University Press, 1953), pp. 21–26. From romantic theory, it is only a short distance, Abrams shows (by citing Mill's essay on poetry), to the point where the "reference of poetry to the external universe disappears . . . except to the extent that sensible objects may serve as a stimulus or 'occasion for the generation of poetry.' " "Thus severed from the external world," he goes on, linking romantic and symbolist theory, "the objects signified by a poem tend to be regarded as no more than a projected equivalent—an extended and articulated symbol—of the poet's inner state of mind" (pp. 24–25). For a different view of this material in *Moby-Dick*, see Bairnard Cowan, *Exiled Waters:*

"Moby-Dick" and the *Crisis of Allegory* (Baton Rouge: Louisiana State University Press, 1982), pp. 121–25.

14. Dryden also discusses this pattern; see *Melville's Thematics*, pp. 98–100.

15. Paul Brodtkorb, Jr., *Ishmael's White World: A Phenomenological Reading of "Moby Dick"* (New Haven: Yale University Press, 1965), p. 27.

16. This is Vincent's phrase from *Trying-Out of "Moby-Dick,"* p. 121.

17. Dryden, *Melville's Thematics*, p. 93.

18. Ibid., p. 94.

19. Ibid., pp. 97–98.

20. While the ideal of diversity, which assists Ishmael in rendering this vision is, as I have argued, also a construct that the mind brings to matter, there is a complementary ideal of plenitude at work in *Moby-Dick* that results in a sense of overflowing of any defined forms: superabundance itself becomes a category of experience. So that I do not think that even with the romantic ideal of diversity considered as a verbal construct, we can omit the aspect of discovery and assimilation of new experience to Ishmael's activity as a narrator.

21. Especially relevant here is Cowan's discussion of Ishmael's "literalism" as a way of reconciling the literary and the literal or naturalistic approaches. Cowan sees Ishmael the narrator in chs. 49–75 as refusing Ahab's allegory of the whale and countering it with a literalism that "is in the service of nature" but which, as Cowan desires to illustrate, "not only opposes culture but contains it and makes culture possible" (*Exiled Waters*, p. 115). Cowan sees Ishmael's approach deriving from Rabelais, whose " 'freedom of vision, feeling, and thought' " derives from " 'his perpetual playing with things' " and " 'invites the reader to deal directly with the world and its wealth of phenomena' " (p. 116; Cowan is quoting Eric Auerbach on Rabelais here; see *Mimesis: The Representation of Reality in Western Literature*, trans. Willard Trask [Princeton: Princeton University Press, 1953], p. 313). However, Cowan insists on our seeing the cultural roots of even Rabelais' naturalism, pointing us to Mikhail Bakhtin's discovery that the "buried traditions that shaped the forms of play and 'triumphant earthly life' of Rabelais" lie in medieval Christianity and its " 'culture of folk carnival humor' " (Cowan, *Exiled Waters*, pp. 116–17; Cowan is quoting from Bakhtin's *Rabelais and His World*, trans. Hélène Iswolsky [Cambridge: MIT, 1968], pp. 10–11). Hence, Cowan indicates that Melville not only finds a model for his naturalism to offset allegorical approaches in Rabelais, but that Rabelais is a source of Melville's grotesque humor as well. In Rabelais' medieval cultural roots, according to Bakhtin, "all that was terrifying becomes grotesque"; "the people play with terror and laugh at it"; and what is frightening becomes "a comic monster." In other words, says Cowan, "The whale itself becomes the 'comic monster' of the folk festival" (Cowan, *Exiled Waters*, p. 119; Bakhtin, *Rabelais*, p. 91).

22. F. O. Matthiessen also views these chapters concerning Stubb's whale as a unit. See *American Renaissance* (New York and London: Oxford University Press, 1941), p. 419.

23. How Melville is able to move to different anatomical aspects of the whale and to continue to suggest various ideas about God is an interesting literary question. What, in other words, are the conditions of his symbolism, the context in

which it finds its life? One factor is Melville's intensive description of the god-like qualities or metaphysical properties attributed to Moby Dick by Ahab (ch. 41) and Ishmael (ch. 42). Another is Melville's assiduous effort to document the sperm whale's "two-fold enormousness" of size and power in "The Affidavit" (45:206). Two others are the use of calculated poetic sentences that speak of the sperm whale in terms of the primary forces of nature or the primal elements of creation and the use of phrases that imply mythic exaltedness to the whale such as "majestic bulk and mystic ways" (27:119) and "most exalted potency" (80:349). As a result, then, of these and other devices, each time Melville examines a physical aspect of the sperm whale, there is a sense in which a theological level of demonstration is taking place about the possible character of nature and God.

24. Leslie A. Fiedler, *Love and Death in the American Novel*, rev. ed. (New York: Dell, 1969), p. 372.

25. Ward, "Cetological Chapters," p. 182.

26. Robert Zoellner, *The Salt-Sea Mastodon: A Reading of "Moby-Dick"* (Berkeley: University of California Press, 1973), chs. 7–12.

27. Brodtkorb, to whom I am indebted here for my language, says that the only idea we get of Moby Dick is a "hurriedly blurred view of the whale as a mysteriously animated object." See *Ishmael's White World*, p. 25.

28. Zoellner, *Salt-Sea Mastodon*, pp. 239–40.

29. Richard H. Brodhead, *Hawthorne, Melville and the Novel* (Chicago: University of Chicago Press, 1973), pp. 22–23.

30. Cowan, *Exiled Waters*, p. 157.

31. Ibid., p. 139.

32. Ibid., p. 145. Cowan, it should be noted, in his discussion of the attempt to go beyond indirect, analogical knowledge, restricts himself to the three chapters I mentioned. I have grouped the scene in ch. 133 also in this same category of "trial" unmediated scenes. I might add that in Cowan's view—and my own— Ishmael finds direct unmediated vision ultimately impossible. In "The Grand Armada" (ch. 87), human presence violates the noumenal opportunity (pp. 155–56); in "The Castaway" (ch. 93), Pip's direct revelation is beyond language and sanity (p. 158); and in "A Squeeze of the Hand" (ch. 94), "removal . . . intellectual reflection on, and not direct vision of, mystery is the only mode in which the truth can be held in the mind" (pp. 159–60); see pp. 139–61 for the full context of Cowan's argument.

33. Brodtkorb, *Ishmael's White World*, p. 146.

34. See Zoellner, *Salt-Sea Mastodon*, p. 259, from whom I am borrowing here. Zoellner shrewdly brings to bear the language from "The Carpenter" (ch. 107) on Moby Dick's behavior in the final chase. This is one of several instances where his chapter, "Noumenal Epiphany: The Three Days' Chase," though diametrically opposite from mine in viewpoint, nonetheless provides essential insights and foci of debate. Other useful discussion by Zoellner concerns the use of qualifying phrases to keep open from the reader the problem of interpretation (pp. 260–61); the significance of the leeward nocturnal flight (pp. 255–58); and the relevance of the sperm whale's blind spot (discussed in "The Sperm Whale's Head") in attempting to understand Moby Dick's behavior in the final chase (pp. 264–65).

35. See, for example, Norman Friedman, "Point of View in Fiction: The Development of a Critical Concept," *PMLA* 70 (1955): 1160–84.

36. Ibid., pp. 1174–75.

37. Zoellner, *Salt-Sea Mastodon*, pp. 254–55.

38. Newton Arvin, *Herman Melville* (New York: Viking, 1950), p. 187.

39. Letter to Hawthorne, June 1?, 1851, in *The Letters of Herman Melville*, ed. Merrell R. Davis and William H. Gilman (New Haven: Yale University Press, 1960), p. 131.

40. Nathaniel Hawthorne, *The English Notebooks*, ed. Randall Stewart (New York: MLA, 1941), p. 432.

41. Samuel Taylor Coleridge, *Shakespearean Criticisms*, ed. Thomas Middleton Raysor (London: Everyman–Dent, 1960), 1:34. Coleridge says in the sentence fragment that seems to have influenced Melville's conception of Ahab, "Shakespeare's mode of conceiving characters out of his own intellectual and moral faculties, by conceiving any one intellectual or moral faculty in morbid excess and then placing himself, thus mutilated and diseased, under given circumstances." For the evidence of Melville's probable reading of Coleridge's Shakespearean criticism, see Merton M. Sealts, Jr., *Melville's Reading*, rev. ed. (Columbia: University of South Carolina Press, 1988), p. 168, #155.

42. Elizabeth S. Foster, "Melville and Geology," *American Literature* 18 (1945): 50.

43. See "Calvinism and Cosmic Evil in *Moby-Dick*," *PMLA* 84:6 (1969): 1613–19; "*Moby-Dick*" *and Calvinism: A World Dismantled* (New Brunswick: Rutgers University Press, 1977); "Calvinist Earthquake: *Moby-Dick* and Religious Tradition," in *New Essays on "Moby-Dick,"* ed. Richard H. Brodhead (London and New York: Cambridge University Press, 1986), pp. 109–40.

44. Admittedly written many years later, Melville's journal entry when visiting the Greek Island of Patmos in 1857 is worth quoting from here, to suggest his resentment at the spirit of rationalism and the "higher criticism" leveled by the German biblical historians at the New Testament: "Was here again afflicted with the great curse of modern travel—skepticism. Could no more realize that St: John had ever had revelations here, than when off Juan Fernandez, could believe in Robinson Crusoe according to De Foe. When my eye rested on arid heigth, spirit partook of the barrenness.—Heartily wish Niebuhr & Strauss to the dogs. The deuce take their penetration & acumen. They have robbed us of the bloom. If they have undeceived anyone—no thanks to them." See *Journal up the Straits*, ed. Raymond Weaver (New York: Cooper Square, 1971), pp. 107–8; entry of February 5, 1857.

45. See Foster, "Melville and Geology," pp. 50–60; also James Robert Corey, "Herman Melville and the Theory of Evolution" (Diss., Washington State University 1968), pp. 10–12.

46. See Foster ("Melville and Geology," p. 54, n. 14) not only for the above judgment on the quality of Melville's knowledge but on other possible sources for Lyell's ideas, such as Louis Agassiz and August A. Gould's *Principles of Zoology* (Boston, 1848) or Gideon Algernon Mantell's *Wonders of Geology*, 6th ed., 2 vols. (London, 1848). In a later article, Foster challenges the claim of Tyrus Hillway (in

"Melville's Geological Knowledge," *American Literature* 21 [1949]: 232–37) that Melville's source for the Lyell material was exclusively Robert Chambers' *Vestiges of the Natural History of Creation*. She shows that only a limited number of the fossils Melville mentions are mentioned by Chambers (see Foster, "Another Note on Melville and Geology," *American Literature* 22 [1951]: 484–85).

47. On July 6, 1844, eleven months after Melville signed aboard the *United States*, the three-volume set of the *Narrative of the Surveying Voyages of His Majesty's Ships Adventure and Beagle* were recorded as transferred from the *United States* to the *Savannah*. See Jay Leyda, *The Melville Log*, 2 vols. (New York: Viking, 1952), 1:180.

48. Sealts, *Melville's Reading*, p. 171, #175.

49. Corey, "Melville," p. 17. It is possible, admittedly, that the common subject matter might, in itself, be enough to explain similarities in language and imagery.

50. See Charles Darwin, *The Voyage of the Beagle*, abridged by Millicent E. Selsam (New York: Harper and Row, 1959), p. 258; Herman Melville, *The Shorter Tales of Herman Melville*, ed. Raymond Weaver (New York: Liveright, 1928), pp. 247–48; also Corey ("Melville," pp. 20–22) who led me to this indebtedness of Melville's.

51. See Darwin, *Voyage of the Beagle*, pp. 115–19 on causes of extinction of species; the idea of competition in nature, however, was not a new idea with Darwin.

52. Foster, "Melville and Geology," p. 65.

53. See Corey, "Melville," pp. 51–52, 87–90.

54. Melville seems to be falling back on the prevalent notion of multiple creations.

55. Corey, "Melville," p. 88.

56. N.a., *Vestiges of the Natural History of Creation* (London: John Churchill, 1844). For a contemporary edition, see Gavin de Beer, intro. *Vestiges of the Natural History of Creation* (New York: Humanities Press, 1949).

57. Ibid., p. 153.

58. Ibid., p. 197.

59. Ibid., p. 154.

60. Herbert Hovenkamp, *Science and Religion in America: 1800–1860* (Philadelphia: University of Pennsylvania Press, 1978), p. 202.

61. Loren Eiseley, *Darwin's Century: Evolution and the Men Who Discovered It* (Garden City: Anchor–Doubleday, 1958), p. 137.

62. Chambers, *Vestiges*, p. 222.

63. A full statement of the theory of recapitulation, from which this phrase is taken, is provided by the American Joseph LeConte: "It is a curious and most significant fact that the successive stages of the development of the *individual* in the higher forms of any group (ontogenic series) resemble the stages of increasing complexity of differentiated structure in ascending the animal scale in that group (taxonomic series), and especially the forms and structure of animals of that group in successive geological epochs (phylogenic series). In other words, the individual higher animal in embryonic development passes through temporary stages, which

are similar in many respects to the permanent or mature conditions of some of the lower forms in the same group. . . . Surely this fact, if it be a fact, is wholly inexplicable except by the theory of derivation or evolution. The embryo of a higher animal of any group passes *now* through stages represented by lower forms, because in its evolution (phylogeny) its ancestors *did actually have these forms*. From this point of view the ontogenic series (individual history) is a brief recapit-ulation, as it were, from memory, of the main points of the phylogenic series, or family history" (*Evolution and Its Relation to Religious Thought* [n.p., 1888], pp. 130–31; quoted by Arthur O. Lovejoy in "The Argument for Organic Evolution before the *Origin of the Species, 1830–1858*," in *Forerunners of Darwin: 1745–1858*, ed. Bentley Glass, Owsei Temkin, and William L. Straus, Jr. [Baltimore: Johns Hopkins University Press, 1959], p. 406).

    64. Chambers, *Vestiges*, p. 231.

    65. Charles Lyell, *Principles of Geology*, 1st American ed., 1837, 1:526. Quoted in Lovejoy, "Argument," pp. 407–8.

    66. *Poissons du vieux gres rouge* was published in 1842–44; Lovejoy ("Argu-ment," p. 407) refers us to Marcou's *Louis Agassiz*, 1:230 for Agassiz's words on the theory of recapitulation.

    67. This is the implication I draw from his passage about "arrested" devel-opment on p. 216.

    68. *The Journals and Miscellaneous Notebooks of Ralph Waldo Emerson*, ed. Wil-liam H. Gilman et al. (Cambridge: Belknap–Harvard, 1960–82), 11:158.

    69. Letter to Samuel Gray Ward, in *The Letters of Ralph Waldo Emerson*, ed. Ralph L. Rusk (New York: Columbia University Press, 1939), 3:283.

    70. *JMN*, 9:211.

    71. Chambers, *Vestiges*, p. 347.

    72. Corey, "Melville," p. 3. I need to give credit here to Corey who, to some extent, precedes me in attributing Melville's tendency to see "parallels" between human and whale mentality to Melville's reading of Chambers. The emphases on the theory of recapitulation and the commonly shared modes of nature are mine.

    73. Tyrus Hillway, "Melville's Education in Science," *Texas Studies in Litera-ture and Language* 14 (1974): 417.

    74. For a summary of many of the reviews and attacks on *Vestiges*, especially that of Asa Gray, see Hovenkamp, *Science and Religion*, pp. 198–204.

    75. Chambers appears to have been unmasked by Francis Bowen, who, Hovenkamp tells us (p. 201), found "similarities in style and argument" between *Vestiges* and an acknowledged work of Chambers entitled *Ancient Sea-Margins*. See Francis Bowen, "Recent Theories in Geology," *North American Review* 69 (1849): 439. When Emerson met Chambers in 1848, he did not appear to know that he was the author of *Vestiges*; see *JMN*, 10:221.

    76. A. R. Wallace, *The Wonderful Century* (New York: n.p., 1898), p. 138. Quoted in Eiseley, *Darwin's Century*, p. 133.

    77. Dirk J. Struik, *Yankee Science in the Making* (Boston: Little, Brown, 1948), p. 305.

    78. Emerson records this as the sales figures in 1848 when he met Cham-bers, with fifty thousand printed for England alone (*JMN*, 10:221). For more on

the extraordinary popularity of the *Edinburgh Journal* and Robert Chambers himself, see Milton Millhauser, *Just Before Darwin: Robert Chambers and "Vestiges"* (Middletown, Conn.: Wesleyan, 1959), pp. 23–25.

79. Letter to Alexander Bradford, in *The Letters of Herman Melville*, ed. Merrell R. Davis and William H. Gilman (New Haven: Yale University Press, 1960), p. 26; Corey, "Melville," p. 33.

80. Corey, "Melville," p. 34.

81. *Chamber's Edinburgh Journal*, March 21, 1846. Quoted in ibid., p. 34.

82. Chambers, *Vestiges*, pp. 224n–225n; see also pp. 340, 347.

83. For another view on the source of coherence in *Moby-Dick*, see James McIntosh, "The Mariner's Multiple Quest," in *New Essays on "Moby-Dick"*, pp. 23–52.

84. Foster, "Melville and Geology," p. 50.

85. Feidelson, of course, argues that the Puritan typological tradition is sufficient to explain Melville's symbolic method.

Chapter 5 Personalism and Fragmentation in Whitman's *Leaves of Grass* (1855–1860)

1. Thomas Wentworth Higginson, *Cheerful Yesterdays* (Boston: Houghton Mifflin, 1898), p. 230.

2. Larzer Ziff, *Literary Democracy: The Declaration of Cultural Independence in America* (New York: Viking, 1981), p. 246.

3. Bronson Alcott, *The Journals of Bronson Alcott*, selected and edited by Odell Shepard (Boston: Little, Brown, 1938), p. 286.

4. *Walt Whitman, Prose Works 1892*, ed. Floyd Stovall (New York: New York University Press, 1964), 2:595. With the exception of the original version of the prefaces to the 1855 edition of *Leaves of Grass*, all references to the published prose of Whitman are from *Walt Whitman, Prose Works 1892*, 2 vols., ed. Floyd Stovall (New York: New York University Press, 1963–64); hereafter cited in parentheses in the text as *Prose* with volume and page number. References to the preface to the 1855 edition of *Leaves of Grass* and to all poems in *Leaves of Grass* are from *Leaves of Grass: Comprehensive Reader's Edition*, ed. Harold W. Blodgett and Sculley Bradley (New York: New York University Press, 1965); hereafter cited in parentheses in text as *LG* with page and line numbers.

5. M. Jimmie Killingsworth, *Whitman's Poetry of the Body: Sexuality, Politics, and the Text* (Chapel Hill: University of North Carolina Press, 1989), p. 107; see also pp. 99, 109, 111.

6. Ralph L. Rusk, *The Life of Ralph Waldo Emerson* (New York: Scribner's Sons, 1949), p. 374; Gay Wilson Allen, *The Solitary Singer: A Critical Biography of Walt Whitman* (Chicago: University of Chicago Press, 1967), p. 206.

7. Betsy Erkkila, *Whitman the Political Poet* (New York and Oxford: Oxford University Press, 1989), p. 38.

8. Irving Howe, *The American Newness: Culture and Politics in the Age of Emerson* (Cambridge: Harvard University Press, 1986), p. 38.

9. Bronson Alcott, "A Selection from His Journal," in *Critical Essays on Walt Whitman*, ed. James Woodress (Boston: G. K. Hall, 1983), pp. 38–39.

10. Frederik Schyberg, *Walt Whitman*, trans. by Evie Allison Allen with intro. by Gay Wilson Allen (New York: Columbia University Press, 1951), p. 50. See p. 50 for a view of Whitman's loneliness in Manhattan in the late 1840s and early 1850s that parallels what I am suggesting.

11. Mrs. Lydia Maria (Francis) Child, *Letters from New York*, 3d ed., American Fiction Reprint Series (Boston and New York, 1845; rpt. Freeport, N.Y.: Books for Libraries Press, 1970), p. 94.

12. Robert K. Martin, "Knight-Errant and Gothic Seducers: The Representation of Male Friendship in Mid-Nineteenth-Century America," in *Hidden from History: Reclaiming the Gay and Lesbian Past*, ed. Martin Bauml Duberman, Martha Vicinus, and George Chauncey, Jr. (New York: New American Library, 1989), p. 181.

13. Even in a work as factual and structured around specific areas of influence as Floyd Stovall's *The Foreground of "Leaves of Grass"* (Charlottesville: University Press of Virginia, 1974), the influence of "personal experience and observation in the streets" receives major emphasis. Stovall says, "It is obvious that the materials of *Leaves of Grass* derive chiefly from Whitman's personal experience and observation in the streets, theaters, and newspaper offices of New York and in the neighboring countryside of Long Island" (p. 150).

14. George B. Hutchinson sees this as the deliberate adoption of the role of the shaman, whose "erotic component of ecstasy . . . answers the special contact difficulties of people whose desires for sensual fulfillment are frustrated in daily life" (p. 28). Hence for himself, full of "terrible, irrepressible yearning," and for the others on the street, Whitman takes on the prophetic, ecstatic role, "fusing the private emotional struggle with public symbols" (p. 27). See *The Ecstatic Whitman: Literary Shamanism & the Crisis of the Union* (Columbus: Ohio State University Press, 1986).

15. This interesting passage from *Democratic Vistas* gives a sense of the transference of expectation for "exaltation" and "absolute fulfillment" from the sexual passions to the senses and the aesthetic capacity animated by the senses. The reader should note the manner in which the long heterogeneous list of images of city life assume a spiritual quality. His spirit is moved to an intuition of the underlying "power, fullness, motion, etc." when the senses speak to his spirit via his "esthetic conscience": "The splendor, picturesqueness, and oceanic amplitude and rush of these great cities . . . costly and lofty new buildings, facades of marble and iron . . . with masses of gay color . . . the flags flying, the endless ships, the tumultuous streets, Broadway, the heavy, low, musical roar, hardly ever intermitted, even at night; the jobbers' houses, the rich shops, the wharves, the great Central Park, and the Brooklyn Park of the hills (as I wander among them . . . musing, watching, absorbing) . . . these, I say, and the like of these, completely *satisfy my senses of power, fullness, motion, &c., and give me, through such senses and appetites, and through my esthetic conscience, a continued exaltation and absolute fulfillment*" (*Prose*, 2:371; italics mine).

16. In "Starting from Paumanok," Whitman explains his view of an ensemble approach to reality:

I will not make poems with reference to parts,
But I will make poems, songs, thoughts, with reference to ensemble,
And I will not sing with reference to a day, but with reference to all days,
And I will not make a poem nor the least part of a poem but has reference to
  the soul,
Because having look'd at the objects of the universe, I find there is no one nor
  any particular of one but has reference to the soul.

(*LG*, p. 23, ll. 172–76)

Whitman wishes to differentiate his approach to poetic subject matter from an approach that focuses on objects or "parts" as ends in themselves. Whitman wants always to be able to apprehend a wholeness by exploring the full contours of events and by mingling both their material and their spiritual dimensions.

While the passage from "Starting from Paumanok" suggests the importance of including spiritual or symbolic aspects of objects, Whitman's primary purpose in his ensemble approach to reality is, I believe, inclusiveness of material reality in its diversity and richness. "Crossing Brooklyn Ferry," in fact, embraces an interesting combination of views of "ensemble" or "scheme" (as he calls it in that poem) in both its spiritual and materialistic aspects. As the phrase "with reference to all days" in "Starting from Paumanok" implies, Whitman saw ensemble in temporal as well as spatial terms; he wanted to relate the present to the past and to the future. "Crossing Brooklyn Ferry" is Whitman's attempt to extend his idea of ensemble into the future. He speaks of

The impalpable sustenance of me from all things at all hours of the day,
The simple, compact, well-join'd scheme, myself disintegrated, every one
  disintegrated yet part of the scheme.

(*LG*, p. 160, ll. 6–7)

Not only in the present, but in the future, Whitman seeks a common link between his "disintegrated" self and the diversity of the scheme. In Stanza 9, he accepts time and materiality and sees they are inseparable from his insight in Stanza 8 that love is the link between himself and future generations; the "dumb, beautiful ministers" of the material world—the harbor that his spirit finds its fulfillment in watching and which future generations will also joyfully watch—are the common denominators between present and future.

17. Donald E. Pease, *Visionary Compacts: American Renaissance Writings in Cultural Context* (Madison: University of Wisconsin Press, 1987), p. 110; see ch. 4, "Walt Whitman and the Vox Populi of the American Masses," especially pp. 108–33. Ziff somewhat anticipates Pease's discussion of the crowd, although he veers toward a larger cosmic context beyond the social scene and its psychological-poetical transactions. He says: "Whitman . . . shows us our potential. . . . And the drama in which he acts for us is ultimately not that between individuals, because

he is all individuals . . . it is the drama of the vital all-in-one and the ultimate reality. The great poems of democracy are the poems of death" (p. 250).

18. Ibid., p. 126.

19. Ibid., p. 128.

20. Ibid., pp. 128–29, 126.

21. Michael Moon, *Disseminating Whitman: Revision and Corporeality in "Leaves of Grass"* (Cambridge: Harvard University Press, 1991), pp. 59–61.

22. See John Kinnaird, "The Integrity of *Leaves of Grass*," in *Whitman: A Collection of Critical Essays*, ed. Roy Harvey Pearce (Englewood Cliffs, N.J.: Spectrum–Prentice-Hall, 1962), pp. 28–29.

23. Paul Zweig makes a similar point: "There is an uncanny parallel between his miscellaneous formless-seeming poems and the oceanlike miscellany of the city, as seen, for example, from lower Broadway." See *Walt Whitman: The Making of the Poet* (New York: Basic Books, 1984), p. 41.

24. Whitman creates the phrase "ensemble-Individuality" as a synonym for "cohesion"; he is trying to convey the successful integration of the mass and the individualistic tendencies of democracy in a balanced fashion. I am borrowing the phrase, used by Whitman in a cultural and political sense, and applying it to the poet and his poetry: there must be a balance, a "cohesion" of "ensemble" (material and spiritual context) and "Individuality" (Personalism) in order for poetry to realize its equilibrium and fullness.

25. Walt Whitman, "Leaves of Grass," in *Walt Whitman: Complete Poetry and Collected Prose*, ed. Justin Kaplan (New York: Library of America, 1982), p. 69.

26. The difficulty of interpreting some of the lines of Section 38 derives from the constant metamorphosis the speaker undergoes and his practice of expressing his new state of mind without explaining its relation to the preceding one. In broad terms, my interpretation dovetails with the lengthy analysis James E. Miller, Jr. gives in *A Critical Guide to "Leaves of Grass"* (Chicago: University of Chicago Press, 1957), pp. 21–28. On specific lines and words, however, I differ from Miller. I see the identification with Christ as existing from the beginning of the section, based on the wording of the 1855 edition; Miller sees it as emerging in the stanza with the three lines beginning "That I . . . " In addition, he sees the speaker in these three lines reproving himself for forgetting the Christ model with its "infinite sympathy and tenderness and granted power" (p. 25) for the unfortunate; I see these three lines as a lament that might be paraphrased, "Would that I could forget the mocker and insults! but I can't because my Christ-impulse overpowers me." Finally, Miller interprets the "overstaid fraction" to refer to that portion of the self that has not yet been filled with transcendent power; I interpret it as referring to the part of the self that had overstayed and been overburdened by its sympathetic impulse.

The one reading that seems to me difficult to support, when considered in context, is the seemingly straightforward reading of the lines "That I could forget . . . " as a self-criticism for forgetting the suffering of others. Given the pervasive motif of identifying with others' suffering in Sections 33–37, it is difficult to suppose that the speaker's "usual mistake" could be that he has ignored their suffering.

27. A set of terms—"pride" and "sympathy"—is put forth in the preface to the first edition of *Leaves of Grass* that parallels the linked terms "individuality-democracy" and "individuality-ensemble," and which serves as a gloss for Section 38. They also reinforce the impression of consistency between the ideas in Whitman's prefaces and his poems. "The soul," says Whitman in the 1855 preface, "has that measureless *pride* which consists in never acknowledging any lessons but its own. But it has *sympathy* as measureless as its pride and the one balances the other and neither can stretch too far while it stretches in company with the other." Although they pull the poet in two directions, prideful individuality and sympathetic identity with others must be entwined. "The inmost secrets of art sleep with the twain. The greatest poet has lain close betwixt both and they are vital in his style and thoughts" (*LG*, p. 716; italics mine).

28. Killingsworth, *Whitman's Poetry*, pp. 25–26; see also pp. 27–31. For Killingsworth's commentary on Section 28, see pp. 35–38. On p. 26 Killingsworth relates these two drives to the same passage in the 1855 preface about "sympathy" and "pride" that I discuss in the preceding note.

29. Kinnaird has a different, interesting thesis: because Whitman's sexual awakening seems to have occurred in his thirties, it was "conjoined with the first intimations of death." It became impossible for Whitman henceforth "to dissociate mind from flesh, sex and death" ("Integrity of *Leaves of Grass*," p. 26).

30. Allen, *Solitary Singer*, pp. 228–31; see also Schyberg, *Whitman*, pp. 142–43.

31. Stovall, *Foreground*, pp. 45–46.

32. Henry Bryan Binns, *A Life of Walt Whitman* (New York: Haskell House, 1969; rpt. 1905 ed.), p. 181.

33. Walt Whitman, *The Uncollected Poetry and Prose of Walt Whitman*, ed. Emory Holloway (Garden City: Doubleday, 1921), pp. 95–96. See Allen's analysis and decoding of "164" as the sixteenth (P) and fourth (D) letters of the alphabet on pp. 420–25. Whitman attempted to conceal the gender and the identity of the individual causing him the distress reflected in his notebook entry of July 15, 1870.

34. See Robert K. Martin, *The Homosexual Tradition in American Poetry* (Austin: University of Texas Press, 1979), pp. xiii–xx, 1–89. Martin's recent vigorous defense of Whitman's homosexuality as the cornerstone of his art was sorely needed. While I am trying to avoid a simple equation of homosexuality with neurosis, my own discussion offers more realism about Whitman's psychohistory than Martin's defense of a tradition makes possible.

35. Somewhat differently, Moon sees concealments and metonymic substitutions in Whitman's writing as the method of a deliberate strategy for liberating repressed sexual—in particular homoerotic—feelings; see *Disseminating Whitman*, pp. 8–9.

36. I take this fine phrase from Eve Kosofsky Sedgwick's book *Between Men: English Literature and the Male Homosocial Desire* (New York: Columbia University Press, 1985), p. 171. Sedgwick contrasts the long-standing decadent subculture of aristocratic English homosexuals with the situation of English middle-class men: "The class of men about which we know most—the educated middle class . . .

—operated sexually in what seems to have been startingly close to a cognitive vacuum. A gentleman "—by which she means an educated middle-class man—" had a good deal of objective sexual freedom, especially if he were single. . . . At the same time, he seems not to have had easy access to the alternative subculture, the stylized discourse, or the sense of immunity of the aristocratic/bohemian sexual minority. So perhaps it is not surprising that the sexual histories of English gentlemen, unlike those above and below them socially, are so marked by a resourceful, makeshift, *sui generis* quality, in their denials, their rationalizations, their fears and guilts, their sublimations and their quite various genital outlets alike" (p. 173).

37. How else are we to reconcile Whitman's extraordinary candor in the "Calamus" poems about his homosexual experience with his lifelong refusal to acknowledge the sexual implications of these poems about himself? (See Allen, *Solitary Singer*, pp. 516–17, 535–36.) Emerson's apparent blindness to the sexual import of these poems (since "Children of Adam" and not "Calamus" were the group of poems Emerson wanted Whitman to remove [see ibid., pp. 237–38]) would seem also to corroborate the claim that homosexuality did not exist as a reality in the public consciousness. Killingsworth has perhaps enriched this issue by suggesting an alternative explanation for Whitman's tendency to conceal or deny truths he seems to hint at. He points us to Whitman's possible identification with the female model of sexual activity—"invagination," which enfolds as it conceals—rather than with the male phallic model, which explicitly asserts and exposes; see *Whitman's Poetry*, pp. 61–65.

38. Karoly Benkert "coined the word 'Homosexualtität' in his argument against extending Prussia's antisodomy law to the newly unified German federation"; see Michael Lynch, " 'Here Is Adhesiveness': From Friendship to Homosexuality," *Victorian Studies* 29 (1985): 88.

39. Ibid., p. 88; see also John D'Emilio and Estelle B. Freedman, *Intimate Matters: A History of Sexuality in America* (New York: Harper and Row, 1988), pp. 120–22, 130–31, 193; and Martin, "Knight-Errant and Gothic Seducers," p. 180. Moon also situates this transition in the disappearance of the preindustrial male relations of "the apprentice-journeyman-master system of training boys to trades" and the emergence of the "relatively brutal and unsatisfying" same-sex relations that arose out of early industrial manufacturing; see Moon, *Disseminating Whitman*, p. 10.

40. D'Emilio and Freedman, *Intimate Matters*, p. 123.

41. Havelock Ellis, *Sexual Inversion*, vol. 2 of *Studies in the Psychology of Sex*, 3d ed. (Philadelphia: F. A. Davis, 1930), pp. 51–53. For an instance of a contemporary gay writer who takes all of Whitman's contacts with men as prima facie evidence of genital sexual activity, see Charley Shively, *Calamus Lovers: Walt Whitman's Working Class Comerados* (San Francisco: Gay Sunshine Press, 1987). Finally, I would like to thank George Chauncey, Jr. of the New York University Department of History for his generous help in providing me with a bibliography on the nineteenth-century American homosexual.

42. See Edwin Haviland Miller, *Walt Whitman's Poetry: A Psychological Journey* (New York: Riverside Studies in Literature, Houghton Mifflin, 1968), especially pp. 21–23, 41–53, 61–62.

43. In the romantic fatalism of Ernest Hemingway's *A Farewell to Arms* history is the cause of the romantics' defeat—when and where the lovers meet. In the universe of the nineteenth-century romantic opera, love leads to death because the impossibility of the ideal union can only be conveyed, economically, in all its tragic richness, through the death of the lovers. But in poetry that seeks to express universal truths about the nature of man, abstract discourse on death and the fact that it may be what life "is all for" is morbid and evasive.

44. Helen Price says Whitman read the poem to her family in 1858 (Richard Maurice Bucke, *Walt Whitman* [Philadelphia: D. McKay, 1883], p. 29). My argument implicitly assumes it was written after the "Calamus" poems.

45. Stephen E. Whicher, "Whitman's Awakening to Death: Toward a Biographical Reading of 'Out of the Cradle Endlessly Rocking,' " in *Walt Whitman: A Collection of Criticism*, ed. Arthur Golden (New York: McGraw-Hill, 1974), p. 93.

46. Whicher thinks "the thousand responsive songs at random" is a reference to "Song of Myself" in which Whitman's correspondence with reality was free of tragic weight (ibid., p. 93). If he is correct, this does not alter the force of what I am saying about how the poem ends: it reminds us that "ensemble-Individuality" in "Out of the Cradle" involves the fusion of a tragic vision with the spontaneous perception of "Song of Myself."

47. Whicher also makes this point (ibid., p. 93).

48. See Char Mollinson and Charles C. Walcutt, "The Emersonian Key to Whitman's 'Out of the Cradle Endlessly Rocking,' " *Arizona Quarterly* 37 (1981): 6–16.

49. Ralph Waldo Emerson, *Nature*, in *Nature, Addresses, and Lectures*, ed. Robert E. Spiller and Alfred R. Ferguson (Cambridge: Belknap–Harvard, 1971), p. 17.

50. For an interesting view of how "Whitman sought to ease his readers out of the confines of routine consciousness by unobstrusively dismantling the linguistic framework" around "Death," the word ecstatic "word up from the waves," see Alan D. Hodder, " 'Wonderful Indirections' and Whitman's Rocking Cradle," *ESQ* 35 (1989): 140.

51. Gustav Bychowski, "Walt Whitman—A Study in Sublimation," in *A Century of Whitman Criticism*, ed. Edwin Haviland Miller (Bloomington and London: Indiana University Press, 1969), pp. 205–6.

52. *Whitman's Poetry*, pp. 42–43.

53. D. H. Lawrence, "Whitman," in *Studies in Classic American Literature* (New York: Viking, 1964), pp. 169–70.

54. See, for example, "There Was a Child Went Forth," *LG*, p. 365, ll. 22–25.

55. To a great extent, I am indebted to Charles C. Walcutt for my analysis of this closing section.

56. W. B. Yeats, *The Collected Poems of W. B. Yeats* (New York: Macmillan, 1956), pp. 335–36.

57. The final stanza merges the subject (the poet and his poems) and the metaphor for the subject (debris) so closely that it is difficult to distinguish between them. My bracketed phrases may be of help to the reader:

Me and mine [my life and poems], [are like] loose windrows, little corpses,
Froth, snowy white, and bubbles,
(See, [me as a corpse and] from my dead lips ooze exuding at last,
See, the prismatic colors glistening and rolling,)
Tufts of straw, sands, [my poems are like] fragments,
Buoy'd hither from many moods, one contradicting another,
From the storm, the long calm, the darkness, the swell,
Musing, pondering, [each poem] a breath, [or] a briny tear, [or] a dab of liquid
    or soil,
Up just as much out of fathomless workings fermented and thrown [as the
    debris],
[Each poem] A limp blossom or two, torn, just as much over waves floating,
    drifted at random [as is debris],
Just as much for us that sobbing dirge of nature [as for the debris],
Just as much whence we come that blare of the cloud-trumpets [as for the
    debris].

58. For other recent readings of this poem, see Moon, *Disseminating Whitman*, pp. 134–58; and Killingsworth, *Whitman's Poetry*, pp. 91–96. Killingsworth
develops a view somewhat related to my own that death provides an "acceptance
of powerlessness as a kind of power" and "the will to reject the forms of power
offered by the 'powers' of the society." He then goes on to see the idea of death
not as a psychological impasse, but as "the metaphor for the psychological processes by which the self is transcended or 'opened up,' made ready to be possessed
by the other" (p. 96). Moon's view of the poem's approach to death is more
elusive: he says it "is not death as Whitman's readers are probably used to thinking of it—as the universal fate of the natural realm including its human inhabitants, as part of the punishment imposed by God on fallen mankind (as Judeo-
Christian tradition would have it)—but merely a death-effect or a range of such
effects, one which includes God in its range." Included in this range of "decom-
position" is not only, according to Moon, "the unwriting of writing generally, but
the unwriting of the culture's dominant writing or scripture, the 'old' (that is,
Christian) Bible" (p. 150).

Chapter 6 Disconnection and Reconnection
in the Poetry of Emily Dickinson

1. See Joanne E. Dobson, " 'Oh, Susie, it is dangerous': Emily Dickinson
and the Archetype of the Masculine," in *Feminist Critics Read Emily Dickinson*, ed.
Suzanne Juhasz (Bloomington: Indiana University Press, 1983), pp. 80–97. Dobson's essay employs an archetypal method to excavate the "elusive masculine
form" in "both Dickinson's life and poetry by viewing it as a single poetic construct, linked by significant similarities of tone and realization" (p. 80). Yet, skillful
as Dobson is, I am unconvinced as I return to reading Dickinson that the masculine animus was the broad animating energy of her genius, just as I am uncon-

vinced by Sandra Gilbert's claim that a mother goddess and "some glimmering consciousness of that deity's powers must have always been with her, presiding over *all* the mysteries she served" ("The Wayward Nun beneath the Hill: Emily Dickinson and the Mysteries of Womanhood," in *Feminist Critics Read Emily Dickinson*, p. 41). In the case of both critics, I find Emily Dickinson more radically disconnected, unable to depend on the wellspring of a male or female poetic resource within her.

2. Edward Hitchcock, *Reminiscences of Amherst College* (Northampton, Mass., 1863), p. 162. Quoted in Richard B. Sewall, *The Life of Emily Dickinson* (New York: Farrar, Straus and Giroux, 1974), p. 24n.

3. Charles Roy Keller, *The Second Great Awakening in Connecticut* (1942; rpt. n.p.: Archon, 1968), p. 42. See also Rev. Heman Humphrey, *Revival Sketches and Manual* (New York: American Tract Society, 1859), pp. 118–259.

4. Sydney E. Ahlstrom, *A Religious History of the American People* (New Haven: Yale University Press, 1972), p. 417; *Second Great Awakening*, pp. 53–54; Humphrey, *Revival Sketches*, p. 206.

5. Keller, *Second Great Awakening*, pp. 43–44; Humphrey, *Revival Sketches, et passim*.

6. Bennet Tyler, *New England Revivals* (Boston: Massachusetts Sabbath School Society, 1846), p. vi.

7. Ahlstrom, *Religious History*, p. 417.

8. Dickinson's mother was converted in 1830 when she was pregnant with Emily. Emily's sister, future sister-in-law, and father all joined the church during the revival of 1850. And her brother, somewhat tardily, joined in 1856 at the urging of his fiancée.

9. Jane Donahue Eberwein, "Emily Dickinson and the Calvinist Sacramental Tradition," *ESQ* 33 (1987): 72–73. Eberwein points to several letters of Dickinson's in which she refers to being present during the communion service; see p. 73.

10. *The Letters of Emily Dickinson*, ed. Thomas H. Johnson (Cambridge: Belknap–Harvard, 1958), Letter 23, 1:67; cited henceforth in the text in parentheses by *L* followed by the number of the letter and the page number of the quotation.

11. *Dickinson*, pp. 360–61.

12. MS notes on religion in the seminary in the Mount Holyoke College Library. Quoted in Sydney R. McLean, "Emily Dickinson at Mount Holyoke," *New England Quarterly* 7 (1934): 31–32. For a history of the revivals at Mount Holyoke Seminary, see also Humphrey, *Revival Sketches*, pp. 268–71.

13. MS letter by Mary C. Whitman in the Mount Holyoke College Library. Cited in McLean, "Dickinson," p. 39.

14. Ibid., p. 37.

15. Charles Anderson and Richard Sewall also construct the 1850 period similarly. Anderson says that Dickinson's "resistance [to revivalism] was clearly connected with the discovery of selfhood, and with the dim awareness that she was an emergent artist"; see *Emily Dickinson's Poetry: Stairway of Surprise* (New York: Holt, Rinehart, and Winston, 1960), p. 258. Of considerable help to me also has been Sewall's thorough treatment of this period; see *Dickinson*, pp. 379–99.

16. Emily Dickinson, *The Complete Poems of Emily Dickinson*, ed. Thomas H. Johnson (Boston: Little, Brown, 1955), Poem 24 dated 1859; cited henceforth in the text in parentheses by the letter *P* followed by the number of the poem.

17. Carroll Smith-Rosenberg, *Disorderly Conduct: Visions of Gender in Victorian America* (New York: Knopf, 1985), pp. 129–64.

18. Jane Donahue Eberwein, *Dickinson: Strategies of Limitation* (Amherst: University of Massachusetts Press, 1985), p. 182.

19. Smith-Rosenberg, *Disorderly Conduct*, p. 33.

20. John Cody, *After Great Pain: The Inner Life of Emily Dickinson* (Cambridge: Belknap–Harvard, 1971), p. 41.

21. Ibid., p. 93.

22. Ibid., p. 46.

23. See also *P* 231, 256, 413, 486, 613, 1119, 1657, 1719.

24. Barbara Antonina Clarke Mossberg, "Emily Dickinson's Nursery Rhymes," in *Feminist Critics Read Emily Dickinson*, p. 50.

25. See Sewall, *Dickinson*, p. 100 and 100n; also Cody, *After Great Pain*, pp. 96–97.

26. For a view of Edward Dickinson's lack of support for "what he knew of his daughter's writing," see Vivian R. Pollak, *Dickinson: The Anxiety of Gender* (Ithaca: Cornell University Press, 1984), p. 238.

27. Sewall, *Dickinson*, pp. 57, 59.

28. Here is a telling excerpt from a letter to Austin in 1851 about the unspontaneous atmosphere in the household: "When I know of anything funny, I am just as apt to cry, far *more* so than to *laugh*, for I know who *loves jokes best*, and who is not here to enjoy them. We dont *have* many jokes tho' *now*, it is pretty much all sobriety, and we do not have much poetry, father having made up his mind that its pretty much all *real life*. Father's real life and *mine* sometimes come into collision, but as yet, escape unhurt! (*L* 65, p. 161; see Sewall, *Dickinson*, pp. 56–57.)

29. Sewall, *Dickinson*, p. 371.

30. R. P. Blackmur, "Emily Dickinson's Notation," in *Emily Dickinson: A Collection of Critical Essays*, ed. Richard B. Sewall (Englewood Cliffs, N.J.: Spectrum–Prentice-Hall, 1963), p. 81. Blackmur says that she "withdrew from the world in all the ways she could manage, and was connected with the world by the *pangs* of the experience she could not abide and yet could not let go. She could not perfect her withdrawal, and she found herself in successive stages of the inability to return. . . . Thus she made the poems of a withdrawal without a return: a withdrawal into spontaneity not experience" (p. 82).

31. Cody, *After Great Pain*, p. 106.

32. After considering whether Dickinson's sexual orientation was ultimately homosexual or heterosexual, Cody makes several interesting statements: "Emily Dickinson apparently was never able to establish for herself a stable sexual orientation, either 'normal' or 'abnormal,' or to assume a consistent adult social role. Consequently she vacillated anxiously in a state of unresolved bisexual potentiality, like a pre-oedipal child, vulnerable from every side" (p. 148) and "attempted to remain sexually ambiguous and uncommitted" (p. 150). He concludes, there-

fore, "that the agonies of renunciation that permeate Emily Dickinson's life and writings had multiple sources in hopeless, incomplete attachments to members of both sexes. In place of real love relationships she apparently evolved disembodied, and therefore nonthreatening, fantasies whose only bridge to their distant and perhaps astonished objects was her poems and letters" (p. 151).

33. This is Sewall's word; see *Dickinson*, pp. 440–41.

34. Ibid., p. 617.

35. See selection provided in ibid., pp. 742–50.

36. Joanne Dobson, *Dickinson and the Strategies of Reticence: The Woman Writer in Nineteenth-Century America* (Bloomington: Indiana University Press, 1989), p. 7. Dobson's book is most notable for its attempt to account for the origins of Dickinson's "extreme stylistic indirection" and her failure to publish not in "unique personal maladjustment but, rather," in a "set of expressive strategies contemporary women's writing offered her" (p. xiv). Dobson describes a "code of reticence" that encouraged women writers "to reveal nothing that would clash with prevailing conventions of morality and personal reticence" (p. xii). Dobson argues that the public expression of experience—"that is to say, the unique experience of the individual woman as opposed to cultural stereotypes of femininity" (p. xii)—thrust women writers into a complex problem of denial or evasive expression.

37. Sandra M. Gilbert and Susan Gubar, *The Madwoman in the Attic: The Woman Writer and the Nineteenth-Century Literary Imagination* (New Haven: Yale University Press, 1979), p. 564.

38. See Karl Keller, "Notes on Sleeping with Emily Dickinson," in *Feminist Critics Read Emily Dickinson*, p. 72.

39. Eberwein, *Dickinson*, pp. 115–16. See also Sewall, *Dickinson*, pp. 330–31 for a discussion of this poem and of the "symbolic use of the materials of childhood and domestic living for the purposes of poetry" (p. 331).

40. My "maid" interpretation has been offered somewhat tongue-in-cheek to suggest the limitations of the dramatic enactment approach of Eberwein and Gilbert. Their approach is not altogether able to exclude the idea of personal expression nor is it able to establish satisfactorily when poems are to be read as character poems rather than autobiographically. In other words, there is a blurry line between character poems and autobiographical poems; and an interpretative method using the dramatic enactment approach, if successful, would need to be able to define when it is appropriate to use it and when it is not. Robert Weisbuch has made a strong case for Dickinson's poems to read generically, rather than in terms of specific dramatic characters or particular circumstances. In his view, Dickinson "does not want us to pin down her symbolic language onto a particular experience but to consider that language as the expression of a pattern which encompasses many diverse experiences. She does not withhold the facts of her private experience but censors irrelevant particularizations to create archetypal autobiographies." See Robert Weisbuch, *Emily Dickinson's Poetry* (Chicago: University of Chicago Press, 1975), p. 38 *et passim*.

41. Letter to Anita Pollitzer, September 11, 1916, in *Lovingly, Georgia: The*

Complete Correspondence of Georgia O'Keeffe and Anita Pollitzer, ed. Clive Giboire (New York: Touchstone–Simon and Schuster, 1990), p. 183.

42. The one attempt to consistently describe a landscape scene, one that even refers to Renaissance painters, is "How the old Mountains drip with Sunset" (*P* 291).

43. These dominant typical qualities found in different poems are the following: sensory impressions expanding into metaphor (*P* 304), expressionism (*P* 658), theatricality (*P* 658), linguistic self-containment (*P* 1601), mystery (*P* 266), and metaphysical awe and ignorance (*P* 522). "The Lilac is an ancient shrub" (*P* 1241) is perhaps Dickinson's quintessential sunset poem encompassing all these traits.

44. See Roland Hagenbüchle, "Precision and Indeterminancy in the Poetry of Emily Dickinson," *ESQ* 20 (1974), especially pp. 41–43. Hagenbüchle creates the noun "transcend" to replace "emblem" or "symbol" for a symbolist poetics when a "metaphor" exceeds its own range of meaning and exists in a state of pure transcendental reference.

45. For another view of this poem, especially the phrase "the Juggler of Day," see Anderson, *Dickinson's Poetry*, pp. 136–38.

46. Jay Leyda, *The Years and Hours of Emily Dickinson* (New Haven: Yale University Press, 1960), 1:xxi.

47. "Yet Do I Marvel," in *Color* (New York: Harper and Brothers, 1925), p. 3.

48. Pollak, *Dickinson*, p. 23.

49. See Joanne Feit Diehl, " 'Ransom in a Voice': Language as Defense in Dickinson's Poetry," in *Feminist Critics Read Emily Dickinson*, pp. 156–75. She focuses on Dickinson's estrangement (my disconnection, although less defined in terms of causality) and protomodernist retreat into language; to these perceptions, which I share, Diehl adds the idea of the female poet struggling to find her own voice and the paradoxical freedom and threat to freedom that total dependence on the "power of the transformative Word" brings (p. 168).

50. Charles Feidelson, Jr., *Symbolism and American Literature* (Chicago: University of Chicago Press, 1953), pp. 184, 169, 35.

51. Herman Melville, *Moby-Dick; or, The Whale* (Evanston: Northwestern–Newberry Edition, 1988), ch. 76, pp. 336–37.

52. David Porter, *Dickinson: The Modern Idiom* (Cambridge: Harvard University Press, 1981), pp. 170–79, 75.

53. Ibid., p. 68.

54. Ibid., p. 79.

55. Sharon Cameron, *Lyric Time: Dickinson and the Limits of Genre* (Baltimore: Johns Hopkins University Press, 1979), p. 5.

56. Ibid., pp. 23, 198, 186.

57. Melville, *Moby-Dick*, ch. 114, p. 492.

58. Ralph Waldo Emerson, *The Collected Works of Ralph Waldo Emerson*, ed. Alfred R. Ferguson et al. (Cambridge: Belknap–Harvard, 1971–), 3:30.

59. This is perhaps the place to explain to those not fully conversant with Dickinson why my analysis of her poems is not highly contextualized in terms of

244 / NOTES TO CHAPTER 6

biographical or historical chronology. Those poems of Dickinson's not included in dated letters have been dated by Thomas Johnson according to handwriting, which he finds to have been similar for periods of time and then to have changed. Not only is this something less than a reliable method, but poems appearing early in her work, say in the 300–400 group, sometimes have the poetic accomplishment and maturity of those poems numbered higher than 1200. Hence the very idea of an early, middle, and late period is of limited usefulness to most critics. (The exceptions I can think of are David Porter's book on Dickinson's early poetry [*The Art of Emily Dickinson's Early Poetry* (Cambridge: Harvard University Press, 1966)] and Yvor Winters' essay on her late, landscape poems; see n. 78.) I find myself, therefore, grouping poems according to subject clusters and nodal viewpoints and deemphasizing the significance of where in the Johnson system they have been dated. Still another approach is perhaps that of critics such as Ruth Miller and William H. Shurr who link poems in terms of the fascicles in which they were bound, although one still must be able to date one or more of the poems to be able to discuss them biographically or historically.

60. I do not mean to imply that wired connections or grids were prevalent during Dickinson's lifetime; rather, I base my remarks on the knowledge that electricity, its identity with lightning, and the danger of electric current were commonplace ideas to her generation.

61. Wendy Barker, *Lunacy of Light: Emily Dickinson and the Experience of Metaphor* (Carbondale: Southern Illinois University Press, 1987), pp. 2, 10–11, 21, 25–29; on the male daylight tradition, see pp. 12–20.

62. Ibid., p. 29; see ch. 4, "Dwelling in Possibility: A Light of One's Own," for Barker's development of her ideas on poetry arising from darkness and creating a new kind of light.

63. Barker only briefly mentions lightning on p. 114. For a view of the artistic and literary sources of Dickinson's use of lightning and thunder imagery, see Barton Levi St. Armand, *Emily Dickinson and Her Culture: The Soul's Society* (London: Cambridge University Press, 1984), ch. 7, "Lone Landscapes: Dickinson, Ruskin, and Victorian Aesthetics," especially pp. 244–52.

64. Ralph Waldo Emerson, "The Over-Soul," in *Collected Works of Ralph Waldo Emerson*, 1:159.

65. We can find poems that define the ideal relations of the self to the following: the soul (*P* 1259), consciousness (*P* 822), art (*P* 855), renunciation (*P* 745), and growth (*P* 750).

66. Sewall places great emphasis on the "columnar Self" as a key idea in understanding how Puritanism influenced Dickinson's sense of calling and self-reliance. See *Dickinson*, pp. 25, 390.

67. The following are the poems I would group in this cluster: 439, 579, 612, 690, 726, 745, 773, 791, 941, 1093, 1223, 1283, 1291, 1430. Other poems dealing with loss and gain as polar or complementary realities, constitutive of each other, I would group separately, although they are clearly related to the above group (313, 355, 359, 364, 376, 379, 405, 430, 512, 522, 534, 550, 571, 572, 574, 682, 684, 689, 711, 801, 1036, 1093, 1125, 1199, 1299, 1382, 1477, 1495, 1717).

68. Cody, *After Great Pain*, pp. 39, 130–43.

69. Richard Wilbur, " 'Sumptuous Destitution,' " in *Emily Dickinson: A Collection of Critical Essays*, p. 130.

70. Wilbur says: "We may say, if we like, with some of the poet's commentators, that this central paradox of her thought is a rationalization of her neurotic plight; but we had better add that it is also a discovery of something about the soul" (ibid., p. 130). Wilbur then quotes and discusses "Undue Significance a starving man attaches" (*P* 439) whose "special" lesson he says is that "once an object has been magnified by desire, it cannot be wholly possessed by appetite" (p. 131).

71. Vivian R. Pollak, "Thirst and Starvation in Emily Dickinson's Poetry," *American Literature* 51 (1979): 49. Pollak quotes Poems 579, 612, and 690 as evidence.

72. Ibid., pp. 41, 34. Pollak points to Poems 579 and 791 as evidence.

73. Ibid., p. 44.

74. Pollak's more recent book, *Dickinson: The Anxiety of Gender*, returns to the subject on pp. 124–32. She retains her judgment that Wilbur goes too far, generalizing the positive aspect of Dickinson's compensatory view and eliding the negative. The only difference (worth noting because I agree with her) is her comment that Wilbur's essay "has stood the test of time particularly well" (p. 127n). His essay does continue to be quite sound and satisfying. I also might note that his division of Dickinson's privation into "three major privations" (she was deprived of an orthodox and steady religious faith; she was deprived of love; and she was deprived of literary recognition [Wilbur, " 'Sumptuous Destitution,' " pp. 128–30]) is somewhat similar to the three "disconnections" I have elucidated. However, I have emphasized lack of paternal love and lack of literary tradition, whereas he has in mind her possible romantic crisis and her lack of literary recognition.

75. See Pollak, *Dickinson*, pp. 115–17.

76. While multiple readings may imply richness as well as incoherence, in the case of "My Life had stood" they do suggest a core of authorial confusion. The poem can be read at face value as a celebration of the power and satisfaction that come from involvement with a woodsman in the independent circumstances of the frontier; or it can be read as the symbolic realization of female artistic power through integration of the woman's masculine "animus" (see Dobson, " 'Oh, Susie, it is dangerous,' " pp. 80–97). Yet the poem can also be interpreted, as Weisbuch has shown, as a warning "against the delusion of achieving self-realization through subservience," as dramatizing "the dangerous delusions of borrowed power"; see Weisbuch, *Dickinson's Poetry*, p. 27.

77. There is an analysis of this poem that does successfully account for these perplexing factors. See Albert Gelpi, "Emily Dickinson and the Deerslayer: The Dilemma of the Woman Poet in America," in *Shakespeare's Sisters: Feminist Essays on Women Poets*, ed. and with intro. by Sandra M. Gilbert and Susan Gubar (Bloomington: Indiana University Press, 1979), pp. 122–34. Blending a Jungian archetypal method with cultural history and feminist psychology, Gelpi does ac-

count for the loss of sexuality and the assertion of aggression in its place. He says, for example, "It is important that the female of the deer is specified, for Dickinson's identification of herself with the archetype of the hero in the figure of the woodsman seems to her to necessitate a sacrifice of her womanhood, explicitly the range of personality and experience as sexual and maternal woman" (p. 126). Also: "But why is the creative faculty also destructive, Eros inseparable from Thanatos? To begin with, for a woman like Dickinson, choosing to be an artist could seem to require denying essential aspects of her self and relinquishing experience as lover, wife, and mother. From other poems we know Dickinson's painfully, sometimes excrutiatingly divided attitude toward her womanhood, but here under the spell of the animus muse she does not waver in the sacrifice" (p. 129). Why, then, do I not acknowledge the coherence of the poem? Because I believe that while Gelpi *explains* the poem in terms of the three approaches I mention above, I do not feel the poem provides us with a fully articulated expression of Dickinson's divided attitude about womanhood, in which she is in control of what she is saying. I would distinguish between the poem as cultural and psychological artifact and the poem as accomplished expression; and I would place "My Life had stood" in the former group.

78. See Yvor Winters, "Emily Dickinson and the Limits of Judgement," in *Emily Dickinson: A Collection of Critical Essays*, pp. 36–39. Poems 258 ("There's a certain Slant of light"), 812 ("A Light exists in Spring"), and 1540 ("As imperceptibly as Grief") receive Winters' imprimatur as combining Dickinson's "greatest power with her finest execution" (p. 36). Winters' intolerance for the idiosyncratic is perhaps the largest reason for the vast number of Dickinson's poems he considers beneath his standards of excellence and for the narrow range of his admiration of her greatness. While it provides a wonderful case study of male elite standards being brought to bear on a female poet, this essay nevertheless also offers a rare instance of a critic trying to make aesthetic judgments and to give reasons for them, something that academic critics, given their primary focus on what poems are saying, usually neglect. The only exception here might be David Porter's *Dickinson: The Modern Idiom*, which has been treated with hostility by feminist critics for his insistence, like Winters', on Dickinson's limitations. See, for example, Suzanne Juhasz's "Introduction" to *Feminist Critics Read Emily Dickinson*, pp. 7–9.

79. Winters, "Dickinson," p. 36.

80. Ibid.

81. For an interesting discussion of the "topological muse of New England," see Lawrence Buell, *New England Literary Culture from Revolution to Renaissance* (London and New York: Cambridge University Press, 1986), pp. 292–93. Buell says: "The challenge of retrieving poetry from a landscape that often seemed as refractory to art as it was to tillage was the great burden, and the great opportunity, for the topological muse of New England."

82. Eberwein, *Dickinson*, pp. 16, 19, 155.

**Chapter 7   Notes on Method; with Some Thoughts on
the Diversitarian Spirit and Democracy**

1. It may sound as though I have come around here to a perspective similar
to that of Carolyn Porter's, which I took issue with in Chapter 3, n. 18. But I was
speaking then as a literary interpreter trying to understand Emerson's motives
from within his own description of his goals. Here I am merely making a historical
observation about Emerson as a figure in the historical setting that I have just
described. In fairness to Porter, I should say that her effort to see Emerson in
relation to emerging capitalism is all the more understandable, given the contexts
I have described. My complaint is that she fails to provide evidence in order to
read economic forces within Emerson's philosophical endeavors.

2. Raymond Williams tries to fashion a dialectical synthesis from the dichot-
omies of "consciousness" and "social reality" in which the sign is not only a social
product but is capable of being internalized and used variously in different human
situations. His formulation does not, however, in my view, quite succeed in specifying enough freedom of individual motive and vision to explain the figures I am
studying. See Raymond Williams, *Marxism and Literature* (Oxford and London:
Oxford University Press, 1977), pp. 39–44.

3. Leo Marx (with Bernard Bowron and Arnold Rose), "Literature, Technology, and Covert Culture," in *The Pilot and the Messenger: Essays on Literature,
Technology, and Culture in the United States* (New York: Oxford University Press,
1988), pp. 130–31.

4. A major turn in recent scholarship is to look at the power bases and rhetorical strategies of different writers competing in the national arena, but to deny
them authority as actually speaking about the problems of the whole culture, even
when they claim to be. I am unwilling to "decenter" New England writers in this
manner.

5. Herman Melville, *Moby-Dick; or, The Whale*, ed. Harrison Hayford, Hershel
Parker, and G. Thomas Tanselle (Evanston: Northwestern–Newberry Edition,
1988), ch. 27, p. 121; Charles Olson, "Call Me Ishmael," in *Modern Critical Views:
Herman Melville*, ed. Harold Bloom (New York: Chelsea House, 1986), p. 14. Clootz
led a deputation of men of different races and nations into the French National
Assembly in 1780 to symbolize all mankind's support of the French Revolution.

6. Ralph Waldo Emerson, "Introductory Lecture" (to "Lectures on the
Times"), in *The Collected Works of Ralph Waldo Emerson*, ed. Alfred R. Ferguson et
al. (Cambridge: Belknap–Harvard, 1971), 1:170. In the end, the primary effect
on Emerson of the multiplicity of the existing political, social, and religious movements was to reinforce his concern with cataloging the moods that inscribed his
inner realm where the core of his relativistic dilemmas dwelt.

7. Stephen J. Greenblatt, preface, in *Allegory and Representation* (Baltimore:
Johns Hopkins University Press, 1986), p. viii. Greenblatt is paraphrasing an idea
in Joel Fineman's essay, "The Structure of Allegorical Desire," pp. 26–51.

8. Ibid., p. viii. Here Greenblatt is alluding to ideas of Paul de Man, whose essay in this volume is titled, "Pascal's Allegory of Persuasion," pp. 1–25.

9. See Chapter 2, n. 15 for scholarship on slavery and the American Renaissance. On urban romantic allegory, see Peter Brooks, "Romantic Antipastoral and Urban Allegories," *Yale Review* 64 (1974): 11–26; Bairnard Cowan, *Exiled Waters: "Moby-Dick" and the Crisis of Allegory* (Baton Rouge: Louisiana State University Press, 1982), pp. 47–59; Walter Benjamin, *Charles Baudelaire: A Lyric Poet in the Era of High Capitalism*, trans. Harry Zohn (London: New Left Books, 1973).

10. Lawrence Buell, *New England Literary Culture: From Revolution Through Renaissance* (London and New York: Cambridge University Press, 1986), p. 117.

11. This is perhaps the point to observe that the interiority of the text itself is clearly suggestive of a continuum that extends on the idealist pole to the semi-autonomous nature of consciousness and to the semiautogenerative meanings of the imagination, once its referential terms have been established. Such a spectrum of materialist and idealist influences on literary creation is at odds with the ideological critic who collapses the difference between internal and external influences and then seems to lose his grasp of internal influences as he finds the hegemonic power of prevailing cultural values dominant within the writer's vision.

12. For a related view, see Michael Moon, *Disseminating Whitman: Revision and Corporeality in "Leaves of Grass"* (Cambridge: Harvard University Press, 1991), pp. 10–11.

13. George B. Hutchinson, *The Ecstatic Whitman: Literary Shamanism & the Crisis of the Union* (Columbus: Ohio State University Press, 1986), p. 24.

14. Susan Edmiston and Linda D. Cirino, *Literary New York: A History and Guide* (Boston: Houghton Mifflin, 1976), p. ix.

15. Fisher sees American culture tending toward the "subtraction of differences" to create cultural homogeneity; my view, at least of nineteenth-century American literature, is that diversity was engaged and emphasized as a uniquely American approach to nature, self, society, and public discourse. In his view of Whitman, moreover, Fisher sees only one pole of his approach—the inclusive one; he fails to see the individualistic pole that leads to difference and atomistic segmentation. See Philip Fisher, "Democratic Social Space: Whitman, Melville, and the Promise of American Transparency," in *The New American Studies: Essays from "Representations,"* ed. Philip Fisher (Berkeley: University of California Press, 1991), pp. 70–111; quoted phrase from p. 72. For a description of Fisher's earlier work on a space of public consciousness created by the media, see my Chapter 1, n. 16.

16. Melville, *Moby-Dick*, ch. 114, p. 492.

17. Emily Dickinson, *The Complete Poems of Emily Dickinson*, ed. Thomas H. Johnson (Boston: Little, Brown, 1955), Poem 1602.

Index

Abrams, M. H., 216n, 226n
Acton, H. B., 224n
Adimari, Ralph, 211n
Agassiz, Louis, 115, 229n
Ahlstrom, Sydney E., 213n, 214n, 215n, 240n
Alcott, Bronson, 121, 220n, 232n, 233n
Allegory, 103, 198–99
Allen, Evie Allison, 233n
Allen, Gay Wilson, 55, 208n, 218n, 220n, 232n, 233n, 236n, 237n
America, nineteenth-century: English vs. American society and, 9–10; fragmentation in, 12, 23–50; ideal of diversity in, 4–5, 248n; metropolitan context in, 23–30; views of self and society in, 12–13, 205–6. *See also* Democracy, American
American Revolution, 32
Anderson, Charles, 240n, 243n
Arac, Jonathan, 27, 208n, 209n, 211n, 212n
Arvin, Newton, 108, 229n
Ashe, T., 207n
Atomistic fragmentation: in Dickinson, 9, 11, 150, 191–92, 199; metropolitan context and, 29–31; as term, 9; in Whitman, 9, 10, 11, 123, 199
Auerbach, Eric, 227n

Bacon, Francis, 70, 221n
Bakhtin, Mikhail, 227n

Ballou, Adin, 37
Balzac, Honoré de, 199
Baptist Church, 33
Barker, Wendy, 170, 244n
Baudelaire, Charles Pierre, 199
Beecher, Lyman, 36, 40, 214n
Beer, Gavin de, 230n
Bell, Michael Davitt, 208n
Benjamin, Walter, 199, 211n, 248n
Benkert, Karoly, 237n
Bentham, Jeremy, 87
Bercovitch, Sacvan, 208n, 210n, 212n
Bernays, Anne, 210n
Binns, Henry Bryan, 236n
Blackmur, R. P., 157, 241n
Blake, William, 47, 83
Blodgett, Harold W., 209n, 232n
Bloom, Harold, 247n
Blumin, Stuart M., 211n
Bode, Carl, 220n
Boston: public space of consciousness in, 208n; religious context in, 37–38, 40–41; Transcendentalist Club in, 44–46, 47
Boston Evening Transcript, The, 38
Bowen, Francis, 231n
Bowron, Bernard, 247n
Bradford, Alexander, 232n
Bradley, Sculley, 209n, 232n
Brewster, David, 221n
Bricker, George H., 213n
Broadway, 28–29, 124–25, 211n

Doan, Ruth Alden, 214n
Dobson, Joanne E., 159, 239n, 242n, 245n
Douglas, Ann, 35, 39, 208n, 214n, 215n
Doyle, Peter, 136
Dreiser, Theodore, 49
Dreyfus, Hubert L., 225n
Dryden, Edgar A., 85, 94–95, 226n, 227n
Duberman, Martin Bauml, 233n
Dürer, Albrecht, 89
Duycknick, Evert, 116
Dwight, John Sullivan, 45, 216n

Eberwein, Jane Donahue, 155, 161, 190, 191, 240n, 241n, 242n, 246n
Economic analysis, 196, 219n
Edmiston, Susan, 248n
Edwards, Jonathan, 55, 218n
Egalitarianism, 5
Eiseley, Loren, 230n
Ellis, Havelock, 138, 237n
Ellis, R. L., 221n
Emerson, Edward Waldo, 218n
Emerson, Mary Moody, 218n
Emerson, Ralph Waldo, 53–81; consciousness and, 62, 64–75, 76–77, 78–79, 80; correspondence and, 72, 78; deconstructionism and, 77–79; Dickinson compared with, 158, 169; disunity and, 73–75; economic context and, 247n; evolutionary context and, 115; existentialism and, 79–81, 223n, 224n; "faith" for, 220n; gap between real and ideal and, 73–75; idealism of, 54, 60, 223n; innovation and, 64–65; modernism and, 202; multiplicity of moods and, 70–73; notion of "balanced soul" in, 77; notion of spirit in, 55, 57–58; polarity and, 60, 67–70, 220n, 221n; protomodernism of, 63, 65, 202; as psychophilosopher, 76, 222n; psychophilosophical context and, 13–14, 50, 63, 216n, 218n, 219n, 220n; rationalism of, 56–58, 60; relativism of, 63, 64–67, 195; religious context and, 32, 40–41, 200; romanticism in, 54–55, 57, 204–5; segmentary fragmentation and, 5, 9, 11, 58, 61–62, 70; sense of experience in, 58–75; "shooting the gulf" image

in, 54, 75–77, 205; skepticism of, 57–58, 73; social vs. psychological reality in, 15, 60–62; temporality and, 55–56; transcendentalists and, 44, 46, 54–55; transition and, 64–67, 77; the unconscious and, 47; unity-in-diversity and, 7, 41; Whitman and, 122, 146, 237n. Works: "The American Scholar" address, 59, 66, 219n; "Chardon Street Convention, The," 214n; "Compensation," 61, 65, 67–70; Divinity School Address, 59; essay on Plato, 77; *Essays: Second Series*, 60–61; "Experience," 61, 65, 71, 74, 76, 78; "Illusions," 65, 72; "Lecture on the Times," 198; "The Method of Nature," 75; "Montaigne; or the Skeptic," 61, 65, 67, 72–73, 75, 76; "Natural History of the Intellect, The," 57, 224n; *Nature*, 55, 75, 218n, 224n; "Nature," 60, 61, 65, 74–75, 76; "Nominalist and Realist," 60–61, 65, 72, 76; "The Over-Soul," 174, 220n; "The Poet," 5, 6; "Self-Reliance," 64–65, 73, 75–76
Emersonian "tradition," 65–67
Emotion: and Transcendentalism, 45–46
England, 4, 9–10
Erkkila, Betsy, 232n
Established churches, weakening of, 32, 33–36, 195, 213n, 214n
European Romanticism: American democracy and, 7–8; influence of, 4–6, 196; nineteenth-century psychophilosophical context and, 42–43. *See also* Correspondence; Diversitarianism
Evangelicalism, 31, 32. *See also* Protestant revivalism
Evolutionary thought, 48–49, 111–18. *See also* Darwin

Feidelson, Charles, Jr., 76, 78, 168, 209n, 216n, 222n, 226n, 232n, 243n
Ferguson, Alfred R., 207n, 216n, 218n, 238n, 243n, 247n
Ferrell, Sarah, 210n
Fiedler, Leslie A., 100, 228n
Fineman, Joel, 247n
Finney, Charles Grandison, 31, 35–36, 212n
Firkins, O. W., 71, 221n
Fish, Stanley, 210n